Global Security

2942

FROM THE LIBRARY OF
DONN STARRY

About the Book and Editors

This overview of world affairs provides a comprehensive assessment of the important trends and events during 1986 and the first half of 1987 that will have a decisive impact on U.S. security. Combining the expertise of an eminent group of regional specialists, economists, and military analysts, *Global Security: A Review of Strategic and Economic Issues* is a concise yet sophisticated reference for scholar and general reader alike.

As in previous editions, the 1986-1987 volume begins with an introduction by the editors reviewing the key events of the period and analyzing their long-term significance. The editors discuss the political rivalries that continue in the Middle East, the economic instability fostered by oil-revenue declines, and the destructive persistence of the Iran-Iraq War. They also examine the primarily domestic problems plaguing East Asia. The book includes a detailed survey of East-West military balance and competition, highlighting changes in both sides' strategic capabilities and evolving balances of conventional power in regions throughout the world. In view of the increasing dominance of economic issues in international events, this edition focuses on such developments as the impact of U.S. international economic policy on national security, the internal programs of reform and revitalization initiated by Mikhail Gorbachev in the Soviet Union, and the external debt crises and economic deterioration facing many Latin American countries.

Events in key parts of the globe are reviewed thoroughly as the contributors analyze regional interdependence in southern Africa and the racial unrest that has gripped South Africa; the internal and regional political and ethnic conflicts facing the nations of South Asia; the varied economic and political dilemmas that confront each country in Latin America; and the growing importance in the security equation of Southern Europe—a region balanced uncertainly between pro-NATO and neutral positions.

Barry M. Blechman and **Edward N. Luttwak** are senior fellows at the Center for Strategic and International Studies, Washington, D.C. Both have made major contributions to the fields of military strategy, defense policy, and issues of national security.

**Published in cooperation with the
Center for Strategic and International Studies,
Washington, D.C.**

Global Security

A Review of Strategic and Economic Issues

edited by
**Barry M. Blechman
and Edward N. Luttwak**

Westview Press / Boulder and London

This Westview softcover edition is printed on acid-free paper and bound in softcovers that carry the highest rating of the National Association of State Textbook Administrators, in consultation with the Association of American Publishers and the Book Manufacturers' Institute.

All rights reserved. No part of this publication may be reproduced or transmitted in any form or by any means, electronic or mechanical, including photocopy, recording, or any information storage and retrieval system, without permission in writing from the publisher.

Copyright © 1987 by the Center for Strategic and International Studies. The views and conclusions expressed in this volume are solely those of the authors and do not represent the positions or policies of the Center for Strategic and International Studies or any agency of the United States government.

Published in 1987 in the United States of America by Westview Press, Inc.; Frederick A. Praeger, Publisher; 5500 Central Avenue, Boulder, Colorado 80301

Library of Congress Cataloging-in-Publication Data
Global security.
  "Published in cooperation with the Center for
Strategic and International Studies, Washington, D.C."
  Includes index.
  1. National security. 2. World politics 1985–1995.
3. United States—National security. I. Blechman,
Barry M. II. Luttwak, Edward.
UA10.5.G573 1987   355'.03   87-14661
ISBN 0-8133-0480-6

Composition for this book originated with conversion of the editors' word-processor disks.

Printed and bound in the United States of America

∞ The paper used in this publication meets the requirements of the American National Standard for Permanence of Paper for Printed Library Materials Z39.48-1984.

6 5 4 3 2 1

Contents

List of Tables and Figures	ix
Foreword, *Amos A. Jordan*	xi
1 The Year in Review, *Barry M. Blechman and Edward N. Luttwak*	1
2 The East-West Military Balance, *James J. Townsend*	22
3 The International Economy with a National Security Perspective, *Gary C. Hufbauer and Kimberly Ann Elliott*	91
4 The Soviet Economy: In Search of Reform, *Herbert S. Levine*	112
5 Southern Africa: Descent into Chaos? *Michael W. Clough*	136
6 NATO's Southern Flank: A Troubled Region, *Alan Platt*	164
7 Latin America: Political Progress, Economic Stagnation, *Sally Shelton-Colby*	186
8 South Asia in 1986, *Stephen P. Cohen*	213
List of Acronyms	237
About the Contributors	243
Other Titles Published in Cooperation with the Center for Strategic and International Studies	245
Index	247

Tables and Figures

Tables

2.1	U.S. nuclear forces	38
2.2	Soviet nuclear forces	43
2.3	Small nuclear forces, 1986	48
2.4	Appropriations for U.S. strategic defense programs	49
2.5	Strategic offensive forces: United States and USSR, January 1987	58
2.6	Procurement of selected weapon systems, 1974–1985	59
2.7	Growth in major weapon systems in the United States	60
2.8	U.S. Navy: Deployable battle forces, 1985–1986	63
2.9	U.S. Air Force aircraft procurement program, fiscal 1986–1989	65
2.10	Potential U.S. forces in Southwest Asia	76
2.11	Relative U.S./USSR standing in the twenty most important basic technology areas	80
3.1	Growth of the U.S. budget deficit	105
4.1	Soviet growth of output and productivity, 1961–1982	113
4.2	Soviet growth of output and productivity, 1983–1986	128
4.3	Growth rates of selected economic indicators for the 12th five-year plan period, 1986–1990	131
5.1	Basic economic data	138

5.2	Economic dependence on South Africa	140
5.3	External trade of Zambia and Zimbabwe that moves through South Africa	141
5.4	The military balance in southern Africa	142
5.5	Racial composition of the South African population, 1985	144
5.6	Explosive devices incidents, annual numbers	148
8.1	Annual funding of the post–FY 1987 program	221

Figures

2.1	A comparison of U.S. defense investment outlays with estimated dollar cost of USSR defense investment, 1965–1985	27
2.2	The U.S. strategic triad, December 1986	31
2.3	Soviet strategic forces, December 1986	39
2.4	Strategic forces preattack static ratio comparison	56
2.5	U.S. and Soviet tactical aircraft production	64
2.6	NATO–Warsaw Pact combat aircraft	73
2.7	NATO and Warsaw Pact maritime forces in the North Atlantic and seas bordering Europe, 1986	74
2.8	NATO–Warsaw Pact comparison	75
3.1	U.S. fiscal and trade deficits	101
3.2	Relative defense expenditures	106
6.1	Major U.S. military installations in Spain	168
6.2	Major U.S. military installations in Greece	177

Foreword

The world, as viewed in the spring of 1987, appears to be a most uncertain and dangerous place. The potentially catastrophic war between Iran and Iraq has continued for seven years, with no end in sight. Were that conflict to spread south along the Gulf, the damage to vital Western interests could be severe. Vicious internal wars savage life in Central America, in southern Africa, in Lebanon, in Afghanistan, in Cambodia; the keys to their resolution remain hidden. Serious confrontations continue between Israel and most of its neighbors, and between India and Pakistan. Although overt hostilities have been avoided in both cases in recent years, the potential for wide-scale conflict remains high; each confrontation is increasingly assuming a nuclear dimension.

Superimposed upon all this is the continuing struggle between the United States and the Soviet Union. Politically, ideologically, economically—covertly and publicly—the two great powers compete for power and influence throughout the globe. Their competition in strategic nuclear arms remains unchecked and is assuming a new dimension in space. Indeed, during the past year, both powers took major steps that severely damaged the fragments of arms control agreements that previously had checked the nuclear competition, at least to some degree. In Europe, in Southwest Asia, in East Asia, the two nations and their allies continue to accrue increments of ever more powerful military capabilities, each seeking to maintain a position of at least military parity, and perhaps to gain the upper hand—should the other falter.

Yet despite their military superiority, or perhaps because of it and its mutuality, the ability of the great powers to influence events elsewhere in the world continues to deteriorate. Even when given a relatively free hand by the other, neither has been able unilaterally to determine the course of local conflicts, such as the internal wars in Central America or southern Africa. Moreover, just as the United States learned in Vietnam, the Soviet Union is beginning to learn in Afghanistan that the price of direct military intervention—in both international and domestic terms—can be very great indeed. Nor have the great powers been able together to resolve certain conflicts, such as the Iran-Iraq War, in whose peaceful settlement they may perceive a common interest. Nor have they together been able to control nuclear proliferation—slow it, yes; eliminate it, no.

Both the United States and the Soviet Union are experiencing internal crises of potentially major proportions. In the USSR, the general secretary, Mikhail Gorbachev, has unleashed a program of reforms and revitalization of unprecedented proportion. Not only the Soviet economy but also its political and governmental institutions, the legal and law enforcement system, the organizations of culture and the arts, and even the party itself have become targets of criticism and subjects of proposals for change. In foreign policy, the new Soviet regime has developed and maintained a public line featuring a nonthreatening posture and repeated initiatives to resolve regional conflicts and to bring about far-reaching measures of arms control.

Although Gorbachev's foreign initiatives are viewed generally with great skepticism, virtually no one doubts his sincere desire to change Soviet society. His ability to do so, however, is open to serious question because, to make change possible, he must undercut the prestige and authority of virtually every institution and every elite within that Soviet society. There is every reason to question the extent to which reform is possible in the USSR, as described in detail in this book by University of Pennsylvania Professor Herbert S. Levine in a penetrating analysis of the Soviet economy. But if the reforms fail, then what of Gorbachev's own future and the durability of his regime? The Soviet regime in five years, two years, or even one year could be quite different from the one now confronted.

In the U.S. case, crisis has been foisted on the president by unruly subordinates, not unleashed by his own initiatives. Never has a U.S. administration fallen so quickly from popular favor. The revelations in November 1986 of the secret arms sales to Iran and the illegal support of the Nicaraguan "Contras" transformed a presidency more popular than any before it into an object of concern in all quarters and derision in some. The report of the president's own Tower Commission in February 1987 made clear the extent of the problems in the National Security Council and its staff, the inability or unwillingness of other executive agencies to prevent either the willful violation of congressional mandates or the amateurish distortion of foreign-policy objectives, as well as the president's own detachment from decisionmaking, even on its most generalized level. Congressional investigations of the Iran/Contra affair in the spring and the continuing investigation of the special prosecutor and his staff guarantee continuing front-page attention to the scandal and, with it, the inability of the administration to regain its footing.

With the administration preoccupied, even crippled in this manner, the nation's domestic problems remained unresolved and its international stance became quiescent. Increasingly, economic issues dominated the news. As the Congress grappled first with the fiscal 1987 and then with the fiscal 1988 budgets, the nation's refusal to face up to the measures necessary to manage the federal deficit became explicit—Senators Gramm, Rudman, and Hollings notwithstanding. Adjustments in the relative value of the dollar caused the trade deficit to diminish somewhat, but not so significantly as to suggest resolution of the underlying structural weaknesses in the nation's economy. The fundamental problems of the international economy have become increasingly clear and their implications for Western security interests increasingly evident.

With these problems in mind, the editors of *Global Security: A Review of Strategic and Economic Issues* decided to emphasize economic issues in the 1986-1987 edition. In addition to the chapter by Professor Levine, this volume includes a review of the international economy by Georgetown University Professor Gary C. Hufbauer and Kimberly Ann Elliott of the Institute of International Economics. A chapter on Latin America by Sally Shelton-Colby features the international debt situation and other economic issues.

Global Security also includes reviews of events in key regions. Michael W. Clough, now at the Council on Foreign Relations, examines the situation in southern Africa, analyzing events both in the Republic of South Africa and in neighboring countries. Stephen P. Cohen, a professor at the University of Illinois, looks at South Asia, assessing interactions between the difficult internal political and ethnic problems that plague every nation in that region and the persistent conflicts that cross national boundaries. And Alan Platt of The RAND Corporation reviews events in southern Europe, a region looming ever larger in U.S. security planning, yet increasingly torn between pro-NATO and less aligned orientations.

Finally, this volume includes an essay in which the editors review the key events of the year and assess their significance. A comprehensive assessment of the military balance between East and West, prepared by James J. Townsend, highlights the most important changes in military capabilities of the two sides.

Global Security was prepared under the direction of Barry M. Blechman and Edward N. Luttwak; both are senior fellows at the Center for Strategic and International Studies. The project was funded by the Alfred P. Sloan Foundation, by Tenneco, Inc., and by the Mosbacher Foundation, Inc. The Center for Strategic and International Studies is a research institution founded in 1962 to foster scholarship and public awareness of emerging international issues on a broad interdisciplinary basis. It is bipartisan and nonprofit. Its areas of research are selected in consultation with its governing bodies, and its work is entirely unclassified.

Amos A. Jordan
President, CSIS
July 1987

1
The Year in Review

*Barry M. Blechman
and Edward N. Luttwak*

During 1986, global perceptions of the U.S. and Soviet governments were drastically overturned. Just when the world had become used to the first successful two-term presidency in Washington since Eisenhower's days—seemingly competent in all major policy areas and capable of maintaining productive relations with Congress—the confused and ill-managed Reykjavik summit, the Republicans' loss of the Senate in spite of exceptional presidential efforts in the congressional elections, and the Iran arms sale revelations shattered the aura of competence and success, undermined the international prestige of the Reagan administration, and presaged a serious reduction in its power to control events.

In Moscow, by contrast, Gorbachev's rule—consolidated within a purged Politburo—decisively broke the pattern of uncommunicative, inflexible, and almost inert leadership that had become the Kremlin norm since the later Brezhnev years. Gorbachev inaugurated a broad array of domestic and international initiatives and introduced two new terms to the Soviet political vocabulary that evoked the prospect of sweeping reforms: *glasnost* (openness) and *perestroika* (restructuring). That change in perceptions was duly reflected in the media. But in the substance of government and politics, there was much more continuity than change during 1986, in both the Soviet Union and the United States.

By the most tangible of criteria—the disposition of the federal budget—the Reagan administration's influence had sharply declined long before the summit, the election, and the Iran-Contra affair. As soon as the administration's budget request for fiscal year 1987 was presented to Congress at the beginning of the year, it became virtually certain that the key demands, for deficit reduction coupled to a substantial increase in defense authorizations, would be substantially rejected.

It was not until much later that the exact numbers were decided, but from the start of the budget season in February it was generally agreed that there was no prospect of congressional acceptance of the $320.3 billion defense request; rather, an unprecedented reduction of some $30 billion was likely. In the end, $291.8 billion was authorized, an 8.9 percent reduction, as compared to 6.1 percent for fiscal year 1986, 5.2 percent for fiscal 1985, and 4.2 percent for 1984. These numbers clearly indicate a trend—a progressive loss of presidential control over the budget process, which is the crucial priority-setting mechanism of public policy in the United States. Symptomatically, the largest reduction of all, amounting to more than 33 percent, was imposed on the request for the Strategic Defense Initiative (SDI) programs, reduced from $5.3 billion to $3.5 billion.

Another resounding defeat for the administration, also entirely predictable before the year-end troubles, was the Goldwater-Nichols Defense Reorganization Act, a package of sweeping reforms vehemently resisted by Secretary of Defense Caspar W. Weinberger; under the circumstances, this was the equivalent of a vote of no-confidence in the administration's management of the Defense Department.

Even those defeats, however, understate the gap between perceptions and substance that the year-end troubles merely reduced. For if one examines the deeper level of governance rather than the surface phenomena of Washington politics, it becomes evident that the strongly positive image of the Reagan administration that persisted through the 1984 reelection obscured very negative realities. By far the most important of these was the position of the United States in the international economy, which cannot but affect its role in international security as well (see Chapter 3 by Gary C. Hufbauer and Kimberly Ann Elliott, on the national security implications of global economic trends).

Whether or not the rising magnitude of the accumulated federal deficit, in excess of a trillion dollars, was and remains harmful in itself is still debatable. What is quite certain is that the deficit's conjunction with a very low domestic savings rate, and the consequent financing of much of it from foreign sources, has resulted in the accumulation of the world's largest external public debt. That debt must now be serviced by interest charges paid for either by otherwise unrequited exports or by the sale of capital assets (which will generate further external payments in the future)—unless additional borrowing takes place, delaying but aggravating the eventual standard-of-living burden of making the necessary transfers abroad. The devaluation of the dollar reduces *pro rata* the accumulated debt in foreign-currency terms but by the same token it depreciates capital assets in the United States that foreigners can buy, and reduces the import-buying capacity of U.S. exports. In other words, devaluation confiscates part of the foreign lending received in the past but aggravates the consequences of borrowing from abroad for current spending, rather than for productive investment.

If public borrowing of the magnitude recently experienced had taken place at a time when the U.S. economy was fundamentally sound, the consequences could only be trivial, just as the "supply-side" publicists have argued, because in the United States the public sector as a whole amounts to less than one-quarter of the total economy; its deficit, in turn, accounts for only a few percentage points of the gross national product.

Unfortunately, the economy is not sound. It is afflicted by a structural malady whose most visible symptom is a long-term decline in international competitiveness, lately dramatized by disappointing *postdevaluation* export figures.

The onset of this condition antedated by many years the Reagan administration, but its positive encouragement of complacency has certainly done nothing to improve the situation. A sinister parallel with Great Britain's economic decline is not improper: It too was masked by possession of an international currency that allowed liberties to be taken with the foreign-trade balance as other countries shipped goods in exchange for sterling-designated paper; it too was characterized by the downfall of classic manufactures and heavy industry, fecklessly slighted as "old-fashioned"; and it too proceeded amidst baseless self-satisfaction (recall Harold Macmillan's slogan of 1959: "you never had it so good"), which anaesthetized British society at a time when there should have been instead a great sense of urgency and alarm.

One need not evoke analogies to register what hard numbers prove— the sharply diminished relative productivity of the U.S. economy, which is slowly but cumulatively impoverishing the United States and its people in real terms, as deflated family income figures clearly show. Masked by inflation during the 1970s and by external borrowing more recently, this process cannot continue for long without leading to a degradation of the standards and institutions of U.S. society in noneconomic ways as well, as the British example again suggests.

Long before any acute societal symptoms are likely to be manifest, the entire position of the United States as a world power will have been eroded. The key to the system of U.S. alliances in place since the aftermath of World War II was the primacy of the United States as both a surplus producer of security and as a net exporter of capital, goods, and services. This dual role enabled the United States to provide concurrently both defensive garrisons in place as well as centralized deterrence from U.S.-based forces without demanding payment *pro rata*. It was this departure from the historically normal collection of overt or disguised tribute by the provider of security that made possible the historically unprecedented duration of the North Atlantic, U.S.-Japanese, and other defensive alliances.

If the U.S. economy fails to recover sufficiently to become internationally competitive once again and reverts to an external surplus position, it is most unlikely that the United States will continue to borrow overseas and also continue to provide forces in place to protect its creditors—unless directly compensated for its military costs and not just for local currency expenditures (as is now sometimes the case, at least in part). Whether it is the necessary resources or the domestic political consent that would be the first to be exhausted, one cannot say; but certainly without one solution or the other, the upkeep of overseas defensive garrisons in Western Europe, Japan, and Korea, the airlift and sealift forces that they require for crisis augmentation and wartime resupply, as well as associated protective forces, simply cannot continue undiminished.

At this time, far from implementing fundamental remedies for an economic decline that clearly has causes of a fundamental nature, no investigation has been made to uncover what those underlying causes might be. Distortions in the capital markets that allocate funds preferentially for manipulative rather than productive purposes, educational shortcomings at many levels, the overstimulation of consumption rather than of saving and production, and even the hidden long-term effects of commercial television are only some of the institutional, societal, and cultural causes that have been mentioned as factors in the present crisis. None are likely to be remedied either by laissez-faire policies or by mere legislative tinkering, but as yet no serious reforms have been proposed, let alone attempted.

In the short term, anticipation of what is to come has included old suggestions from novel and unexpected quarters (e.g., Henry Kissinger) for reductions in the U.S. forces stationed in West Germany and Japan and of course the reduction in defense authorizations already mentioned. Most harmful of all, so far, has been the continuing decline in funds for economic security assistance and in loan guarantees for foreign military sales extended to poorer allies in difficulties. Nor has the United States, in its reduced economic state, been capable of confronting the Latin American debt crisis, whose direct consequence has been to block the recovery in U.S. exports in the largest potential market, and whose indirect political consequences could be catastrophic for the stability of the region. Overall, crisis-prevention efforts by way of economic assistance continue to be slighted as compared to crisis-management capabilities by military means, even though the cost ratios are similar to those between preventive and therapeutic medicine.

Whereas newly negative perceptions of the Reagan administration have merely corrected exaggerated images of success, newly positive perceptions of Gorbachev's leadership of the Soviet Union have overstated its meager results so far. That Gorbachev has been party general secretary for only two years at this writing is not as significant an excuse as it might have been in other circumstances: By the time Gorbachev secured his control of the Politburo, the critique of the status quo established under his predecessors was already fully developed, a reform agenda for the economy had been broadly ventilated, and suggestions for change in other areas of Kremlin policy (including the conduct of public relations overseas) had been accumulating for almost a full decade. Hence Mikhail Gorbachev has not been in the usual position of a reforming successor who must first expend much time and energy in breaching the barrier of complacency. Brezhnev in his dotage, Andropov in his illness, and Chernenko in his debility obviously did not launch a reform program; but among Soviet economists and diplomats (e.g., Abel Aganbegyan), technically minded military leaders (e.g., Marshal Nikolay V. Ogarkov), and military-minded technical managers (e.g., those in aerospace), there was no complacency to breach. Rather, much anxiety—and an increasing tendency to propose fairly radical reforms even by way of public media accessible to Western observers—had been expressed. It is against that background that Mikhail Gorbachev's record must be assessed. (On the Soviet economy in detail, see Chapter 4, by Herbert S. Levine).

At the 27th Party Congress in February 1986, Gorbachev received much praise for the improved performance of the economy since his advent to power. Industrial statistics were cited to show that in the last quarter of 1985, output had increased at an annualized rate of 3.5 percent. Scrutiny of the possible causes reveals that the weather (the coldest winter in two decades) had depressed the basis of comparison (namely, the last-quarter 1984 figures); that two days of holiday were suppressed ("postponed") during the second half of 1985; and that investment had been increased by 2.7 percent during 1985 (in a pre-Gorbachev decision), as compared to a growth rate of 1.9 percent in 1984. What Gorbachev can claim full credit for are his anti-alcohol and work discipline campaigns, as well as his replacement of twenty-five presumptively "stagnant" (if not corrupt) ministers and state committee chiefs with economic portfolios, and of five Central Committee departmental chiefs with supervision over economic sectors, including machine-building and construction.

Such *administrative* measures can have, and apparently did have, a one-time positive effect; in February 1987, figures were published according to which the temperance campaign had not only increased productivity but also reduced mortality rates. Still, a "work harder/

drink less" campaign of exhortation is a weak substitute for *structural* measures, that can have a continuing effect by providing incentives for an improvement in worker productivity that does not fall off—as mere exhortation must. Instead of structural change, however, one more wave of bureaucratic reorganization has occurred, with a recasting of the agro-industrial supervisory system, the formation of new industrial bureaus, and more of the same. But the Soviet economy has been on a treadmill of reorganization for many years—under Brezhnev as well—without any perceptible beneficial effects in the long term.

For a regime that speaks so much of *perestroika* (restructuring), the absence of genuine structural reform has been quite remarkable. Gorbachev has been cited as having vehemently criticized *Gosplan*, the central-planning bureaucracy, which is the administrative instrument of state control over the economy; but he has not abolished *Gosplan*, as indeed he cannot until the only alternative, a market economy, is first put in its place. Hence Soviet factory administrators (they are not managers in any real sense) continue to receive minutely detailed *Gosplan* orders that specify what is to be produced at what numerical rate; they are not allowed to decide for themselves—and indeed they could not, given the absence of a responsive market whose prices would be the only valid indicators of what should be produced—of what quality, and in what volume.

To be sure, decrees have been published that widen the sphere of collective and even private enterprise. At first glance, they suggest that sweeping changes should result, but a more detailed scrutiny reveals that as much is being taken away as is being given.

In regard to private enterprise, for example, practices already very widespread have been legalized: State employees who used to perform auto repairs, construction work, tailoring, and other services illegally ("on the left" as the Russians say), and in their spare time, may now do so officially, so long as their state work is not slighted and they declare their private income and pay rather high taxes. Full-time private practice is still not allowed, however; nor is the employment of others. And in a fatal omission, no provision has been made for the legal purchase of the necessary tools and supplies by the newly legalized artisans. In the past, tools and supplies were obtained "on the left" also, directly or indirectly through the theft of state property, which was seemingly tolerated up to a point as a sort of fringe benefit. In the present much more regulated climate, illegal appropriations have been greatly restricted by all accounts; at the same time, there are still no Western-style hardware or "do-it-yourself" stores to provide what is needed legally. Similarly, in the latest decrees, Soviet collectives (i.e., cooperative enterprises) have even been authorized to transact business directly with foreign entities without having to go through the Ministry of Foreign Trade and the intermediate state-trading offices established in each sector. But the ruble remains nonconvertible, and no market has been established to apportion scarce hard currency by competitive ruble bidding. Hence, in practice, this aspect of the reform must remain a dead letter, except insofar as collectives choose to export directly, earning foreign currency that would presumably have to be remitted to the state bank for exchange at the inflated official rate, which should in turn make most exports unprofitable.

To be sure, external trade is only a minor factor for the Soviet economy in general and thus for most enterprises; thus the persistence of central planning is by far more important in nullifying the administrative reforms enacted so far. But the disjunction between the liberalization of external dealings and the failure to create a foreign-currency market that would make them profitable are characteristic of Gorbachev's innovations as a whole in addressing externalities rather than the substantive core of each question.

The explanation commonly offered is that substantive reform is blocked by an uncooperative bureaucracy, and there is undoubtedly some truth in that: Certainly a great many in the middle and higher layers of the state bureaucracy must resent the upheavals and mass firings of the new regime, which has explicitly repudiated "the stability of cadres" that Brezhnev has ensured and, of course, there are the usual factors of inertia and fear of the unknown at work. But there also exists a much greater obstacle to substantive economic reform that many commentators appear to overlook: The present system, though increasingly unsuccessful in ensuring meaningful growth in conditions of rapid technological change, has been successful indeed in guaranteeing Moscow's highly centralized political control over a vast land of very diverse population.

Whatever its defects as an economic instrument, the *Gosplan* has been effective as a political instrument in subjecting economic activity in every part of the Soviet Union to Moscow's detailed control: It largely preempts the nominal autonomy of the republics, and above all it enables the Communist party itself to function in its postrevolutionary *managerial* role. It is only because the party's cadres have detailed output targets to administer, rather than entrepreneurial tasks ill-suited to political operatives, that these cadres have been able to function in significant and materially rewarding roles as the managers of collective and state farms, industry large and small, wholesale and retail distribution entities, and infrastructural services. Insofar as illegal activities proliferated under the old regime, in reaction to the rigidities and errors of central planning, they did not erode the center's political control. On the contrary, they provided ample justification for periodic intervention in the affairs of republic-level party and government structures by the central authorities and for the reassertion of party discipline over the state apparatus in general.

If, however, Soviet economic life were to be genuinely liberalized, as the Chinese rural economy has been, the political consequences would presumably resemble those manifest in the Chinese countryside: With the transfer of managerial roles, prestige and material rewards would transfer from party cadres to entrepreneurs, the party itself would decline, having no clear role left to it other than (1) propaganda among an indifferent population and (2) the supervision of the *administrative* state bureaucracy at the local level—a most unrewarding task compared to the control of economic activities, with their ample opportunities for patronage and privilege.

In other words, an economic transformation such as the one Gorbachev shows every sign of desiring cannot proceed very far without a political transformation as well. This fact has undoubtedly been recognized in principle by Moscow's new ruler, as evidenced by his coupling of the political *glasnost* with the economic *perestroika*, along with the liberalizing signals emanating from the Kremlin, notably including the recall of Dr. Andrei D. Sakharov from exile, the release in early 1987 of several hundred of the best-known dissidents from the Gulag, and the relaxation of the censorship over long-suppressed books and films. As Soviet exiles remind us, however, unknown numbers of unadvertised dissidents continue to languish in jail, and the police system continues to repress as before. Nor has the relaxation of censorship extended beyond borderline cases of cultural, rather than political, expression.

There has been much debate about the real content of Gorbachev's liberalization and about its intended purpose; some commentators, of course, have suggested that it is nothing more than a propaganda exercise aimed at Western opinion. That is certainly true in regard to the sensitive emigration question, because new regulations presented as more permissive have turned out to be less so upon close examination. ("Family reunification," rather than freedom of movement, remains the only accepted criterion, and its scope has been drastically reduced by the redefinition of families to mean only nuclear families.) Nor has the advertised increase in the numbers of people allowed to leave taken place as of this writing. But with this exception, Gorbachev's liberalization measures are clearly aimed at impressing the domestic intelligentsia as much as foreign opinion, if not more so. The real question is not the "sincerity" of the Gorbachev liberalization, whether economic or political, but rather its objective scope and limits under the current political system of the Soviet Union.

In regard to the economy, the limit to the possible scope of liberalization is set by the degree to which the submersion of party cadres by a new elite of entrepreneurs is acceptable—and this, inevitably, is the very same limit that was decisive in halting the progress of Chinese reforms. Actually, that limit is much more restrictive in the Soviet case because in many parts of the Soviet Union, *Russian* party cadres would be displaced by non-Russian entrepreneurs.

In regard to Soviet politics, the limit to liberalization is set by the twin imperatives of dictatorship and centralization: Unless Gorbachev means to abandon the Leninist system and launch a democratic revolution (which no observer deems possible), he must inevitably continue to rely on a system of control ultimately based on police repression. Unless he means to surrender Russian primacy in the USSR and accept nationalist secessions from the empire (another impossibility), Gorbachev must continue to impose Moscow's control over all parts of the Soviet Union, including areas with large non-Russian populations.

It may be seen therefore that questions about Gorbachev's "sincerity" are beside the point. The scope for liberalization, economic as well as political, has final boundaries set by the fundamental nature of a nonelective, nonascriptive political system whose claim to legitimacy derives entirely from the authority claimed in turn by the Party, as keeper of a supposedly scientific and all-inclusive doctrine of governance. To the extent that entrepreneurs (even if party members)—rather than party officials *as such*—are allowed to make decisions, to the extent that individuals (even if party members) are allowed freedom of expression in any sphere according to their own individual preference as opposed to the collective will of the Party, the authority of the Party—the sole basis of the regime's legitimacy—must be diminished.

In Hungary, a large erosion of the party's authority and a very large reduction of the sphere of state control have been perfectly compatible with the stability of the regime, because Moscow's capacity for compulsion stands behind the Hungarian party leadership. But there is no greater power determined to protect the system behind the Kremlin leaders, and the compatibility of regime stability with the liberalization must therefore be much more narrow in their case. Just how much liberalization can be risked is no doubt the central issue of inner-party politics, and in this connection arises a subterranean but decisive debate, in which the Alma Ata riots of July 1986 may be cited as a warning. Now that the man at the top can no longer impose his will by administrative methods alone, as Stalin did, it is the gatherings of the higher cadres from time to time that will give subjective answers to key questions (which may differ from Gorbachev's view), just as in 1964 an inner-party consensus diverged from the liberalizing course that Khrushchev had set, leading to its interruption and substantial reversal, along with Khrushchev's removal. That precedent, incidentally, suggests that Gorbachev's security of tenure should not be taken for granted, especially because Gorbachev has made many promises that will be hard to keep (e.g., large pay raises for many classes of professionals) while plainly making life uncomfortable for many more party leaders than he can possibly remove.

The Prospects for Arms Control

A direct implication of the present conjunction of a weakened Reagan administration and a Soviet leadership that is perilously dynamic rather than securely inert is that the level of activity in arms control negotiations is greatly enhanced even as the chances of agreement are reduced. The former consequence reflects the added incentive for display on the world scene created by authority problems at home, and the latter, the difficulty of securing internal consensus on agreements in the state of weakness implied by those same problems.

The explicit obstacle to agreements on limits or reductions in nuclear weapons of intercontinental range—and, indeed, for a time, an obstacle to all agreements—has been the Soviet insistence on the precondition that U.S. efforts to develop strategic defenses based on advanced technologies be stopped, or at least confined to exploratory research. The determination with which this demand has been pressed by Moscow is certainly understandable, given the chronology of the last great technological competition in the strategic-nuclear realm over ballistic missiles as well as the uncannily parallel chronology of SDI competition:

- The Soviet Union started serious developmental work on land-based and submarine-launched ballistic missiles before the United States.
- The U.S. defense establishment, otherwise preoccupied bureaucratically, did not emulate the intensity of the Soviet effort until 1957 (i.e., after the spectacular demonstration of Soviet rocketry of the *Sputnik* launch).
- Within only five years, the United States had overtaken the Soviet effort in both land-based and submarine-launched ballistic missiles, gaining a sharp advantage that peaked by 1967 and was not wholly lost until the late 1970s. In other words, the Kremlin leaders had to operate in a state of inferiority in the important category of ballistic-missile weapons of intercontinental range for at least fifteen years, a leadership lifetime even for leaders of exceptionally long tenure.

Similarly:

- The Soviet Union's broad effort to develop ballistic missile defenses included serious developmental work on technologies utilizing "new physical principles" (e.g., directed energy) before the United States.
- The U.S. defense establishment, otherwise preoccupied bureaucratically, did not begin to respond until 1977, following a reappraisal of the potential of directed-energy weapons. (In that year, the decision was made to increase the funding of such programs by more than 300 percent.)
- Within five years, the United States had overtaken the Soviet effort and launched a large research program that appeared to be making considerable progress, thus presaging another long period of advantage for the United States in regard to these military capacities, if the competition continues to unfold.

As the disadvantaged competitor so far, the Soviet Union obviously considers it irrelevant whether SDI capabilities are worth having, whether they would be "cost-effective" or indeed effective at all, let alone desirable in the total strategic context. (Was the progression from manned bombers to intercontinental ballistic missiles [ICBMs] desirable for the United States?) Actually, if Soviet leaders believe their own insistent claims that U.S. SDI defenses could be neutralized by much cheaper countermeasures (as they could undoubtedly be circumvented by nonballistic forms of delivery, such as manned aircraft and cruise missiles), they should logically allow—even encourage—the U.S. SDI effort to proceed at full blast, given the resulting "opportunity benefit" to the Soviet Union in all other sectors of the overall military competition.

But these, of course, are not the terms of the question for Soviet leaders, who are certainly not agitated by the prospect that the United States would waste its resources on ineffectual SDI forces, and who are unlikely to fear preemption by a "first-strike" combined with SDI in this fourth decade of the nuclear era, when almost everyone has thoroughly come to understand the consequences of even a few small-scale nuclear detonations. Instead, it is in the political meaning of the matter that the most probable explanation of the intensity of the Soviet attitude must be found: Having so recently overcome a long-lasting disadvantage in ballistic-missile weapons of intercontinental range and continuing to face inferiority in manned bombers, Soviet leaders now face the possibility of another lifetime of disadvantage in SDI-type capabilities—and that is something that they are clearly eager to avoid.

As it is, the publicity that has attended the U.S. SDI program has already deprived the Soviet Union of the political benefits that it briefly obtained from the belated but impressive results of its costly, heavy ICBM programs. Until SDI came along, the weightiest term in the vocabulary of strategic power was the SS-18, now almost forgotten even though its physical capabilities are greater than ever, along with those of other, more recent ICBMs. The political costs already imposed and the much broader costs that the U.S. SDI programs could impose (notably including the diversion of particularly scarce Soviet high-technology resources from economic to military modernization) are surely of greater moment in Soviet eyes than the putative instabilities of a strategic regime that includes novel forms of ballistic-missile interception.

Such considerations do not, of course, constitute compelling arguments for the allocation of U.S. resources to SDI efforts, let alone the vast resources that a full-scale deployment would require. Among other things, there is the fact (not perhaps intuitively obvious) that high-confidence defenses against cruise missiles and low-altitude bombers would be almost as demanding as those now projected against ballistic missiles: The high-contrast parabolic trajectories of long-range ballistic missiles in nonreflective space are inherently much easier to acquire and track than the paths of aircraft flying within reflected terrain or ocean clutter. In other words, it is quite wrong to imagine that strategic ballistic missile defenses could be converted into strategic defenses *tout court* through a marginal supplementary effort; the dimensions of the combined effort are likely to be considerably greater than any chosen estimate for an SDI defense alone. (That much is suggested by the huge capital costs—in excess of $100 billion—of Soviet strategic air defenses, which are nevertheless deemed insufficient to intercept more than a modest proportion of U.S. bombers.)

Regardless of whether the prospective devaluation of Soviet ballistic-missile forces of intercontinental range justifies a full-scale SDI deployment that has many other implications as well, or even the current SDI research and development expenditures by the United States, it is almost certain that the Soviet leaders will continue to insist on SDI prohibitions as the pre-condition for agreed reductions in the existing nuclear forces of intercontinental range. Equally, it is improbable that the pre-condition will be acceptable to the Reagan administration or that congressional restrictions on SDI will suffice to render the issue moot. Hence, at this writing, any substantive U.S.-Soviet accord on nuclear weapons of intercontinental range seems unlikely, notwithstanding the procedural progress reported from time to time in the Geneva talks. (Projections of U.S. and Soviet nuclear forces are included in the discussion of the East-West military balance in Chapter 2, by James J. Townsend.)

That, of course, does not rule out limitations or reductions in other categories of nuclear weapons, notably including those of intermediate range, the so-called INF weapons. Soviet leaders had indicated a willingness to conclude a separate agreement on INF weapons during much of 1986, until the Reykjavik summit; by the spring of 1987, they had again decided that a relaxation of the SDI pre-condition was justified by broader political considerations—in particular, Moscow's attempt to revive a full-blown détente with Western Europe in order to obtain a much-needed infusion of capital and technology. Certainly such a policy stance is more likely to achieve that medium-term goal than the opposite course briefly pursued, whereby INF limits were mortgaged to SDI prohibitions to intensify Euro-U.S. tensions for the sake of the long-term goal of fragmenting the North Atlantic alliance. If nothing else, the political transformation of Western Europe caused by the drastic decline of the Communist parties of France, Italy, Spain, and Portugal and by the persistence of conservative majorities in Britain and West Germany, has greatly weakened Moscow's political influence in Europe—even though the Atlantic alliance is as troubled as it has ever been by fresh doubts about the competence of U.S. leaders, the persistent eccentricity of U.S. views on terrorism and the means to oppose it, and chronic trade disputes. (See Chapter 6, by Allan Platt, on the current problems in U.S. relations with the nations of southern Europe.) In any event, in August 1987 an INF agreement appeared almost certain before the end of Reagan's term.

Regional Questions

This book contains separate reviews of major issues and events in Southern Africa (Chapter 5 by Michael W. Clough), Central and South America (Chapter 7 by Sally Shelton-Colby), and South Asia (Chapter 8 by Stephen P. Cohen). What follows is devoted to some salient Middle East and East Asian questions.

The Middle East

The Middle East certainly presents a dramatic contrast to the substantial, if uneven, progress of the European economies, the recovery of European self-confidence since the nadir of the oil-price crisis, and the continued, if very slow, consolidation of the European Community. Inter-Arab rivalries are as deep as they have ever been, the Iran-Iraq War persists most destructively, and there has been no real progress in either extending the scope of the Israeli-Egyptian accords or bringing other Arab participants into the peace process.

With oil prices showing no signs of reverting to their pre-glut levels even in current dollars, let alone on the basis of an import-weighted basket of currencies (in which the yen looms large), Arab economies are stagnant at best—a condition fairly comfortable in the thinly populated United Arab Emirates; much less so in Saudi Arabia, where foreign-currency reserves continue to decline; and very negative for the indirect beneficiaries of the oil boom, notably Egypt, Jordan, and Syria, where remittance and subsidy income has drastically declined.

The potential for political instability is compounded by the wholesale repatriation from the oil-producing states of immigrant Arab (as well as non-Arab) workers, who have returned to Egypt and Jordan with disappointed expectations and often with acute resentment against the capitalist-traditionalists (and U.S.-aligned) oil-country elites, to find their own economies in distress. Egypt faces an especially acute hard-currency shortage, caused by the unhappy conjunction of the loss of remittances, the decline in its own oil revenues, and reduced Suez Canal tanker tolls. Given the condition of the U.S. external balance, no corresponding increase in U.S. economic aid is feasible, and both Germany and Japan have ignored U.S. hints that they should step into the breach by providing the needed help. Syria is not the beneficiary of U.S. solicitude, but its economic distress is just as acute and much less likely to be assuaged: The Soviet Union is in no position to provide the hard-currency relief that the country urgently needs.

Lebanon's continuing tragedy is of diminishing impact on the international scene, and each rendition of its repetitive hostage drama arouses less attention than its predecessor. Likewise, notwithstanding recurrent, if small-scale, turmoil in the West Bank and Gaza, that inner core of Arab-Israeli strife is of diminishing international significance as the power of the Palestine Liberation Organization (PLO) continues to decline. But the Iran-Iraq War continues to exact a high cost for the international economy by precluding a possible 10 million barrels a day of oil output; it continues to be locally destructive on a much larger scale than any previous warfare in the region; and it continues to generate acute anxiety throughout the world as well as in the adjacent countries.

The Iran-Iraq War. Iraq's ability to withstand Iranian attacks is in doubt each time news comes out of a renewed Iranian offensive, and the mere continuation of the fighting automatically implies the possibility of an Iranian victory—because Iraq has been unable to contest the initiative on the ground, which remains wholly with Iran. For a time during 1985–1986, Iraq appeared to have found a war-winning remedy in the aerial attack of Iran's oil-loading facilities, which promised to extinguish Iran's war-making capacity at its financial source.

There was a sudden and yet to be explained surge in the precision and determination of air attacks by Iraqi-marked aircraft against the Kharg Island terminal complex in August 1985 (ineffectually attacked so often before by pilots who hurriedly scattered their ordnance); shortly afterward, there was a long-range strike of similar precision against the remedial transshipment facilities that the Iranians had quickly improvised at the head of the gulf, beyond the maximum range of Iraqi air power in the absence of a refueling stop in Saudi Arabia or the Emirates. Iran's oil income declined abruptly to very little, and for a while its warmaking capacity was sustained only by the drawing down of foreign-exchange reserves. But Iraqi air power reverted to its normal level of competence, and the Iranians were able to reconstitute their export capacity. As of this writing, Iran is lifting some 2 million barrels a day, thereby earning enough foreign exchange to sustain the war at its normal level of hard-currency expenditure.

Moreover, having abandoned at least temporarily its attempt to circumvent frontal warfare on the ground, Iraq has been using its air power most to bomb urban areas—a practice that has no material impact on Iran's war-making capacity and whose psychological effect may well stimulate continued popular support for the war.

With Iran periodically attacking on a large scale while Iraq is content to parry the blows, some of Iran's attacks inevitably succeed at the tactical level. Sooner or later a blow is likely to succeed at the operational level as well, thus yielding victory and a breakthrough in one sector of the front. But unless that breakthrough were to engulf the Baghdad region, the one vital center of Iraqi resistance, even an operational-level victory need have no decisive result at the strategic level. If, for example, Basra were to fall to the Iranians, Iraq's war fighting capacity would not be *materially* reduced. Although it is the country's second-largest city, it is neither a significant producer of war materials nor an entry point for their importation from abroad. (Because of Iran's effective blockade, Iraq's supplies come overland through Jordan and Turkey, and Iraq's premier port is no longer Basra but rather Jordan's Aqaba[1] on the Red Sea.) It has been suggested that the fall of Basra may result in a collapse of morale in army and country or in the fragmentation of the regime's hitherto formidable stability under Saddam Hussein's dictatorial grip. But such a psychological collapse is more likely at the early stage of a war and not after six years of psychological conditioning under its harsh discipline; certainly there would be no sudden shock because Basra has been threatened for years.

Every war eventually consumes the human and material means needed for its continuation, finally bringing about an end to active hostilities, even if that end is not first achieved by diplomacy. This process, however, has not progressed very far in the Iran-Iraq case. Iran's casualties have been high, but not high enough to reduce the number of troops it can field; Iraq's casualties, much fewer but exacted from a much smaller population, have similarly not resulted in a decline in troop levels. And in spite of declining oil revenues, there is no sign that the Saudi, Kuwaiti, and Gulf subsidies that allow Iraq to continue fighting will fall below the required level. Iraq is fighting a capital-intensive, high-cost war, with a huge consumption of ammunition and extensively mechanized forces that require constant expenditures for spare parts and replacement equipment; even so, Iraqi war costs at approximately $1 billion per month or so do not exceed the inflow of oil revenues and subsidies.

Hence, despite greater international concern of late, the most plausible estimate is that the war will continue unless either the Iraqi or Iranian leadership changes: The fall of Saddam Hussein would certainly open the way for negotiations, whereas the death of the Ayatollah Khomeini might simply lead to a one-sided suspension of further offensives, if not to the opening of peace talks.

East Asia

The East Asian scene is now dominated by the domestic travails that variously affect China, South Korea, and the Philippines. In each case, the determining factors are internal; although the international context is important, it is not the dynamic factor in the situation.

China's Latest Political Reversal. In China, the process of liberalization has come to an end. It may resume, of course, but having for the nth time repudiated its own course and attacked the very forces it had previously stimulated into action (i.e., independent entrepreneurs, the educated classes, innovative economic managers, and outspoken voices in the press), the Beijing party leadership can hardly expect a prompt renewal of cooperation and activity.

On the contrary, because of the long history of previous reversals and the harsh and protracted persecutions that they engendered, the consequences of what may remain a limited interruption and marginal reversion of the process of liberalization may nevertheless be catastrophic for China's modernization. Those who believed the leadership once again on this last go-around, consciously accepting the risk of subsequent attack as "capitalist roaders" and "agents of bourgeois infiltration," now live in fear even if they are not actually persecuted. If given the chance again they are likely to steer clear of renewed exposure.

For such elements—the very people on whom the hopes of modernization must rest—the lesson of the 1986 convulsion is that the Chinese Communist party will not in fact allow a progressive liberalization and that the only safe course is to remain as passive as possible within roles ideologically approved even by the most conservative interpretation. That option, of course, is not compatible with the needs of Chinese economic modernization; other side-effects include the reduced probability that Chinese students expensively educated overseas will return, a loss of confidence in Hong Kong that will diminish the capital and skills eventually destined to remain for China's disposition in 1997, and the collapse of Beijing's effort to persuade Taiwan of the sincerity and durability of its promises of liberality and autonomy.

No doubt all these are tolerable costs for party cadres who witnessed the astonishingly rapid collapse of party authority—and their own prestige—in the more liberalized rural regions, and who had every reason to anticipate an extension of the process to the urban areas and industry as well, if the liberalization had continued. After all, they had the example of the areas nearest to Hong Kong before them, where not only the state but also the party had fulfilled the Marxist promise by withering away. Disregarded, impoverished, and increasingly powerless, the local cadres were classic exemplars of a displaced ruling class. Their counterparts elsewhere in China obviously mean to preserve their privileged positions, even at the cost of China's modernization. The lesson for what may await in Gorbachev's Soviet Union need not be belabored.

Political Stability in Korea and the Philippines. In South Korea, as in the Philippines, processes of democratization not as different as they might seem superficially are progressing by fits and starts under drastically different economic conditions, with high growth and rising prosperity in Korea as opposed to the indebtedness and stagnation in the Philippines. For all the attention it receives, the communist insurgency of the Philippines remains localized in very few parts of the country; the major phenomenon is the restructuring of a new political community based on national parties rather than on congeries of local power holders that combine the roles of quasi-feudal chieftains, gang leaders, and entrepreneurs. An irresponsible press, a personalized tradition, the admixture of cultism with political participation, and, above all, a weak economy are greatly complicating the process, in which the destructive role of communist guerrillas remains marginal and would be even more so were it not for the lack of discipline and competence in the armed forces. The level and direction of U.S. and other aid flows remain of critical importance.

Likewise, the much-advertised acts of police repression in South Korea are only marginal episodes because they are taking place in the context of a progressive democratization of the political system, which they do as much to accelerate (when police excess results in a backlash) as to retard. Opposition leaders once exiled or banned from all political activity are now running increasingly well-organized parties that can recruit cadres in substantial numbers from the ranks of a large and growing middle class and that obtain funding from the many business people who support political change. In recent demonstrations, a key bottleneck for opposition organizers was the shortage of parking space not only in downtown Seoul but also in provincial capitals such as Kwanju; and, indeed, car-bound motorists played a role in the proceedings. It is true that a definite radicalization has taken place among university students, but the political allegiances thus formed are generational and ephemeral for each successive age cohort, resembling student activism in Japan.

Above all, the boundaries of the political quarrel between government and opposition are shrinking relentlessly with the progression of the calendar: It seems more and more evident that there will be no repudiation of President Chun's promise to resign for good at the end of his term in 1988, and the likelihood of genuinely free elections is presaged by the lack of effective governmental interference with the progress of party organization, the spread of branches throughout the country, and the development of intraparty communications.

Japan's Disguised Economic Crisis. There is no political turmoil in Japan, but notwithstanding the boom in all aspects of the financial superstructure, the Japanese economy has reached a critical turning point. In the more traditional and heavy industries there is an outright crisis: Shipping, shipbuilding, and, therefore, steel as well as the associated ancillary industries are in sharp decline, with major bankruptcies, accumulating indebtedness, and rising unemployment in cities such as Kitakyushu and Nagasaki. The more recently developed, and indeed hyper-developed, export-oriented automobile and consumer-electronic industries are either losing their market shares or sacrificing profit, or moving production overseas as the yen (150 yen per dollar) makes profitable domestic production impossible in most cases. Smaller firms manufacturing components, as well as those that produce more traditional products (textiles, porcelain, etc.), can neither afford continuing losses nor move production overseas, and bankruptcies among them are sharply increasing.

Thus the highly efficient industrial base that subsidized Japan's highly inefficient agriculture—as well as the state-owned railways and other state services of unequaled quality and correspondingly high cost—is now eroding rapidly. Because this situation follows upon the climax of the same export boom that brought about the drastic currency realignment, while prices have been falling for Japanese raw material imports, and because saving propensities have been very high, while the subsidization of agriculture and market patterns have indirectly increased land values to astronomic levels, Japan's industrial crisis has begun with huge foreign-exchange reserves, equally huge accumulated personal and pension-fund savings, and a society replete with nominal real-estate fortunes.

For the time being, this situation is resulting in a great outflow of capital overseas, chiefly to the United States. The question for the Japanese is whether to invest in transferred production facilities or simply to purchase real estate or financial instruments. But not all Japanese can become rentiers or managers of Japanese-owned factories and banks overseas. There is the definite prospect of rising unemployment for industrial workers in the many smaller firms that do not guarantee lifetime employment, as well as for those now working in state services that are to be denationalized and in the associated service sectors. In that context, continued tolerance for Japan's uniquely high agricultural price structure is bound to diminish: Astronomic food prices will no longer be willingly paid by workers laid off or reemployed in lower-paying service jobs.

For the ruling Liberal Democratic party (LDP), a dangerous conflict of interests has thus been created between equally indispensable farm and urban electorates—hence the powerful incentive to find a new basis for Japan's international economic policy. A revolution in public finance to generate very large public investment in infrastructures and an equally revolutionary restriction of agricultural subsidies to free suburban land for much-needed housing (so as to expand the construction sector) could alleviate the situation, but even so, only a reversion to a "realistic exchange rate" in terms of comparative prices could avert the accelerating decline of Japan's export-based industrial economy. But that is impossible so long as the nontariff blockade against foreign imports continues undiminished. Otherwise it would merely trigger a long-accumulated protectionist reaction in the United States, Western Europe, and elsewhere. Now that sectoral analyses of the distribution system for goods as varied as cigarettes and petrochemicals have finally and belatedly dispelled the illusion that Japanese markets are accessible, except in carefully delimited or even purposefully chosen instances (BMW automobiles, high-priced French fashions, etc.), a decline of the yen would unleash a protectionist counterblockade that was averted in the past only by a network of unfulfilled promises, expensive lobbying, and Japanese reliance on the short span of attention—and outright deception—of successive U.S. administrations and European governments. The claim, for example, that Western salesmanship has been monolingual and lacking in energy (an explanation frequently echoed by Japan's lobbyists) has now been exploded by belated comparisons with Korean and Taiwanese export efforts. Both countries have been just as unsuccessful in exporting to Japan, in spite of the fluency in Japanese, the notorious dynamism of their salesmen, and the low prices; indeed, Korean and Taiwanese consumer goods can be found in shops all over the world, except in nearby Japan.

Having failed to persuade the bureaucracy to restrict the import blockade sufficiently to prevent the drastic revaluation of the yen, and being unwilling to attack agricultural protectionism (the great bastion of their political support) and too timid even to contemplate the redirection of economic activity to meet housing needs, acute as they are, Japan's feeble LDP leaders (only nominally equivalent to their foreign counterparts, as the spectacle of ministers routinely overruled by the bureaucracy clearly shows) have thus far exercised no more real control over Japan's internationally disruptive export industries than their prewar predecessors exercised over Japan's internationally disruptive military bureaucracies. Unless they can now take the initiative, Japan's economy and, therefore, society will slide leaderless into a deep and uncharted crisis, a crisis already presaged by rising unemployment figures in a setting where unemployment is the cause of the deepest possible anguish.

Envoi

The dominant contemporary phenomenon on the world scene is the acute contrast between the diminution of political leadership in most of the major countries and the tidal force of economic, technological, and cultural trends in what is increasingly a global society. Only the least informed continue to believe in the essential competence of government to confront problems that are only rarely encompassed by the limits of their jurisdiction, and that greatly exceed the limits of their powers and expertise. And only the most feckless continue to trust in holistic philosophies of governance. The collapse of faith in collectivistic systems has now extended to most parts of the world, with the symptomatic exceptions of Cuba, Ethiopia, and Nicaragua, where the repressive by-products of collectivism are more seriously desired by the respective regimes than any illusory societal benefits. But in the noncollectivistic world, the confusion is no less even if liberties are not thereby sacrificed: The attempt to continue to regulate in detail causes the diverse dysfunctions lately manifest in Japan, whereas wholesale deregulation causes the profoundly destructive diversion of capital and human skills to unproductive financial manipulations, as in the United States and Britain.

As for the true scope of the international influence of the Soviet Union and the United States, ever more dubiously called "superpowers," this is best revealed by their signal inability to impose even a temporary cease-fire in the Iran-Iraq War, which they both deplore, albeit for opposite reasons—a failure that stands in sharp contrast to the decisive interruptions they successively imposed on Arab-Israeli and other wars in previous decades.

2
The East-West Military Balance

James J. Townsend

The year 1986 was marked by continuity in U.S. and Soviet conventional defense programs and by growing uncertainty over the future of the strategic balance. According to many observers, the same year marked the end of the SALT era in nuclear arms control, with both sides breaking, or on the verge of breaking, the limits set down in 1972 and 1979. Agreement on intermediate nuclear forces in Europe, elusive throughout 1986, seemed possible in 1987, and prospects for a strategic arms treaty were virtually nil. The Strategic Defense Initiative (SDI) had shifted the focus of U.S. strategy away from preserving the traditional deterrent framework, casting a long shadow over U.S. strategic forces, arms control, and even conventional military programs.

The fat years for U.S. defense spending came to an abrupt halt, with zero real growth the optimistic prediction for the balance of the 1980s. According to Senate Armed Services Committee Chairman Sam Nunn, zero real growth in the Defense Department's fiscal year (FY) 1988 budget was the "best case," and a 1 percent increase above inflation would be "almost miraculous."[1] House Armed Services Committee Chairman Les Aspin echoed the same sentiments, saying that for the defense budgets of the rest of the decade, "The only question is whether they will be zero or zero-plus-inflation." The result will be cancellation or delays in a number of major weapons programs. Scaling down its expectations, the Reagan administration in January 1987 sought only a 3 percent real increase in defense spending for FY 1988, but even that modest increase was not to be attained.

Defense spending increases in Western Europe have also become unlikely. The United Kingdom, for example, is planning only 1.6 percent growth in 1987–1988 and 0.9 percent in 1988–1989, meaning there will be reductions in Britain's real defense spending when inflation is taken into account. With the sole exception of Norway, every NATO nation will surely miss the alliance's goal of 3 percent annual real growth in defense expenditures, and the extra 4 percent deemed necessary for high-technology conventional weapons improvements will certainly not be forthcoming. This record is worse than that of 1985, when only six of the sixteen NATO nations met the 3 percent goal.

In the Warsaw Pact countries, meanwhile, Soviet General Secretary Mikhail Gorbachev has increasingly made his presence and personality felt, but without revealing his own agenda for Soviet and Pact military policy. There has been no evidence of shifts in military spending patterns since the Gorbachev accession. The 27th Party Congress of the Communist party of the Soviet Union in February and March 1986 announced neither reorganization of the armed forces nor doctrinal innovations. Gorbachev's speeches have exhorted greater productivity and raised expectations for economic growth and technological modernization, but so far without the necessary concrete steps to back them up. The general secretary has proven to be a master in the theater of arms control, seizing the initiative on more than one occasion and putting the Reagan administration on the defensive. The disarmament drama reached its denouement in the October summit in Reykjavik, Iceland when Reagan and Gorbachev tried to outdo one another with arms reduction schemes and later blamed one another for the resulting—and inevitable—failure of the summit process.

The following sections outline the principal measures of the East-West military balance, with particular emphasis on developments in 1986. Appearing first is an introduction on measuring the military balance, with caveats about the yardsticks usually relied upon in net assessment. Nuclear and conventional forces are examined separately, followed by a section on Soviet military research and development.

How to Measure the Military Balance

Numbers are just starting points for serious analyses of the military balance, and not all numbers are equally valuable. Military budgets by themselves are poor indicators of the balance because although they measure the resources devoted to military capabilities, they provide no assessment of how well, or for what purpose, those resources are utilized. A nation can convert its resources—by varying degrees of efficiency—into military power. Spending does not necessarily produce results, as a comparison of Soviet and U.S. investment in agriculture illustrates. Nor does excessive spending guarantee that appropriate forces will be built for the contingencies that will be faced. It has been argued, for example, that the centrality of NATO requirements leads not only to U.S. weapons and forces less suitable for interventions elsewhere but to more expensive forces as well.

There is a great distance between resource inputs and battle outcomes. Nonetheless, estimates of Soviet defense spending are often used to justify Western military budgets, although these inputs provide at best an indirect measure of military power and, indeed, may even mislead analysts seeking to assess relative capabilities. Even less useful for estimating the balance are comparisons of the relative Eastern and Western defense burdens—the percentages of total resources devoted to military purposes.

The art of measuring the balance of power is called "net assessment." It should encompass not only military but political, economic, and social factors as well. And, net assessments must follow the three unities of time, space, and action.

Net assessment requires the skills of a novelist as much as those of an accountant. Indeed, contemporary novels have contained the most widely read net assessments, from General Sir John Hackett's *The Third World War: August 1985* to Tom Clancy's *Red Storm Rising*. These are hardly dispassionate academic studies. Rather, they are thoughtful and provocative case studies. Hackett's book contained warnings about the thin Western margin of security in order to persuade readers of the need for increased NATO defense spending. Clancy's novel promoted high-tech electronic warfare.

The need for objective net assessments is great. Analyses of the military balance—whether well or poorly executed—are not only critical to decisionmaking on military program details; they also filter into the mindsets of policymakers, influencing their thoughts and actions on a wide range of foreign-policy issues. As the United States witnessed in the late 1970s, net assessments can influence popular perceptions as well, thus decisively affecting national politics. Changes in net assessments also affect perceptions in other countries. Leaders in those countries understand—perhaps more acutely than their superpower counterparts—shifts in the balance of power. Such key regional powers as India and China often play the great powers against one another. Erstwhile client states in Africa, Asia, and Latin America also concern themselves with the regional implications of the East-West balance.

The most logical place in the U.S. government to look for data on the military balance is in the intelligence community, particularly the Central Intelligence Agency (CIA) and the Defense Intelligence Agency (DIA). Both agencies provide analyses of foreign military developments to U.S. government officials. In regard to net assessments, however, the intelligence community operates at a disadvantage. Analysts who specialize in the study of Soviet or Warsaw Pact armed forces do not necessarily follow the trends in U.S. forces. There are few specialists with expertise in both the "blue" and the "red" sides of the equation.

The compartmentalization of classified military information necessary for security also exacts a price in denying any single analyst a comparative perspective of military developments. Only limited attention is paid to net assessment by U.S. intelligence agencies. The result of that limited attention is the focus of the annual publication, *Soviet Military Power*, prepared by the DIA. This document eschews overall force comparisons and limits comparisons to individual U.S. and Soviet weapon systems.

Moreover, the accuracy of publicly available information on weapons in both the East and the West should no longer be taken for granted. After flirting with the idea of an extensive disinformation program in 1986, the U.S. Defense Department and CIA determined that the costs of a disinformation effort would outweigh its benefits. In an ominous footnote to this decision, however, the Department of Defense (DoD) has stated that it will retain its policy of providing disinformation on specific military programs and activities, particularly on strategic defenses and weapons development programs. The goal of such deception of the Western media would be to mislead the Soviet Union on the likely performance of U.S. weapon systems.[2]

There is more than one military balance to be examined in comparing Eastern and Western military alliances. There are regional balances (e.g., the NATO-Warsaw Pact balance in Europe), the naval balance, the balance of strategic capabilities, and others. In peacetime, deterrence requires adequate forces to convince an adversary that the risks of engaging in conflict outweigh the likely benefits. In military terms, creating this perception is inherently an easier task than actually building the forces needed to prevail in a conflict. Politically, however, maintaining such a deterrent is difficult, particularly for democracies where a consensus on defense issues must be sustained and where constituencies typically do not wish to contemplate the possibility of war. The NATO deployment of Pershing II and cruise missiles is a typical case, in that tremendous amounts of political capital had to be expended before the alliance could deploy a very modest number of weapons. Once a conflict in which national values are threatened begins, however, political consensus usually ceases to be a problem, even in democracies otherwise ambivalent about external threats.

Balances can be further divided into categories of short-term and long-term assessment. The military balance usually changes only slowly. Resources devoted to defense change only gradually within a given period of time; planning horizons are five—or more—years long. Although technological innovation can lead to revolutionary changes, this does not often occur. Prophecies of technological "revolutions" in warfare have not been borne out by combat experience. New doctrines are seldom promulgated for weapons that do not yet exist (with the notable exception of the freshly minted doctrine of "assured survival" based on the assumed existence of space-based strategic defenses). Similarly, weapons are not developed until a requirement has been identified. Instead, scientific research and doctrinal thought tend to evolve side by side until new weapons can be fitted into in a convincing framework. This has been the case with the U.S. Army AirLand Battle concept, for example, and the related NATO Follow-On Forces Attack concept. Both these doctrines were made possible by the development of improved sensing capabilities and guided munitions, which are able to strike Warsaw Pact targets before they could reach the immediate battle zone.

The military balance also changes slowly because new weapons require lead times of ten to fifteen years from conception to deployment. If a weapon does not exist on paper today, chances are it would not be deployed in significant numbers in the year 2000. Indeed, most of the U.S. force structure for the next century already rolls, flies, or floats today.

For the short term, it is pointless to count that which is not ready for action. The quality of existing troops and their numbers, equipment, training, and readiness are the determinants of combat effectiveness in the short term. Over the long term, however, the development and procurement of new equipment can become more important than the readiness of existing forces, as the money devoted to training, manpower, and operations must be spent again each year. Because manpower is less expensive in the Soviet Union and Eastern Europe than in the West, and because exercises and training are less frequent and intense, the East is able to maintain larger forces; in addition, a greater proportion of defense spending is devoted to procurement than in the West, thus creating a stock of equipment that grows each year.

The values of U.S. and Soviet defense investment are shown in Figure 2.1. The defense spending increases of the early 1980s have closed the gap in investment that had opened in the 1970s. A steady increase in Soviet spending on military research and development, growing at roughly 4 percent per year, has accompanied these investment trends over the past ten years. The goal of increased research and development (R&D) spending is to provide greater technological options to Soviet military decisionmakers.

When the other Western allies are taken into account, the picture is less bleak. According to U.S. intelligence estimates, although the Soviet Union spends more on defense than the United States, NATO has consistently outspent the Warsaw Pact. The Warsaw Pact makes a relatively small contribution to Soviet science, research, and development, whereas Canada, Western Europe, and Japan are responsible for technological innovation and cooperative production arrangements.

FIGURE 2.1. A Comparison of U.S. Defense Investment Outlays with Estimated Dollar Cost of USSR Defense Investment, 1965–1985

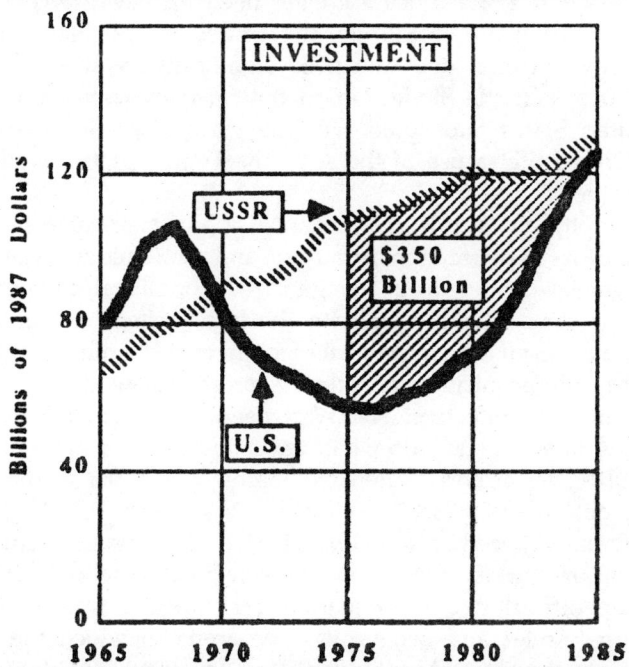

Source: Under Secretary of Defense, Research, and Engineering, *The FY 1987 Department of Defense Program for Research and Development* (Washington: Department of Defense, 1986), p. II-3.

The Fallacy of Symmetry

A common misconception about the military balance is the idea that equal forces on each side create a "balance"—that is, a military stalemate. The most exalted manifestation of this fallacy is in the area of nuclear arms control. Here, equal quantitative limits on weapons are enshrined, due to the belief that those limits can produce equal security or stability. The real balance, however, results not from side-by-side or even force-against-force comparisons, rather it results from the comparison of the capabilities of a force to the demands of a mission it must fulfill. Estimates of military power are sterile without consideration of the use to which forces are to be put.

Quite dissimilar forces can yield a stable military balance. One can argue that U.S. nuclear superiority in the 1950s (even in the face of Soviet conventional superiority in Europe) produced such a balance, deterring Soviet aggression in Europe. On the other hand, equal forces can result in a dangerous disequilibrium. For example, owing to geography, the United States has a greater need for naval forces than the Soviet Union. To reinforce Europe, the United States relies on sealifts while the Soviet Union does not need significant naval forces to fight a war in Europe. If the Soviet Union built a navy comparable to that of the United States and could win the war at sea—or even simply deny the United States use of the sea—the United States would lose a war in Europe.[3]

As geography confounds the elegance of symmetrical comparisons, so do inequalities in population, resources, and economic systems. Equally important, the two sides do not wage their geopolitical competition by means of the same rulebook or with the same criteria of success.

Taken to its logical extreme, a goal of symmetry in military capabilities could lead to the acquisition of military forces that would be useless—or at least not cost effective. The West need not match the number of Soviet tanks; rather, it must do whatever is necessary to deter or prevent a successful Soviet armored offensive against a member of the Western alliance, if deterrence fails.

Net assessment based only on quantitative measures inherently favors attrition warfare, measuring off weapon against weapon as it does. It is much more difficult to derive equations for maneuver warfare, factoring in operational styles and geography. The arena in which the attrition model remains the most plausible is that of the strategic balance, where such measures as probabilities of warheads arriving on target can be readily calculated and the number and location of key targets is known in advance. Recent changes in strategic warfare, especially the advent of mobile missiles, bring even this application of attrition theory into question. For conventional warfare, this simple attrition paradigm is woefully inadequate. Comparisons of arsenals at the theater level offer little to help predict the outcome of an event such as a battle. Moreover, force levels considered outside their operational and tactical frameworks are almost meaningless.

The Intellectual Fallacy

Analyzing the military balance casts military programs into a framework that is much more intellectual in nature than the dynamics of the processes that actually create military programs and policies. Bureaucratic interests and politics, which contribute nothing to the combat effectiveness of forces, are a significant—sometimes dominant—factor in military policy. Estimates of the prospective military balance tend to underestimate the role of inertia, arguably the most potent force in all human undertakings. Also lacking is the "friction" of the battlefield—a term coined by Karl von Clausewitz, and a factor that tends to make even simple tasks difficult. On the twentieth-century electronic battlefield, given the firepower and other capabilities available to both sides, this friction no doubt would be greater than even Clausewitz could imagine.

In cases where there is a near match between two sides in quantitative terms, the outcome of conflict is unpredictable: The uncertainties previously described would overwhelm any differences discerned. Moreover, there are thresholds below which net assessments are not useful, particularly at the lower end of the conflict spectrum. Only when one side enjoys a large material preponderance can the outcome of conflict be predicted from the static balance. Yet even here prediction is questionable, as the wars in the Middle East and the Falklands attest.

Nuclear Forces

Nuclear weapons have become the icons of military power in the twentieth century. Their advent has made the East-West military balance a concern not only for its protagonists but also for the entire world. The balance of strategic capabilities of the superpowers spills over into international relations more generally as well. Since World War II, the United States and its European allies have depended on nuclear weapons to deter an attack from the Soviet Union. The relatively cheap cost of nuclear weapons, as compared to conventional forces, allowed Western Europe to spend more on economic development in the 1940s and 1950s, without jeopardizing its security. Even after the USSR acquired its own nuclear capability, the lure of relying on nuclear weapons remained irresistible. Despite recurrent expressions of public concern, this dependence on nuclear weapons has not ended; indeed, it shows little prospect of being replaced by a new security arrangement in the near future. The credibility of NATO's deterrent, however, has been progressively undermined by the growth of Soviet nuclear forces.

Throughout the nuclear era, the technologies of offensive nuclear capabilities have outraced efforts to develop defenses against them. Both the United States and the Soviet Union deployed defenses against bombers in the 1950s and early 1960s, but the United States dismantled most of its system when the Soviet Union's bomber force was eclipsed by Soviet ICBMs against which defenses seemed ineffective. The USSR continues to deploy a very very large air defense system, but U.S. officials are confident that American bombers would be able to penetrate that system with relative impunity. In recent years, of course, the possibility of effective missile defenses has again been raised, and both nations are pursuing major research programs to explore these possibilities—programs that now dominate arms control negotiations and that may drastically alter the basis of both the planning for and the prevention of nuclear war. In this section, developments in superpower offensive capabilities (as well as those in third countries) during the past year will be reviewed. Also included will be a summary of the superpowers' efforts to develop defenses against nuclear weapons.

Offensive Capabilities

Overall, current trends in strategic, theater, and tactical nuclear weapons favor the East. The problem for the West has not been a lack of resources, technology, or even political will. Rather, the failure has occurred on a political level: The Western consensus on nuclear weapons has virtually disappeared. The very existence of these weapons has been repeatedly challenged on moral grounds. Major political parties in the United Kingdom, the Federal Republic of Germany, and other countries have renounced the existing NATO nuclear doctrine and urged the dismantling of nuclear forces. A similar attack on nuclear deterrence has come from proponents of strategic defenses, whose technological exuberance supports the belief that current nuclear forces will soon be obsolete.

The United States

The United States maintains a balanced triad of nuclear delivery systems—land-based missiles, submarine-launched missiles, and bombers (see Figure 2.2). Nuclear weapons can serve several purposes, from conveying national prestige to the accomplishment of military missions in a conflict should deterrence fail. U.S. military objectives for nuclear forces include:

- deterrence of nuclear attack on the United States;
- deterrence of nuclear or conventional attack on U.S. allies; and
- maintenance of a capability for the prosecution of limited and flexible military operations for strategic purposes.[4]

The first objective is the least demanding. Most observers believe that maintaining a nuclear capability that would survive a Soviet attack and destroy Soviet population centers and industry in retaliation is sufficient to deter a Soviet attack. If this assessment is accurate, very few weapons would be needed to fulfill this requirement. Command and control requirements also would be minimal for such a spasmodic retaliatory response. In the extreme, some (including former President Jimmy Carter) have argued that the number of nuclear weapons aboard

FIGURE 2.2. The U.S. Strategic Triad, December 1986

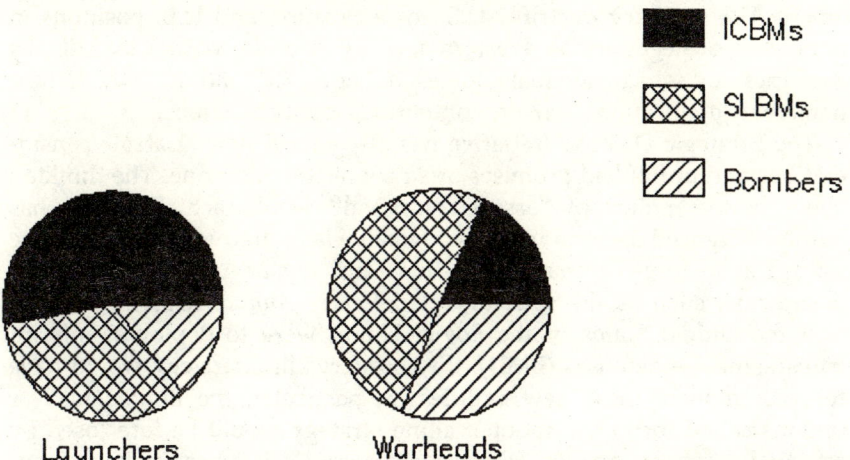

Source: Arms Control Association, "Strategic Nuclear Forces of the United States and Soviet Union," Press Release (February 6, 1987).

a single ballistic missile submarine would suffice to inflict an unacceptable retaliatory blow on the Soviet Union.

Deterring an attack on NATO is not likely to be as simple. The most fundamental difficulty is credibility. Although it appears plausible that U.S. leaders would retaliate with nuclear missiles against a country that attacked their own homeland, the implementation of such a response appears less likely on behalf of an ally because the Soviet Union would match the retaliation with an attack against the United States itself. Extending deterrence to allies requires force levels high enough to exercise limited options in the theater, while retaining the necessary retaliatory forces. The independent British and French nuclear forces add an extra measure of uncertainty to the calculations of a potential aggressor.

The ability to conduct limited strategic operations is the most difficult objective of all. It would call for robust command, control, and communications; for weapons that could survive a Soviet first-strike; and for flexible targeting capabilities. The U.S. force posture has never been able to meet the requirements to carry out such operations—known collectively as countervailing strategy—since the U.S. doctrine began to call for limited nuclear options fifteen years ago. The number of Soviet targets exceeds the levels of U.S. nuclear forces by a wide margin. "To retaliate," according to a briefing at the Strategic Air Command Headquarters in Omaha, "it would take more than double what we have on the ramp now."[5]

Indeed, over the past fifteen years, gaps have widened progressively among U.S. military doctrine, U.S. force posture, and U.S. positions in arms control negotiations. Western security is underwritten by military doctrines for which adequate forces do not exist and for which fundamental justifications remain contentious political issues.

The Strategic Defense Initiative has also raised new strategic considerations and unfulfilled promises of a new nuclear doctrine. The thinking about how a policy of "assured survival" would actually work has hardly advanced beyond rhetoric. Nonetheless, harbingers of a move toward a defense-dominant world have already begun to color official documents, such as the secretary of defense's *Annual Report*.

If the United States or the Soviet Union were to deploy significant ballistic missile defenses (BMD), the countervailing strategy would have to accommodate these new realities. In particular, the limited nuclear options called for in the countervailing strategy would be foreclosed by effective defenses, causing Western nations to rely once again on conventional forces for their defense.

In 1986, two major new U.S. strategic weapons made their long awaited debuts—the MX missile and the B-1 bomber. Progress was also made in other elements of the strategic modernization program, including submarine-launched ballistic missiles and command, control, and communications.

Intercontinental Ballistic Missiles. The problem of intercontinental ballistic missile (ICBM) vulnerability, raised in the 1980 campaign as the issue of the "window of vulnerability," remains unsolved. The President's Commission on Strategic Forces, chaired by General Brent Scowcroft, advocated in 1983 the development of a mobile single-warhead ICBM that would present less lucrative targets to the Soviets than heavy, silo-based missiles with multiple warheads, such as the MX ("Peacekeeper"). The idea met approval on Capitol Hill and became the U.S. Air Force small ICBM program (also dubbed "Midgetman"). As 1986 drew to a close, however, both Peacekeeper and Midgetman remained in limbo.

The first ten MX ICBMs became operational at Warren Air Force Base, Wyoming in December 1986. As of December 1986, the Peacekeeper had undergone fifteen successful flight tests, with five more tests planned for 1987.[6] All fifty of the missiles currently authorized are scheduled to be deployed in refurbished Minuteman III silos by December 1988. Twelve MX missiles have been authorized in the fiscal 1987 budget, with another twenty-one proposed for fiscal 1988.[7] A plan was unveiled in the fiscal 1988 defense budget to deploy a second series of fifty Peacekeeper missiles in a rail-mobile basing mode, to be released from their central garrisons on military bases and moved via national railroads during time of crises. Two MX missiles would be deployed aboard each train. This rail-mobile basing scheme was proposed only after months of deliberation, during which the Air Force reportedly favored placement of the missiles in an array of closely spaced, superhard silos.[8] This basing option—the dense pack deployment plan—had been rejected by Congress in 1982.

Officials continue to debate the design of the proposed small ICBM. As noted, the Scowcroft Commission in 1983 called for a small, mobile ICBM with a single warhead. The commission recognized that a single-warhead missile was less cost-effective than a multiple-warhead system. Because each single-warhead missile would constitute a low-value target, however, it offered advantages in reduced vulnerability and greater stability.

Congressional supporters, such as Les Aspin, chairman of the House Armed Services Committee, favor a 37,000-pound single-warhead missile. The Air Force, on the other hand, would prefer a 52,000-pound system capable of carrying two warheads.[9] The Air Force claims that it needs 1,500 ICBM warheads capable of destroying hard targets in order to implement the countervailing strategy against Soviet targets. To achieve this, 500 single-warhead small ICBMs, along with 100 MX missiles, each with 10 warheads, would be required. The prospect for congressional authorization of Peacekeepers beyond the already approved 50, however, is exceedingly dim. Therefore, to attain the required number of warheads, the deployment of small ICBMs would have to be increased to 1,000. If a two-warhead small ICBM were developed, however, the total number required could be kept to 500 missiles.

Meanwhile, the existing Minuteman ICBM force continues to be upgraded. Prompted by improvements in the Soviet ABM ring around Moscow, the U.S. Air Force is beginning full scale development in 1987 of a passive decoy system for the Minuteman III.[10] To counter Soviet ABM systems, decoys will be deployed on the Minuteman III and a maneuvering reentry vehicle is currently under development. The last year for the Titan ICBM is 1987 and the last seven operational missiles of this class will be retired by the end of the same year.

In short, the ICBM leg of the U.S. strategic triad is being modernized steadily, but more slowly than called for in the plans of either the Reagan or Carter administration. The vulnerability of silo-based missiles persists, and no mobile basing scheme has been found that meets political and military standards of acceptability. Congress has intervened extensively in the ICBM modernization programs, as well as in related arms control negotiations, resulting in additional complications. The eventual resolution of the issue remains uncertain.

Submarine-Launched Ballistic Missiles. Whereas ICBM programs have borne the bulk of political debate and congressional scrutiny, the sea-based leg of U.S. strategic forces has quietly become the strongest component. The vulnerability of ICBMs to Soviet missiles—as well as to U.S. indecision—has made submarine-launched ballistic missiles (SLBMs) the strongest leg of the triad. SLBMs presently account for some 5,760 warheads of the 7,800 total U.S. strategic ballistic-missile warheads.[11] In a recent editorial, members of the Scowcroft Commission characterized sea based forces as "the heart of our survivable deterrent."[12]

New *Ohio*-class or Trident ballistic-missile submarines continue to be deployed at the rate of one per year. At the end of 1986, there were seven operational Tridents and an eighth Trident was undergoing sea trials. Each submarine carries twenty-four missiles, with an average of eight warheads per missile. Although there is a question about the number of ICBMs to be introduced and future strategic requirements, current plans call for the deployment of a total force of twenty-five to twenty-seven Trident submarines.

As the new Tridents (and bombers equipped with cruise missiles) have been deployed, the United States has faced the decision of whether to retire the older Poseidon submarines in order to remain in compliance with SALT limitations. In September 1985, President Reagan ordered the early retirement of a Poseidon submarine to stay within SALT ceilings. In May 1986, two additional Poseidons were retired for military and budgetary reasons. In the fall of 1986, the administration ordered two additional Poseidons to be overhauled rather than retired, however, ensuring that the United States would be in violation of the SALT II limit when bombers became operational in December.

SLBMs will not only be the ultimate retaliatory weapon but—with the deployment of more accurate missiles, reentry vehicles, and guidance systems—will also be capable for use in counterforce missions. The Trident II (D-5) missile began flight tests in January 1987. The first Trident II missile will be deployed in 1989 on the ninth Trident submarine and eventually will be retrofitted on the first eight as well. Proposed Department of Defense funding calls for the procurement of 66 Trident II missiles in both fiscal 1988 and 1989. The United Kingdom will also acquire the Trident II missile, which will become operational in 1991.

Bomber Force. The United States moved forward with its two manned strategic bomber programs in 1986. As a growing number of Soviet ICBMs become mobile, manned aircraft may grow in importance as components of the only strategic system that can find and destroy such mobile targets.

The B-1B has been introduced into operation, with 28 (of 100 planned) aircraft delivered to the Air Force (ahead of program schedule) as of

January 1987. Both the cost and performance of the aircraft in the first year have been disappointing, however. More than one-half of the operational B-1Bs experienced fuel seepage in their fuselage and wing tanks.[13] Additional problems have arisen in the electronic warfare suite of the aircraft, in its terrain-following radar, in its flight controls, and in its missile-launching systems. As a result, the Air Force suspended more than $250 million in progress payments to B-1B contractors.[14] Operating costs for the B-1 are high—even by strategic bomber standards; complaints were frequently voiced over the B-52's cost of $7,000 per flying hour, and the B-1 costs $21,000 per flying hour.[15]

Development has continued on the Advanced Technology Bomber (ATB). This follow-on to the B-1B will be deployed in the early 1990s, with a planned force level of 132 aircraft by 1996.[16] The ATB is probably the largest "black" program in the U.S. defense budget, and its secrecy so far has remained intact. Another highly classified program is the Advanced Cruise Missile, a replacement for existing cruise missiles that will share some of the ATB's stealth characteristics.

Faced with improved Soviet air defenses, the ability of the B-52 to penetrate Soviet air space will lessen in the late 1980s. Accordingly, air-launched cruise missiles (ALCMs) have been fitted on many aircraft in the B-52 fleet. So far, 90 B-52G aircraft have been modified to carry 12 air-launched cruise missiles each. An additional 95 B-52s will be fitted with ALCMs. By the 1990s, all B-52s with a strategic mission will be equipped with cruise missiles.

On November 28, 1986 the United States deployed the 131st B-52 bomber armed with cruise missiles, exceeding the limits of the SALT II treaty for the first time. Reagan announced that he would no longer be bound by the unratified SALT II treaty in May, but reserved the option of remaining under the SALT limit until a final decision was made—only days before the bomber deployment. The Air Force plans to finish the modification of all 194 B-52s to carry cruise missiles by the second quarter of fiscal 1990.

Command, Control, and Communications. The Reagan administration's strategic modernization program also provides for improvements in warning sensors, communication systems, and command centers to support strategic forces. This is an uncontroversial and invisible part of the strategic budget, but is vital to the implementation of present doctrine.

Two new Pave Paws phased-array radar systems—one in Georgia and the other in Texas—will become operational in FY 1987, closing the SLBM-attack warning gap. A similar radar will come on-line at Thule, Greenland in 1987. The Ground Wave Emergency Network is designed to replace the current reliance on telephone lines for communication among sensor sites, the National Command Authority, and strategic forces. The first phase will be operational in FY 1987, with the entire system (including links to ICBM forces) scheduled for completion by the end of the decade.

The strategic bomber force will be equipped with miniature terminals for receiving very low frequency communications. These signals can be transmitted over long distances and are less susceptible to nuclear effects than satellite or high-frequency communications. The MilStar extremely high frequency (EHF) satellite system would provide secure two-way voice communications between commanders and forces. The system is now in advanced development. New electronic equipment is also being procured for command centers that will be resistant to electromagnetic pulse effects.

Nonstrategic Nuclear Forces. All 108 Pershing II intermediate-range ballistic missiles (IRBMs) and 464 ground-launched cruise missiles (GLCMs) are scheduled to be deployed in Europe by the end of 1988, nine years after the unanimous NATO decision on Long-Range Theater Nuclear Forces and eleven years after Soviet deployments of SS-20s began. At the end of 1986, all of the Pershing IIs and 208 of the ground-launched cruise missiles had been deployed in the Federal Republic of Germany (FRG), in the United Kingdom, and in Italy. The remaining GLCMs will be stationed in the Netherlands, Belgium, and the FRG.

By January 1986, the United States had withdrawn all atomic demolition munitions from Europe, in accordance with NATO's October 1983 Montebello decision to reduce tactical nuclear weapons in Europe by 1,400 warheads by 1990. When the decision is fully implemented, there will be 4,600 U.S. tactical nuclear warheads in Western Europe.

Supreme Allied Commander General Bernard W. Rogers announced programs to improve the security and survivability of NATO nuclear forces. For instance, storage vaults are being developed for gravity bombs that will be collocated with their delivery aircraft in hardened shelters. Training and tactics for dispersal and concealment of Pershing II and GLCM systems off-base are also being emphasized.

The command and control systems for nonstrategic nuclear weapons are being upgraded. Two new communications systems for nonstrategic nuclear forces in Europe and the Pacific are nearly complete. An ultrahigh frequency (UHF) satellite system is operational in the Pacific, with its European counterpart scheduled for completion in 1987. Work has begun on another system, a high-frequency (HF) network, which will provide communications resistant to jamming in Europe and part of the Pacific theater starting in 1989.[17]

At the end of 1986, there were about 150 to 200 nuclear-armed Tomahawk long-range sea-launched cruise missiles (SLCMs) deployed aboard approximately 25 attack submarines and surface ships. Deployments of nonnuclear Tomahawks also began in 1986, reaching a total of 441 by December.

In sum, U.S. nuclear forces were augmented in 1986 by the introduction of a new ICBM and a new bomber, by the continuation of its ballistic-missile submarine program, and by further deployment of GLCMs in Western Europe. The force totals reflected in Table 2.1 show the change in force from December 1985 to December 1986. Even more important is the potential for future force growth because of the U.S. decision to break the SALT II limitations. This decision was not taken until late 1986, and its impact on force posture is not yet known. Congress may also check any efforts to expand the force posture, through either budgetary limitations or cuts in particular programs, such as the MX. Although the first steps away from SALT II limitations may be halting ones, the absence of an offensive arms agreement opens the way for major increases in nuclear weapons. As indicated in Table 2.1, the number of warheads per missile is climbing dramatically. Moreover, the new weapons (MX, Trident II, B-1B, and ATB) will additionally offer improved accuracy.

The USSR

The Soviet Union traditionally has not built strategic forces around the concept of a balanced triad, as has the United States. Land-based intercontinental ballistic missiles have been the overwhelming mainstay of Soviet nuclear forces up to now (see Figure 2.3). The programs now under way, however, are leading to greater diversification of Soviet strategic nuclear forces. New SLBMs, strategic bombers, and cruise missiles will be deployed in the late 1980s and early 1990s. Although ICBMs will still account for more than half of Soviet strategic warheads, a growing number will be deployed in mobile basing modes.

According to the Defense Intelligence Agency (DIA), the Soviets will be able to increase their inventory of offensive strategic warheads from about 9,000 at the end of 1986 to some 12,000 within three years and possibly to 16,000 by the mid-1990s.[18] This growth, combined with a slowly changing U.S. target base (that is, new U.S. ICBMs and other targets), will result in potentially improved Soviet coverage of those targets. Lee and Staar estimate that Soviet requirements for warheads capable of destroying hardened targets, for example, could be reduced by about one-third through the early 1990s if no significant growth occurs in the U.S. target base.[19]

Intercontinental Ballistic Missiles. The Soviet ICBM force at the beginning of 1987 consisted of 1,398 missiles, 72 of which were mobile SS-25s, first deployed in 1985. The SS-25 is roughly the size of the

TABLE 2.1

U.S. Nuclear Forces (Number of Launchers)

INTERCONTINENTAL BALLISTIC MISSILES

	1985	1986	1996
Titan	14	4	0
Minuteman II	450	450	450
Minuteman III	550	550	450
Peacekeeper	0	10	100
Small ICBM	0	0	500
	1,014	1,014	1,500

SUBMARINE-LAUNCHED BALLISTIC MISSILES

	1985	1986	1996
Poseidon (C-3)	288	256	128
Trident I (C-4)	360	384	152
Trident II (D-5)	0	0	384
	648	640	664

BOMBERS

	1985	1986	1996
B-52G (ALCM)	98	98	0
B-52G (pen.)	69	69	0
B-52H (ALCM)	14	34	96
B-52H (pen.)	82	62	0
FB-111	61	61	0
B-1B	0	15	100
ATB	0	0	132
	324	339	328

(Table continues)

TABLE 2.1 (continued)

MEDIUM- AND INTERMEDIATE-RANGE MISSILES

	1985	1986	1996
GLCM	128	208	364
Pershing 2	108	108	108
	236	316	472

Note: Projections assume no arms control restraints.

Source: International Institute for Strategic Studies, The Military Balance 1986-87 (London: IISS, 1986), p. 222; Organization of the Joint Chiefs of Staff, Military Posture FY 1988 (Washington: GPO, 1987), p. 19; Congressional Budget Office, Modernizing U.S. Strategic Offensive Forces: The Administration's Program and Alternatives (Washington: GPO, May 1983), p. 3, 93; Arms Control Association, "Strategic Nuclear Forces of the United States and Soviet Union," Press Release (April 10, 1986); Arms Control Association, "Strategic Nuclear Forces of the United States and Soviet Union," Press Release (February 6, 1987).

U.S. Minuteman ICBM, and is armed with a single warhead with a yield of about 50 kilotons.[20] The SS-25 is replacing the earliest version of the SS-11, and the new missile is being deployed in units of 9 launchers at former SS-7 ICBM sites.[21] In November 1986, Japanese sources reported that deployment of the mobile SS-24 ICBM had begun,

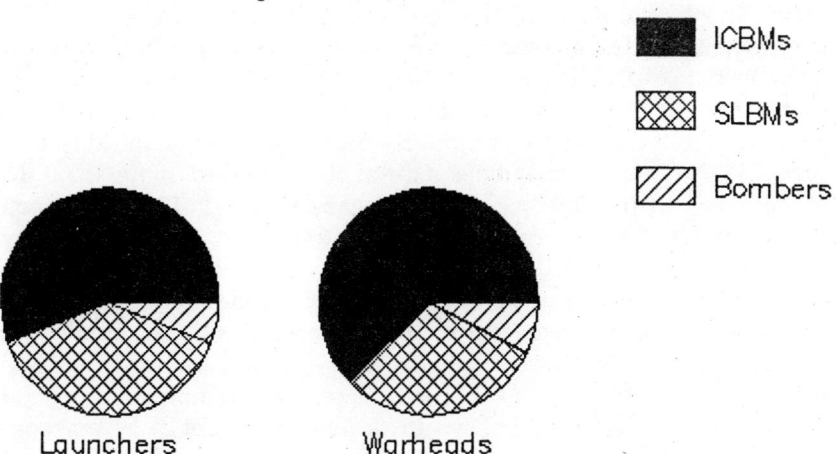

FIGURE 2.3. Soviet Strategic Forces, December 1986

Source: Arms Control Association, "Strategic Nuclear Forces of the United States and Soviet Union," Press Release (February 6, 1987).

with 10 launchers in place.²² The development of a second type of new ICBM (in addition to the SS-25) violates a provision of the SALT II agreement. Several R&D efforts are already under way for new ICBMs beyond the SS-25 and SS-24, including a liquid-fueled replacement for the very large MIRVed SS-18. The new missile is believed to carry even more warheads than the 10 carried by each SS-18. This program suffered setbacks in 1986, however, when test missiles exploded in April and August. Some Western experts blamed the failure on the guidance system.

The remainder of the Soviet missile force consists of silo-based SS-11, SS-13, SS-17, SS-18, and SS-19 missiles. Of these silo-based launchers, some 818 have been rebuilt since 1972.²³ By the mid-1990s, if present trends continue, the SS-19 will be the only remaining Soviet missile of this fourth generation. The rest of the force will consist of the new SS-18 follow-on and of SS-24 and SS-25 ICBMs.

Submarine-Launched Ballistic Missiles. The Soviet Union operates the world's largest submarine force, with more nuclear submarines and more strategic missile submarines than in all other navies combined. There are currently 62 modern, nuclear-propelled strategic missile submarines in Soviet service, armed with some 950 ballistic missiles. The current construction effort is producing more than two new submarines of this type every year. And, a significant increase in the submarine production rate is possible because of existing shipyard facilities.²⁴

Despite the size of Soviet ballistic-missile submarine efforts, the United States still enjoys a considerable lead in the number of SLBM reentry vehicles. U.S. submarine and missile technology remains superior to that of the Soviet Union, particularly in its ability to reduce the noise created by the submarines, thus enhancing the submarine's ability to hide. Moreover, U.S. antisubmarine warfare capability is markedly superior to that of the Soviets.

The latest Soviet ballistic-missile submarine is the Typhoon. It is 561 feet long, about the length of the U.S. Trident submarine and displaces some 25,000 tons when submerged—about one-third more than the Trident. The fourth Typhoon-class boat began sea trials in 1986. According to Captain John Moore, editor of *Jane's Fighting Ships*, 14 Typhoons may eventually be constructed.²⁵

The Typhoon nuclear-powered fleet ballistic missile submarine (SSBN) payload consists of twenty SS-N-20 weapons, the largest SLBM yet produced. The SS-N-20 is reported to carry six to nine warheads and to have a range of some 4,500 nautical miles. The missile is said to have encountered some problems in development, but it became operational in 1983 and went to sea that year in the first Typhoon submarine.²⁶ In September 1986, a test launch of an older SS-N-8 SLBM strayed more than 1,000 miles from its course, crashing in Manchuria.

There is no evidence that the Soviets will slow their rate of submarine missile development and construction; thus, in the absence of an arms agreement, the USSR is likely to maintain a force of at least sixty modern, nuclear-propelled strategic missile submarines for the foreseeable future.[27]

Bombers. Modernization of the air-breathing leg of Soviet strategic forces is also proceeding. The Soviet Union is producing the H version of the Tu-95 Bear bomber, armed with the AS-15 air-launched cruise missile, to replace the Mya-4 Bison. Over the past year, some fifteen Bison bombers have been replaced, and twenty new Bear bombers introduced.

An advanced long-range bomber, the Blackjack, remains in development. The Blackjack has not reached operational status as early as had been predicted in the West, perhaps indicating some developmental problems. Nevertheless, the Blackjack is forecast to replace all Bison bombers and all but a few existing Bear A, B/C, and G model bombers by the mid-1990s, thus accounting for half the Soviet heavy bomber force. The other half will consist of the Bear-H just described.

The Soviets also have been producing the Backfire intermediate-range bomber at a rate of thirty per year. There are now 260 Backfires in service, including those assigned to Soviet naval aviation (in operational units). The Backfire, as the most modern bomber in the Soviet arsenal, has an unrefueled combat radius of 4,000 kilometers. When fitted with a refueling probe, however, the Backfire is capable of intercontinental missions. Indeed, the U.S. Joint Chiefs of Staff include the Backfire in their count of strategic offensive forces, although it is excluded from SALT II limitations.

The Soviets are developing an aerial refueling tanker version of the Il-76 aircraft to support the strategic bomber operations. The Il-76 conversion—called "Midas" by NATO—will be comparable to the twenty-year-old U.S. KC-135. Enhanced aerial refueling capability will increase the utility of the Backfire bomber as well.

Strategic Command, Control, and Communications. The proliferation of mobile ICBMs, SLBMs, and bomber forces places new demands on command, control, and communications for the USSR. Assistant Secretary of Defense Donald C. Latham reported that the Soviet Union is developing a counterpart to the U.S. E-6A submarine communications relay aircraft. The Soviets are also developing an extremely low frequency submarine communications system.

Nonstrategic Nuclear Forces. There are now 441 SS-20 intermediate-range ballistic missiles deployed against targets in Europe and the Far East, an increase of about 40 launchers from 1985. First deployed in 1977, the SS-20 is a mobile missile with three reentry vehicles. Each launcher is equipped with a reload missile, potentially doubling to 2,646 the number of SS-20 warheads that would be available in a conflict. About 100 older SS-4 silo-based intermediate-range missiles are operational but scheduled for retirement.

The modernization of Soviet short-range nuclear forces also continued in 1986, stirring new concerns in Western Europe. Some 575 Scud short-range ballistic missiles are positioned against NATO targets, with 100 more stationed along the Sino-Soviet border and in the Far East. These missiles have been replaced with the SS-23 Spider, a more accurate missile with a greater range, first deployed in 1985. The SS-23, with a range of 300 miles, can reach most targets in the central European front from Warsaw Pact territory. About 900 smaller missiles, the free rockets over ground (FROGs), have been replaced by the modern SS-21 Scarab. As of late 1986, the reequipping of the Soviet Central Group of Forces with SS-21s and SS-23s was complete, and East European forces began receiving SS-21s.

According to the Department of Defense, as many as four new Soviet long-range cruise missiles are now in development. A ground-launched variant of the AS-15 ALCM (the SSC-X-4) as well as a sea-launched derivative (the SS-NX-21) are reportedly near deployment.[28] The CIA estimates that the USSR will eventually deploy some 1,500 nuclear SLCMs. A larger cruise missile, the SS-NX-24, will be flight-tested from a converted Yankee-class cruise-missile attack submarine. The new missile could become operational by the end of 1987. A ground-launched version of the larger missile may also be developed. Although these cruise missiles will initially be deployed with nuclear warheads, improvements in guidance and munitions could allow them to pose a nonnuclear threat to such key targets as airfields and nuclear weapon sites.

The modernization of Soviet nuclear forces continued steadily in 1986, with growth in force levels particularly evident in SLBMs: More than 200 new SS-NX-23 warheads were deployed, and 100 new ALCMs were carried on Bear-H bombers. The Soviet inventory of Backfire bombers also grew by 5 aircraft in 1986. A detailed breakdown of Soviet nuclear forces is presented in Table 2.2.

Other Countries

Although the United States and the Soviet Union control more than 95 percent of the global arsenal of nuclear warheads, the remaining nuclear potential is hardly inconsequential. The destructive power of even relatively small numbers of weapons available to the other nuclear powers is substantial, and both the quality and diversity of these small nuclear forces are likely to increase through the 1990s. For example,

TABLE 2.2

Soviet Nuclear Forces

INTERCONTINENTAL BALLISTIC MISSILES

	1985	1986	1996
SS-11	448	448	448
SS-13	60	60	60
SS-17	150	150	150
SS-18	308	308	308
SS-19	360	360	360
SS-24	0	0	300
SS-25	72	72	300
	1,398	1,398	1,926

SUBMARINE-LAUNCHED BALLISTIC MISSILES

	1985	1986	1996
SS-N-5	39	39	0
SS-N-6	304	272	160
SS-N-8	292	292	268
SS-N-17	12	12	0
SS-N-18	224	224	240
SS-N-20	80	80	440
SS-NX-23	32	48	n/a
	983	967	1,108

BOMBERS

	1985	1986	1996
Bear-H	110	110	0
Bear-H (ALCM)	40	50	n/a
Bison	30	15	0
Backfire	270	275	n/a
Blackjack	0	0	100
	450	450	100

Note: Projections assume no arms control restraints.

Sources: International Institute for Strategic Studies, *The Military Balance 1986-87* (London: IISS, 1986), p. 222; Organization of the Joint Chiefs of Staff, *Military Posture FY 1988* (Washington: GPO, 1987), p. 19; Congressional Budget Office, *Modernizing U.S. Strategic Offensive Forces: The Administration's Program and Alternatives* (Washington: GPO, May 1983), p. 3, 93; Arms Control Association, "Strategic Nuclear Forces of the United States and Soviet Union," Press Release (April 10, 1986); Arms Control Association, "Strategic Nuclear Forces of the United States and Soviet Union," Press Release (February 6, 1987).

France would be capable of inflicting as many as 81 million fatalities in an all-out assault on the Soviet Union; it could also wipe out two-thirds of the USSR's industrial capacity. Following the introduction of the Trident in the early 1990s, Britain would be capable of killing as many as 68 million and incapacitating up to half of all Soviet industry.[29] Indeed, the fact that these forces are deployed by two NATO nations makes them impossible for the Soviet Union to ignore.

Third-country nuclear forces complicate assessments of the strategic balance as well as the resolution of arms control negotiating issues. European nuclear forces have come under discussion at summits attended by President Reagan and General Secretary Gorbachev. One of the principal differences between the United States and the Soviet Union is the issue of how (if at all) to account for the British and French forces in arms control negotiations. Similarly, Soviet military requirements hinge on the threat from China—a problem that the United States no longer takes explicitly into account.

Research by the United States and the Soviet Union into ballistic-missile defenses has provoked protests by the smaller nuclear powers. Neither a U.S. nor Soviet space "shield" would be welcomed by the Europeans. The former is perceived as weakening the U.S. nuclear commitment to Europe; the latter would render useless the retaliatory forces of Britain and France.

United Kingdom. Britain's dedicated nuclear forces consist of 210 aircraft (30 Buccaneer S2s and 180 Tornado GR-1s) and 4 submarines carrying a total of 64 Polaris submarine-launched ballistic missiles. In addition, certain shorter-range British aircraft, Lance missiles, and artillery guns could be used to deliver nuclear ordnance.

In September 1986, the keel was laid for the HMS Vanguard—the first of four planned British Trident submarines. Although no deployment schedule has been announced, it is expected that the Vanguard will become operational in 1991. Each missile can carry up to 8 warheads, and each submarine can accommodate 16 missiles. As yet, however, the British government has not disclosed the details concerning the number that will actually be carried. When the Polaris systems are replaced by Trident D-5 missiles, the number of British strategic nuclear warheads will increase sharply, and up to 672 Trident warheads will be available, depending on the number of submarines on station within range of their targets.[30]

Both the Labour and the Alliance parties have opposed the Trident program. Prime Minister Margaret Thatcher, however, was reelected in 1987, some three to four years before the first British Trident would go to sea; the program will certainly be completed. Spending and production will reach their peak in 1988, with some 25,000 British workers employed in its production. Moreover, the British firm Vickers has negotiated a clause in its contract for the first Trident, guaranteeing 125 percent of the contract's value if cancellation occurs before the order for the second submarine is placed.[31]

The British very low frequency (VLF) communications system for submarines is also currently being updated, with a more capable extremely low frequency system in development.

Still unclear is the extent to which (if at all) present British nuclear targeting policy is related to that of the United States. Targeting policy for a British-only retaliatory strike against the USSR would be very different from a targeting policy created to integrate with U.S. planning. Until recently, this question has been moot because the British forces have been so small that, beyond countercity attacks, they offered little capability. In the 1990s, however, this question will become more relevant.

France. In late 1986, France announced a new five-year, $71 billion defense budget, emphasizing nuclear modernization programs. New strategic programs include the S-4 land-based missile and the M-5 submarine-launched missile. French testing of nuclear devices in the South Pacific also continued in 1986.

French strategic nuclear forces now consist of 18 intermediate-range ballistic missiles, more than 100 nuclear-capable aircraft, and 6 ballistic-missile submarines. The potential vulnerability of land-based systems has led France, like Britain, toward increased emphasis on submarines.

The lightweight S-4 land-based missile will enter development in 1987, eventually replacing the 18 S-3 missiles deployed in silos on the Plateau d'Albion. Plans for mobile deployment have been discontinued for the time being, but a mobile deployment scheme could be adopted later.

The sea-based Force Oceanique Strategique (FOST) consists of 5 Redoubtable-class submarines and 1 Inflexible-class submarine. The Redoubtable-class boats, first deployed in 1977, carry 16 single-warhead M-20 missiles. The Inflexible-class submarine is armed with the first French MIRVed missile, the M-4 SLBM, with 6 reentry vehicles. The addition of this submarine in 1985 doubled the number of French SLBM warheads.[32] The M-4 will be fitted to four of the older submarines by the early 1990s, and a seventh submarine will be delivered in 1994. New tests of the M-4 missile were conducted in 1986, revealing a range of some 3,730 miles—longer than Western defense experts originally believed. Development of a follow-on SLBM—the M-5—equipped with 12 reentry vehicles was announced in the 1987 five-year plan. Construction of a new class of ballistic-missile submarine, the NG-class, will begin within four years and will enter service in the late 1990s.

The political consensus behind French nuclear forces has been remarkably consistent. This commitment is reflected in the high priority that nuclear forces are given in the French defense budget. For the period 1984–1988, for example, 31.7 percent of French expenditures on military equipment is devoted to nuclear weapon programs.[33]

China. Testing of several new Chinese nuclear systems was revealed in 1986, although details remain sketchy. Early in 1986, the People's Liberation Army (PLA) conducted exercises simulating the use of tactical nuclear weapons.[34] These maneuvers fueled speculation that the PRC had, for the first time, developed tactical nuclear weapons. Tests were also conducted of both land- and sea-based cruise missiles. Research and development are under way for the second generation of Chinese ballistic missile submarines.

Little is known publicly in the West about Chinese nuclear forces, their size, technical characteristics, or the doctrine governing their use. Compared to those of the Soviet Union and the Western nuclear powers, the Chinese arsenal is relatively old and small, containing a total of only 300–400 warheads, a large number of which are deployed on delivery systems designed in the 1950s and early 1960s. Only a few of these missiles can reach beyond the Asian theater, although the newest Chinese ICBM, the CSS-4, can reach not only Moscow but targets throughout the northern hemisphere.

Moreover, nuclear weapons have apparently escaped the severe cutbacks made in Chinese military programs; instead, they have assumed the highest priority within the defense budget. Development of nuclear weapons fits well with China's goals of technological modernization and development of space systems. Indeed, the Chinese space program is closely aligned with military ends. Although China has not yet deployed a missile with multiple warheads, in 1981 it tested a rocket that launched three satellites, thus demonstrating the essentials of MIRV technology.

Development of China's missile programs continues. China is working its own version of the Soviet designed FROG-7 nuclear-capable tactical missile. It has also begun flight tests of a new version of its CSS-2 intermediate-range ballistic missile. Four more Han-class ballistic-missile submarines are under construction (four have already been built), each of which carries six missiles.

Israel, South Africa, India, and Pakistan. Although Israel has long been on the list of nations capable of building nuclear weapons, this status has been veiled in secrecy and cultivated ambiguity. The Israeli government claims that it will not be the first to introduce nuclear weapons in the Middle East. The implicit corollary, however, is that it has the capability to make atomic devices and use them if necessary.

Bold new revelations about Israeli nuclear capabilities were made in October 1986, in an episode stranger than any espionage novel. Mordechai Vanunu, an Israeli citizen who claimed to have worked at the Dimona nuclear facility in the Negev Desert, appeared in London with a story to peddle. Subsequently, Vanunu was abducted in Rome by members of the Israeli Shin Beth security organization and taken back to Israel to stand trial for treason.

The story, however, was picked up by the London *Sunday Times*, along with photos and illustrations. According to the *Sunday Times* article, Israel has stockpiled between 100 and 200 nuclear weapons and has the capability and components to build atomic weapons of advanced designs—and perhaps neutron or hydrogen weapons as well.

South Africa, India, and Pakistan also are believed to be on the verge of possessing nuclear weapon capabilities. It can be expected that all three countries will have operational nuclear forces by the end of the 1990s.

The nuclear forces of countries other than the United States and the Soviet Union are expected to more than double within the next decade. With the British deployment of the Trident II SLBM, the Soviets will face the best nuclear weapon system in the world from nuclear forces independent of the United States. Table 2.3 summarizes the nuclear forces of third nations as of December 1986.

Strategic Defenses

In an assessment of the strategic balance ten (or even five) years ago, strategic defense would have rated a footnote at most. The ABM Treaty of 1972 effectively foreclosed the deployment of missile defenses beyond the relatively insignificant level of 100 ABM launchers. Although the USSR maintained a large air defense system, the United States had virtually none. Today, more is written about strategic defense than about any other strategic program. President Reagan's Strategic Defense Initiative has reopened the issue of strategic defense, and, as a result, limiting that initiative has become the number-one arms control priority of the Soviet Union.

Both the United States and the Soviet Union are pursuing major R&D programs in strategic defense technologies. Some U.S. analysts have warned of the possibility of a sudden, perhaps imminent, Soviet break from the ABM agreement and of the deployment of a nationwide missile defense by the USSR. Soviet fears of similar moves by the United States have also arisen, reinforced by the Reagan administration's broader interpretation of restrictions under the ABM treaty. Political pressures for early U.S. deployment of strategic defenses reached new heights in

TABLE 2.3

Small Nuclear Forces, 1986

System	Number Deployed	Year Deployed	Range (km)
UNITED KINGDOM			
Aircraft			
Tornado	170	1981	2800
SLBM			
Polaris A-3	64	1967	4600
TOTAL	234		
FRANCE			
Aircraft			
Jaguar A	45	1974	1600
Mirage IIIE	30	1964	2400
Mirage IVA/P	22/8	1966/86	3200
Super Etendard	38	1981	2800
Land-Based Missiles			
SSBS S-3	18	1980	3500
SLBM			
MSBS M-20	80	1977	3000
MSBS M-4	16	1985	4400+
TOTAL	257		
CHINA			
Aircraft			
Tu-4 Bull	10-30	1966	6100
Il-28 Beagle	10-20	1974	1850
Tu-16 Badger	100	1966	5900
Land-Based Missiles			
CSS-1 (DF-2)	40-60	1966	1100
CSS-2 (DF-3)	85-125	1972	2600
CSS-3 (DF-4)	10*	1978	7000
CSS-4 (DF-5)	10*	1980	12000
SLBM			
CSS-N-3 (JL-1)	24-26	1983	2200-3300
TOTAL	289-381		

ISRAEL

100-200 weapons have been reported.
Potential delivery systems include tactical aircraft
and Jericho surface-to-surface missiles.

* estimate

Sources: International Institute for Strategic Studies, The Military Balance 1986-87 (London: IISS, 1986), pp. 142-143, 202-203.

TABLE 2.4

Appropriations for U.S. Strategic Defense Programs
(in millions of dollars)

	FY 1985 Actual	FY 1986 Planned	FY 1987 Proposed	FY 1988 Proposed
Strategic Defense Initiative				
Development:	1,398	2,759	4,803	6,291
Air Defense				
Development:	103	106	53	77
Procurement:	140	182	193	263
TOTAL	243	288	246	340
Space Defense				
Development:	198	200	278	226
Procurement:	22	10	33	334
TOTAL	220	210	311	560

Source: Caspar W. Weinberger, *Annual Report to the Congress Fiscal Year 1987* (Washington: GPO, 1986) p. 223.

early 1987. President Reagan was said to personally favor an early deployment of even a limited strategic defense system.

United States

The United States is pursuing all three elements of strategic defense—defense against ballistic missiles, air defense, and space defense—although not in a balanced way. Ballistic-missile defense receives the preponderance of funds, whereas air defense—the one program for which proven technologies exist—is funded at such a low level that its budget could be a rounding error for the Strategic Defense Initiative (see Table 2.4).

Strategic Defense Initiative. The SDI research program made considerable progress in 1986, diplomatic efforts to involve U.S. allies in the program were positive, and enthusiasm for early deployment of an antiballistic missile system grew. At the same time, the January 1986 explosion of the Space Shuttle Challenger and the April 18 Titan rocket explosion seriously set back launch schedules, in turn delaying scheduled experiments for the SDI program. These failures were so great that a U.S. firm has contracted with China for the launch of two satellites by the end of 1987.

At present, the SDI both contributes to and detracts from U.S. military strength. On the positive side, the SDI emphasizes the technological advantages that the United States enjoys and plays on the Soviet leadership's profound fear of a possible Western breakthrough in the arms competition and thus creates the only meaningful leverage the United States has had in arms control negotiations in recent years. If cost were no consideration, the development of a strategic defense might very well be the most effective way to reverse trends in the military balance. The SDI would discount the Soviet Union's primary advantage in its strategic forces—the ballistic missile.

Unfortunately for the United States, however, the cost of pursuing a strategic defense may nullify these advantages, especially as the time for deployment draws near. There is no way to precisely estimate the cost of a strategic defense system with any degree of confidence because the specifications have not yet been determined. There are a range of options, from the modest to the extravagant, that the United States could pursue. One private study released in 1986 predicted that a comprehensive space-based defense against ballistic missiles and aircraft would cost $770 billion to build and operate for ten years.[35] Already, given the overall zero ceiling on growth in defense spending, any increase in spending for SDI crowds out other defense programs. Moreover, if the United States appears to be inevitably headed for a ballistic-missile defense, the Soviet Union could give up hope of an offensive arms accord and either increase its own offensive force or deploy a strategic defense itself. Either step would appreciably raise the cost of a strategic defense program.

There is continuing confusion over the purpose of the SDI. In a June 1986 report to the Congress, the administration described the goal of the SDI as follows:

> The goal of the SDI is to conduct a program of vigorous research and technology development that may lead to strategic defense options that would eliminate the threat posed by ballistic missiles, and thereby:
>
> - Support a better basis for deterring aggression;
> - Strengthen strategic stability;
> - Increase the security of the United States and its Allies.
>
> The SDI seeks, therefore, to provide the technical knowledge required to support an informed decision in the early 1990s on whether or not to develop and deploy a defense of the U.S. and its Allies against ballistic missiles.[36]

Toward these ends, the SDI organization is pursuing research efforts in five broad areas: surveillance, acquisition, tracking, and kill assessment (SATKA); directed-energy weapons (DEW); kinetic-energy weapons (KEW); systems analysis and battle management (SA/BM); and survivability, lethality, and key technologies. The SDI organization reported progress in each of these areas in 1986.

In particular, SDI research in 1986 was marked by several milestones. In July, a successful test of a ground-launched interceptor against a hypersonic target was conducted. The system was the U.S. Army flexible lightweight agile guided experiment (FLAGE), aimed at building a defense against short-range missiles. In September 1986, a dramatic test of the kinetic-energy-weapons guidance system used to destroy ballistic missiles was conducted. The test used 38 radars, 31 satellite communications links, and 6 aircraft airborne around the world. During the test, a Delta rocket booster was successfully detected, tracked, and ultimately destroyed by a 6,500-mph collision with a maneuvering kinetic-kill vehicle.[37]

The SDI also made diplomatic progress in the past year. The United States has successfully pushed for cooperation with NATO and other allies on SDI research. As of February 1987, agreements had been signed with the United Kingdom, the Federal Republic of Germany, Japan, Italy, and Israel. A number of research contracts with foreign firms have already been drawn up by the SDI organization.

Antisatellite Warfare. The United States has successfully tested the Air-Launched Miniature Vehicle (ALMV) for use against low-altitude satellites. The weapon would be launched by a specially configured F-15 tactical aircraft. The ALMV destroyed a target in space in a 1985 test. In September 1986, the missile's infrared guidance system was tested, using a distant star as a "target." The system is not yet in production, and further testing against objects in space has been prohibited by Congress during fiscal 1987.

Air Defenses. Since the SDI program was launched, one of the most persistent criticisms has been its concentration on ballistic missiles and its neglect of the bomber and cruise missile threat to the United States and its allies. The DoD has responded that the air-breathing threat would be dealt with in due course, but little concrete progress has been reported. In the spring of 1986, however, this rhetoric took shape as the Air Defense Initiative (ADI). Although it is funded at a much lower level than BMD programs, the ADI program announced its goal to provide a level of protection against bombers and cruise missiles similar to that of the SDI against ballistic missiles. Air defense requirements are being drawn together into a new framework called Strategic Defense Architecture 2000, which is intended to serve as a planning document for the rest of the century.

There are 16 air defense squadrons protecting North America—11 Air National Guard, 4 U.S. Air Force, and 1 Royal Canadian Air Force. The United States has 300 interceptor aircraft and 100 air defense radars for strategic defense. The interceptor aircraft, which include F-106s, F-

4s, and F-101 fighters, are largely 1950s and 1960s aircraft. Three of the four USAF squadrons have been modernized with F-15 interceptors. In fiscal 1987, the fourth Air Force squadron will be disestablished. Similarly, the network of surface-to-air missiles that complemented the interceptors was phased out in 1975. As the USSR modernizes its bomber force, U.S. air defense forces are becoming increasingly vulnerable to the Soviet threat—especially from new air-launched cruise missiles, which can be launched some 1,500 miles from their targets.

In October 1986, the Air Force selected the F-16 fighter for the continental air defense fighter mission. The F-16 was chosen over the Northrop F-20 Tigershark, an aircraft developed with $1.2 billion of Northrop investment. Some elements of the SDI program may yield breakthroughs that would also be useful in air defense. Special advanced air defense research in 1987 includes new surveillance systems, weapons, fire control systems, sensors, and survivability measures.[38]

The USSR

The Soviet Union has been interested in strategic defense for a considerable period of time. Indeed, the Soviets have been more consistent in their investment in strategic defense with respect to deployment as well as R&D. According to then CIA Deputy Director Robert M. Gates, the Soviet Union has spent some $150 billion in the last ten years on strategic defense.[39] The Soviet program is a balanced one, with early deployment of systems combined with periodic upgrades of their capability.

Prompted by U.S. research in defensive technology, the Soviet Union has stepped up work on countermeasures. These include conventional approaches such as penetration aids and decoys, greater use of bombers and cruise missiles, and depressed-trajectory SLBMs. Suppression of enemy defenses is also being examined, including the potential of ground-based directed-energy weapons designed to disable targets in space.

The Soviet space program is devoted in considerable measure to military applications. Space-launching capability could become a critical factor in any U.S. or Soviet move to deploy a full-fledged space defense. In July 1986, a new Soviet heavy launch vehicle, the SL-16 booster, was tested. The booster carries a payload of some sixteen tons, more than twice the limit in manned Soviet space flights.[40]

Ballistic Missile Defense. The Soviet directed-energy research program suffered a major setback in late May or early June 1986, when the Soviet airborne laser laboratory, a modified Il-76 aircraft, was destroyed in a fire. According to the Pentagon, this was the only testbed of this type.

Research into laser weapons is reportedly conducted on a large scale in the Soviet Union. The DoD has estimated that the cost of the Soviet effort would be about $1 billion per year if pursued in the United States. The Soviets lead the West in ground-based lasers, although development of an operational laser weapon is not likely to occur before the late 1990s.

The Soviet Union has enlisted the participation of its Warsaw Pact partners in its strategic defense research efforts. The German Democratic Republic (GDR), Czechoslovakia, and Hungary are involved in projects including precision engineering, image processing, and instrumentation. The largest portion of this research is carried out in the GDR. East European countries are also involved in Soviet computing initiatives, with important spillovers for strategic defense.

The USSR maintains the world's only operational antiballistic missile system, consisting of 64 nuclear-armed Galosh interceptor missiles designed to defend Moscow. Modernization of this system is currently under way; the new interceptors planned will bring the total to 100, as allowed by the ABM treaty. A second defense layer of silo-based nonnuclear interceptors is being added, and the radar system for early warning and battle management is being updated. Six new large phased-array radars have been built to replace the Hen House early warning radars. The sixth new radar, built at Krasnoyarsk in Siberia, violates the ABM treaty provisions governing ABM radars. It is neither within a 150-kilometer radius of the Soviet capital nor on the periphery of the country oriented outward. The Galosh system, old or modernized, is not large or capable enough to disrupt U.S. attacks on Moscow or, for that matter, French or British nuclear strikes. All three countries have active programs to develop decoys and other penetration aids to mislead the ABM system.

ASAT. The Soviet Union maintains the world's only operational antisatellite system, although it is far less capable than the U.S. system now being developed. There have been no apparent Soviet tests of the system since 1983. The Galosh ABM interceptor may have ASAT capabilities as well. Research on ballistic-missile defenses will provide additional ASAT capabilities through a variety of kill mechanisms, such as land-based lasers.

A report that surfaced in the West German press in October 1986 indicated that three U.S. satellites had been disabled by ground-based lasers in the Soviet Union. Although this seems unlikely, the Soviets have established laser research centers at Shary-Shagan and Troitsk and are conducting experiments in directed-energy weapons. According to the U.S. Department of Defense, the USSR could develop a prototype laser antisatellite weapon by the end of the 1980s and field operational units by the mid- to late 1990s.⁴¹ Such lasers might also have applications against cruise missiles or anti-aircraft missiles.

Air Defenses. The Soviet Union currently has nearly 12,000 SAM launchers, 10,000 air defense radars, and more than 1,200 interceptor aircraft.⁴² The strategic SAM force consists of SA-1, SA-2, SA-3, and SA-5 missiles (which were designed in the 1950s and 1960s), with fewer than 800 of the SA-10 type. Over half these interceptors are older MiG-23 and Su-15 aircraft. The new MiG-29 and Su-27 fighters will soon be introduced into Soviet air defense squadrons.

Arms Control

In arms control, the year 1986 produced no new agreements or other concrete progress, but rather a bewildering array of the most far-reaching proposals since the 1948 Baruch Plan. The Reykjavik summit between Reagan and Gorbachev puzzled nearly all observers—including some of the participants. Gorbachev opened the bidding in Iceland by proposing 50 percent cuts in all strategic forces, along with demands that both sides abide by the ABM treaty for ten years. Apparently without staffing or counsel beforehand, President Reagan agreed to the proposal, adding the elimination of all nuclear-armed ballistic missiles in a ten-year period. By the time the media spectacle ended, both leaders had laid claim to proposals to eliminate all strategic nuclear weapons. Although it is tempting to dismiss this as mere lip service to disarmament, the idea of deep cuts is apparently now taken seriously by both nations' senior leaders.

In testimony before the House Armed Services Committee in November 1986, Admiral William J. Crowe, chairman of the Joint Chiefs of Staff, expressed concerns about the proposals put forward at Reykjavik. Crowe testified that eliminating all ballistic missiles would require restructuring of the U.S. deterrent (building new weapons systems) and strengthening conventional forces. One of the new systems mentioned by the chairman was a supersonic, submarine-launched cruise missile. Crowe said that although he would not favor the elimination of all strategic weapons, he would favor eliminating ballistic missiles. While a formal study by the Joint Chiefs on the implications of cutting ballistic missiles had not yet been released in February 1987, preliminary findings indicated that the United States and NATO would be worse off after the elimination of ballistic missiles. According to the study, the U.S. industrial base could not close the conventional gap with the Soviet Union in ten years, even if more defense funds than are now projected were appropriated.

This sentiment was also evident in regard to theater nuclear weapons in Europe. In testimony before the House Armed Services Committee, Supreme Allied Commander General Bernard W. Rogers stated in 1986 that removal of intermediate nuclear forces in Europe would leave NATO worse off than in 1979, when the decision to deploy the new NATO missiles was reached. Rogers stressed the continuing need for nuclear weapons to maintain a credible deterrent.[43] According to Rogers, withdrawing the Pershing II and ground-launched cruise missiles deployed in Europe would leave NATO with only the F-111 fighter-bombers stationed in the United Kingdom to deliver nuclear weapons. Due to improvements in Soviet air defenses, additional aircraft will now be required to ensure the viability of the "flexible-response" strategy.

In February 1987, U.S. and Soviet arms negotiators renewed their efforts and identified goals that had been lost in the confusion of Reykjavik. According to reports from Geneva, procedural issues—such as the composition of working groups—have been solved, and frameworks on areas of agreement are being drafted. Nonetheless, fundamental disagreements remain, especially over the tradeoff of delaying the deployment of the SDI in exchange for cutting the numbers of Soviet heavy ICBMs. Both sides appear to have retrenched, moving away from the ambitious Iceland proposals.

A new item on the nuclear arms agenda was raised in 1986. In a letter from Chancellor Helmut Kohl to President Reagan in October, the West German government urged the United States to follow up any accord on medium-range weapons with negotiations addressing the shorter-range systems, particularly SS-21s, Scud-Bs, and SS-23s. The West Germans expressed concern that if shorter-range systems are ignored, a gray area that the Soviets could exploit could be created. These missiles could also pose a threat to NATO using only conventional and chemical warheads. In an agreement on short-range systems, NATO is likely to insist on the right to match some 1,000 such missiles in the Soviet arsenal.

Strategic Balance

Because deterrence depends on how the opponent views a situation, the strategic balance must be considered through Soviet eyes as well as in relation to U.S. models of effectiveness. Although Soviet views of strategic capabilities are not easy to discern, it is clear that the Soviets regard nuclear weapons from a perspective different from that of the United States. U.S. and Soviet concepts of the utility of nuclear weapons and their role in future conflict are quite different. Soviet perceptions are critical in determining Western requirements because it is the Soviet

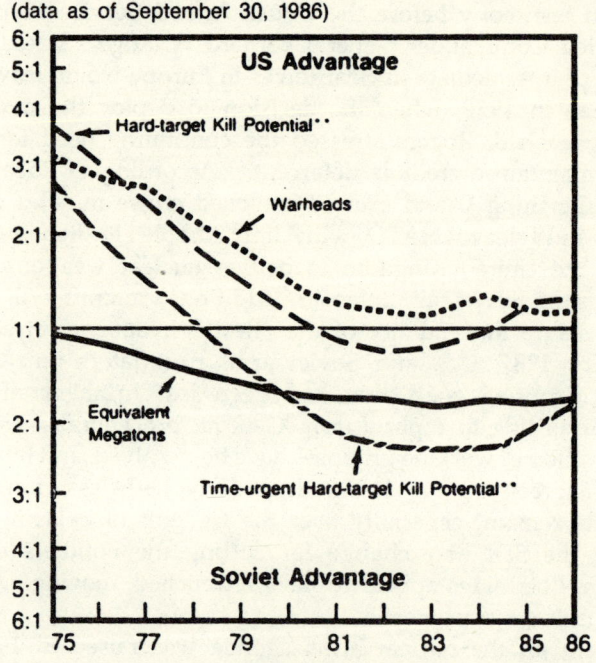

FIGURE 2.4. Strategic Forces Preattack Static Ratio Comparison (data as of September 30, 1986)

* Total active inventory (includes FB-111 and BACKFIRE)
** Hard-target kill potential represents ability to destroy targets reinforced to withstand some effects of a nuclear blast.
Calculations are based on potential against identically hardened targets.

Source: Organization of the Joint Chiefs of Staff, *Military Posture FY 1988* (Washington: GPO, 1987), p. 34.

leadership who must be deterred. To be effective, Western forces must make clear to Soviet officials that Soviet plans for the use of nuclear weapons could not be carried out effectively and that dire consequences would ensue if those plans were implemented. Yet, much of what passes for analysis of the strategic balance is a mere reiteration of force data, with no reference to scenarios of when or how the weapons might be used and, thus, no real assessment of the impact of those forces.

In most debates, static measures of weapon inventories are used to indicate the strategic balance (see Figure 2.4). But such measures are only the starting point for any serious analysis of strategic forces. The most important static measures are numbers of launchers, warheads, and throw-weight. Launchers are the vehicles that carry nuclear weapons to their targets (e.g., missiles and aircraft). Because they are large, easily recognized, and can be readily counted through satellite imagery, launchers have been the standard counting unit in both SALT treaties.

A launcher may carry more than one warhead, as in the case of missiles with multiple independently targetable reentry vehicles (MIRVs). Some launchers can be used to fire additional missiles in a relatively brief period of time; they are said to be "reloadable." Bombers introduce a complication in arms control counting rules because their large payload capacity makes a number of alternative bomb and missile-load alternatives possible; yet the highest loading level may not be practical from an operational point of view.

Throw-weight measures the effective payload of a missile and thus provides a single index covering the size and number of reentry vehicles (warheads and penetration aids) it can carry. Throw-weight of missiles can be estimated by observing missile tests. Although there is no direct equivalent to missile throw-weight for bombers, weapons payload is sometimes used for this purpose.

The overall composition of the two sides strategic forces are compared in Table 2.5. The United States retains its lead in SLBM warheads and bombers—a lead offset by a similar Soviet preponderance in ICBMs. The United States also enjoys a qualitative lead in SLBMs and bombers and at least equal ICBM quality. Historically, the Soviets have led in throw-weight and number of launchers, while the United States has maintained an edge in the number of warheads and accuracy. These U.S. advantages are dwindling, however, as shown in Tables 2.6 and 2.7. The preattack static ratio comparison shows the ratio of U.S. to Soviet nuclear weapons capability. To the extent that some strategic forces are vulnerable, the ratio would shift even more sharply in favor of the side that strikes first.

Nuclear scenarios must consider factors beyond the arsenals of the adversaries. For instance, the target bases of the United States and USSR are quite different. Generally, the targets in the United States are softer, fewer, and less dispersed than those in the Soviet Union.[44] In addition, the location of many large U.S. cities near the coastline decreases warning time for attacks from submarines.

Because the goal of the United States is to deter the Soviet Union from a range of actions, the most critical assessment of the nuclear balance is that of the Soviet Union. This difference is fundamental because the Soviets are likely to base their estimates on different scenarios, objectives, measures of effectiveness, and perhaps different assessment processes.[45] Unlike their U.S. counterparts, Soviet strategic planners do not seem overly concerned about a surprise attack on their nuclear forces. The Soviet scenario of a surprise attack, rather, centers on the

TABLE 2.5

Strategic Offensive Forces: United States and USSR, January 1987

INTERCONTINENTAL BALLISTIC MISSILES

System	U.S. Launchers	Warheads		USSR Launchers	Warheads
Titan	4	4	SS-11	448	448
Minuteman II	450	450	SS-13	60	60
Minuteman III	550	1,650	SS-17	150	600
Peacekeeper	10	100	SS-18	308	3,080
			SS-19	360	2,160
			SS-24	?	
			SS-25	72	72
	1,014	2,204		1,398	6,420

SUBMARINE-LAUNCHED BALLISTIC MISSILES

System	Launchers	Warheads		Launchers	Warheads
Poseidon	256	2,560	SS-N-5	39	39
Trident I	384	3,072	SS-N-6	272	272
			SS-N-8	292	292
			SS-N-17	12	12
			SS-N-18	224	1,568
			SS-N-20	80	720
			SS-NX-23	48	480
	640	5,632		967	3,383

BOMBERS

System	Launchers	Warheads		Launchers	Warheads
B-52G	167	2,142	Bear	160	940
B-52H	96	1,276	Bison	15	60
FB-111	61	366	Backfire	270	540
B-1B	15	120			
	339	3,904		445	1,540

Sources: International Institute for Strategic Studies, The Military Balance 1986-87 (London: IISS, 1986), p. 222; Organization of the Joint Chiefs of Staff, Military Posture FY 1988 (Washington: GPO, 1987), p. 19; Arms Control Association, "Strategic Nuclear Forces of the United States and Soviet Union," Press Release (February 6, 1987).

TABLE 2.6

Procurement of Selected Weapon Systems, 1974-1985

	United States	USSR
Surface-to-air missiles*	11,700	105,000
Long- and intermediate-range bombers	8	400
Fighters	4,050	7,800
Helicopters	2,050	6,500
Submarines	44	110
Major surface combatants	98	90
Tanks	8,400	27,000
Artillery	2,200	22,000

* Does not include naval or portable SAMs.

Note: These numbers reflect gross additions to weapons inventories and do not reflect retirements because of obsolescence or SALT restraints.

Source: Central Intelligence Agency and Defense Intelligence Agency, "The Soviet Economy Under a New Leader," a report presented to the Subcommittee on Economic Resources, Competitiveness, and Security Economics of the Joint Economic Committee, U.S. Congress (March 19, 1986), p. 6.

escalation of an increasingly tense political-military situation, in which adequate warning time to raise Soviet nuclear forces to a wartime level of readiness would not be available.[46]

General Purpose Forces

Assessments of the East-West military balance, which tend to be heavily hardware oriented, may be a carryover from strategic net assessment. In the case of the strategic balance, this narrowness of vision is tolerable, as human factors play a comparatively small role once launch orders have been made. In theater warfare, however, consideration of hardware alone is, at best, inadequate. The importance of human factors has been demonstrated by aerial combat experience, in which training and pilot skill—particularly situational awareness—have been decisive. Some analysts have gone as far as to argue that the Israeli pilots would have fared equally well in their air engagements even if they had swapped aircraft with their enemies.

Despite their inadequacies, force counts are the starting point for estimates of the conventional balance as well as the nuclear balance. One measure of conventional force trends is procurement. As indicated

TABLE 2.7

Growth in Major Weapon Systems in the United States

	FY 1980	FY 1985
Close Combat		
M-1 Tanks	34	3,021
Bradley Fighting Vehicles	0	1,936
Hellfire Missiles	0	111
Helicopters		
AH-64 Apache	0	45
AH-1S Cobra	538	990
UH-60 Blackhawk	0	584
Air Defense Missiles		
Patriot	0	612
Stinger	0	584
Artillery		
Multiple-Launch Rocket System	0	204
Copperhead	0	8,541

Source: Caspar W. Weinberger, *Annual Report to the Congress Fiscal Year 1987* (Washington: GPO, 1986), p. 49; International Institute for Strategic Studies, *The Military Balance 1986-87* (London: IISS, 1986).

in Table 2.6, the USSR has outproduced the United States in most major weapons by as much as nearly 10 to 1 in the past dozen years.

United States

The U.S. defense buildup of the 1980s made itself evident in all the services. As shown in Table 2.6, the quantity of new weapons reaching the field was impressive. In addition, intangibles such as troop morale were also greatly improved since 1980. Readiness was at its highest level since the Vietnam War, and manpower quality was steadily improving.

Ground Forces. The U.S. Army and Marine force structure did not change in 1986. The Army component consists of eighteen active divisions and ten reserve divisions. The Marine Corps has three active divisions and one reserve division. The active divisions rely on reserve forces for up to a third of their fully mobilized strength. U.S. allies contribute a significant amount of support in Europe and South Korea.

The trend toward lighter units continued in 1986. Ten of the Army's active divisions are not "light," including four light infantry divisions that completed reorganization in 1986. Marine Corps divisions are, by their nature, "light" divisions. The trend toward lighter units has been motivated by a shortfall in airlift and sealift. The new divisions have greater firepower for close combat, but less mobility or endurance than standard divisions.

The M-1 Abrams tank and the Bradley fighting vehicle (BFV) continued to be introduced in Army operational units in 1986. The M-1 is being funded at the level of 840 tanks per year through fiscal 1988, along with similar numbers of the BFV. M-1 deliveries in 1986 brought the Army to more than one-half of its total force goal of 7,467 M-1s, which will be achieved in the 1990s. The Marine Corps also procured some 600 assault amphibian vehicles and light-armored vehicles in fiscal 1986.

Although manpower levels and ground vehicle modernization continue as planned, aviation programs have been strongly affected by budget cuts. Army aircraft procurement will decline from $1.62 billion in fiscal 1986 to $1.12 billion in fiscal 1988 to $713 million in fiscal 1989. Army acquisition objectives for AH-64 Apache attack and OH-58D observation helicopters have been cut from 675 and 578 to 593 and 135, respectively. The first figure represents less than half the 1,206 Apaches the Army originally sought.[47] In addition, procurement of the UH-60 Blackhawk will be stretched out under the budget cuts. The Marine Corps helicopter fleet update will also be delayed. The Marines will receive six of the fourteen CH/MH-53 helicopters requested in fiscal 1988 and seven of the fourteen requested in 1989.[48]

These stretch-outs and cutbacks are significant, but they pale against the magnitude of the development programs under way for the helicopters of the future—the light helicopter experimental (LHX) and the U-22. The Army faces the obsolescence of some 5,000 helicopters designed in the 1950s and 1960s, including the UH-1 Huey and AH-1 Cobra. To replace the fleet of utility and scout-attack helicopters, the Army is developing the LHX for a total price tag near $40 billion. The LHX program schedule was accelerated in October 1986, moving the date for initial operational capability from 1998 to 1995.[49] Weight and cost targets for the aircraft have been increased, and risk reduction measures have been implemented to facilitate the shorter development schedule.

The other large rotorcraft program, the Navy V-22 tiltrotor, also continued in development. In May 1986, U.S. Naval Air Systems Command announced the award of the $1.7 billion V-22 full-scale development contract to the team of Bell Helicopter Textron and Boeing Ventol. The first flight of the aircraft is expected in June 1988. The Marine Corps will acquire 552 MV-22s to replace the CH-46 and some CH-53A/D helicopters in the combat assault mission. Variants of the V-22 will be used by all of the services, including search and rescue, special operations, and transport.

The first phase of the Army's $11 billion forward-area air defenses (FAAD) has been approved for an operational capability in 1991 in Europe.[50] The plan has four phases: development of command, control, and intelligence C^3I; non-line-of-sight; line-of-sight forward heavy and line-of-sight rear; and combined arms initiatives. The concept calls for employment of airborne and terrestrial sensors (both active and passive), along with a variety of air defense weapons—from a fiber-optic guided missile (FOG-M) to air-to-air missiles for helicopters to a surface-to-air gun to replace the canceled Sergent York (Divad) system.

In June of 1985, the President's Chemical Warfare Review Commission concluded a review of the U.S. chemical munitions stockpile. The commission concluded that current stockpiles were inadequate and that the deterioration of old munitions presented a possible safety hazard. These findings strengthened the case for binary weapons (weapons that combine two harmless chemicals to produce a chemical agent), thus helping gain congressional approval for binary artillery shells and bombs. The 155-millimeter binary chemical artillery shell is ready for production, and the Bigeye chemical bomb is in advanced development, with operational testing scheduled for 1987.

In addition to offensive measures, the commission recommended improved protection measures, better detection and warning devices, improved prophylaxis, and casualty treatment. Seventy-five percent of the fiscal 1987 chemical warfare budget is for defensive equipment needs.[51]

In one respect, however, NATO's procedures for chemical warfare took a step backward in 1986. At the June Summit of Western Industrial Nations in Tokyo, President Reagan agreed to Chancellor Helmut Kohl's proposal that the United States withdraw its older chemical weapon stocks from West Germany and *not* replace them with the new binary weapons. The new weapons will be retained in the United States, except in a crisis, which would require moving the chemical weapons to Europe.

Naval Forces. The U.S. Navy edged toward its goal of 600 ships, with over $11 billion devoted to shipbuilding in fiscal 1987. Due to the long lead times, however, the force structure does not yet reflect this increase in investment. The only new ship deployed in 1986 was an additional Trident ballistic-missile submarine. Table 2.8 shows the number of each type of ship in 1985 and 1986.

The readiness of the Navy has improved considerably since fiscal 1980. Stocks of naval munitions and other expendibles have increased as much as 100 percent; training has increased, as measured by the size and number of exercises and by flying hours. There were 48 Joint Chiefs of Staff (JCS) exercises in fiscal 1980 and 86 in fiscal 1986.

TABLE 2.8

U.S. Navy: Deployable Battle Forces, 1985-1986

	1985	1986
Ballistic Missile Submarines	38	39
Strategic Support Ships	6	6
Aircraft Carriers	13	13
Battleships	3	3
Cruisers	32	32
Destroyers	69	69
Frigates	113	113
Nuclear Attack Submarines	97	97
Diesel Attack Submarines	4	4
Patrol Combatants	6	6
Amphibious Ships	62	62
Mine Warfare Ships	3	3
Combat Logistics Ships	54	53
Support Force Ships	54	55
TOTAL	554	555

Note: Data as of December 31, 1985 and December 29, 1986.

Sources: Caspar W. Weinberger, *Annual Report to the Congress Fiscal Year 1987* (Washington: GPO, 1986), p. 179; Caspar W. Weinberger, *Annual Report to the Congress Fiscal Year 1988* (Washington: GPO, 1987), p. 166.

The Gramm-Rudman budget cuts of 4.9 percent from the Navy budget, which were threatened in 1986, caused only minor revision of the Navy's five-year shipbuilding plans. Outright cancellation of ships is rare once plans have been approved. Future budget cutbacks, however, could result in stretch-outs. Worse yet, ships may be built without the money to arm and equip them. Initial outlays for naval construction are relatively low compared with total project costs, thus making possible the prospect that many programs started in the late 1980s might never be completed.

Air Forces. Despite the defense budget increases, the number of aircraft procured each year by the United States has declined. As shown in Figure 2.5, over the period 1981-1985, the United States produced an average of 355 aircraft per year for a total of 1,775, whereas the Soviet Union maintained an average rate of 640 aircraft per year for a total of 3,200 produced.

Research on the advanced technology fighter has continued, although operational status will not be achieved until near the year 2000. In addition, development has continued on the F-19 Stealth fighter. In August 1986, the *Washington Post* reported that 50 F-19 Stealth fighters

FIGURE 2.5. U.S. and Soviet Tactical Aircraft Production

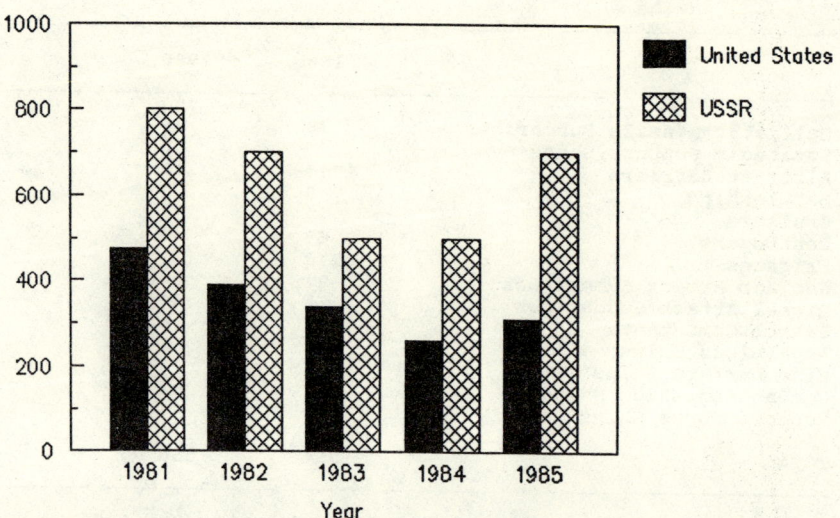

Source: Organization of the Joint Chiefs of Staff, *Military Posture FY 1987* (Washington: GPO, 1986), p. 52.

were operational in Nevada. These fighters are designed to minimize detectability, particularly when flying at night or in bad weather. They would be assigned to special missions in which surprise is at a premium. Although development has been secret, a plastic model of the F-19 has appeared in toy shops around the country. Department of Defense officials, however, have refused to comment on the authenticity of the model.

Aircraft procurement will suffer from the latest round of budget austerity. The Air Force procurement will shrink from $21 billion in fiscal 1986 to $17 billion in fiscal 1989, as shown in Table 2.9. These cutbacks, combined with increasing unit costs, will exacerbate the problem of modernizing air power.

Command, Control, Communications, and Intelligence. The U.S. Department of Defense and related agencies are conducting a number of programs to enhance U.S. command, control, communications, and intelligence capabilities. New doctrines such as AirLand Battle and Counter Air 90 are predicated on the creation of better C^{3}I.

One of the possible mismatches between doctrine and force posture is in battlefield surveillance capability. Current U.S. and NATO doctrine require timely and accurate intelligence on the status of the battlefield and targeting data.[52] The USAF/Army Joint Surveillance Target Attack

TABLE 2.9

U.S. Air Force Aircraft Procurement Program,
Fiscal 1986-1989 (in millions of dollars)

1986	1987	1988	1989
21,417.6	17,355.6	14,191.4	17,221.4

Source: Department of Defense, <u>Department of Defense Budget for Fiscal Years 1988 and 1989: Procurement Programs (P-1)</u> (Washington: DoD, January 1987), F-i.

Radar System (Joint STARS) is the centerpiece of AirLand Battle surveillance. Designed to provide an aerial view of the land battle similar to that provided by airborne warning and control system (AWACS) for the air battle, Joint STARS will detect enemy forces behind main battle lines and transmit data on their location to aircraft and ground weapons. Joint STARS is a wide-area, multimode radar system that will look beyond the forward line of own troops (FLOT), detecting and locating targets such as fixed and moving vehicles, command posts, assembly areas, and low flying aircraft, even in the inclement weather that prevails for the greater part of the year in central Europe. The major components of the Joint STARS radar are identical to those used in the Army Mohawk system, providing commonality for procurement and support of these systems. The first flight tests for Joint STARS are scheduled for summer of 1987, with the system reaching limited operational capability in September 1991.

Budget stringencies are causing cutbacks in programs intended to modernize C^3I and other electronic programs. In March 1986, for example, the Air Force canceled the Lockheed Precision Location Strike System (PLSS) scheduled for deployment on 10 TR-1 aircraft. This system would have provided real time data links from the TR-1 to weapon systems allocated to attack the target. According to Air Force Chief of Staff General Charles A. Gabriel, the Air Force has "other ways" to perform this task, including Joint STARS. In February 1987, the Air Force canceled plans to put new electronic countermeasure systems on its F-111s, citing higher-than-expected costs.

The USSR

Major changes in the Soviet command structure became evident in 1986. As early as 1985, the USSR began activating high commands within the theaters of military operations (TVDs) with high ranking commanders in chief. Marshal Nikolai Ogarkov, former head of the General Staff, was reported to have been appointed commander of the TVD against NATO's central region.[53]

There was no evidence of changes in Soviet defense procurement in 1986; that is, major modernization programs continued to produce several new weapons systems for the armed services. Systems newly introduced include a jet fighter, a large transport aircraft, and a combat helicopter. The emphasis on quality has also continued, closing the gap between Soviet and Western technology in aircraft, ships, and missile systems.

Ground Forces. Soviet ground force units are being reorganized into expanded tank and motorized rifle divisions. These new units are being configured for greater mobility and firepower. Modernization of Soviet ground forces equipment continued in 1986. Over one-third of the 52,600 main battle tanks in the Soviet arsenal have been replaced by the latest models from the T-64/72/80 series.[54] During the late 1980s, additional tanks will be fielded to bring the Soviet force to nearly 60,000. Other armored-vehicle programs have also proceeded, including the limited deployment of the BTR-80 wheeled armored personnel carrier.

The Soviet helicopter has assumed a new importance on the battlefield and will be used for a greater variety of missions. In addition to its application on the NATO battlefield, the helicopter has been essential to Soviet operations in Afghanistan. An indication of the significance the Soviets attach to helicopters is their insistence on the need for effective antihelicopter, as well as antitank, defenses. Traditionally, Soviet defense efforts have been concentrated against tanks, which were regarded as the major threat to the success of Soviet military actions. In the future, however, enemy helicopters will also become important targets. Helicopters and new helicopter technology have also received attention in the Soviet military press.[55]

The Mi-26 (which takes the NATO code name Halo) heavy lift helicopter created a sensation in the West when it appeared at the 1984 Farnborough Air Show. The Mi-26 is a product of the Mil Design Bureau. It evolved under the design leadership of Marat Tishenko, director of the design bureau since Mikhail Mil's death in January 1970 and creator of the Mi-24 attack helicopter series. The Mi-26 is the holder of five world records (including one for lifting a 33,000-pound load to 18,000 feet). With 8 rotor blades spanning 105 feet and powered by 2 engines (11,400 horsepower each), the Mi-26 is without technical or functional parallel in the West.

There is little evidence of advanced technology or technical innovations in the Mi-26. The design is consistent with the Mil Design Bureau's practice of employing established technology to minimize risk. Despite this cautious design philosophy, however, Soviet industry has produced its share of aircraft developmental failures and these include several major helicopter efforts. The Mi-26's conventionally articulated rotor architecture, semi-monocoque airframe, steel tube spar/fiberglass pocket rotorblades with symmetrical airfoils, and boosted push/pull rod control system though massive are skillfully engineered, but reflect Western design practices of the mid-1960s. Only the transmission design is innovative.[56]

The Soviets have developed a tactical doctrine for employing combat helicopters based on the capabilities of the Mi-24 Hind. They are also conducting major training and tactical experimentation efforts designed to integrate tank, motorized rifle, and attack helicopter units and to explore new ways of using helicopters independently and with operational maneuver groups (OMG). These efforts have been most evident since 1976.[57]

Development of the Hind probably began in the middle to late 1960s, with the first operational model surfacing in the early 1970s. According to one Warsaw Pact news source, the Hind was developed on the basis of the Sikorsky Blackhawk, with the mission of carrying a dozen troops.[58] The Mi-24 incorporates many of the design features of the Mi-8 Hip, including the same engines and the same five-bladed main and three-bladed antitorque rotor systems.

In 1986 the replacement for the Hind—the Mi-28 Havoc antitank helicopter—was reported to have entered service with the Soviet Groups of Forces in Eastern Europe. The Mi-28 is comparable to the U.S. AH-64 Apache and is armed with the AT-6 Spiral antitank guided weapon and a nose-mounted cannon. The Havoc appears to be a logical development following the Mi-24 Hind D/E and reputedly shares common propulsion, rotor, and other components with the Hind.[59]

Yet another Soviet helicopter in development is the Hokum. It is reportedly capable of speeds up to 210 mph and will have a dedicated air-to-air mission.[60] Its purpose is to achieve rotary wing air superiority over the battlefield.

Increased Soviet use of remotely piloted vehicles for surveillance and target designation is also forecast for the 1990s, although no details have been made public.[61] The Soviet Union has long been interested in the use of unmanned systems, but it lags behind the West in their application, especially where advanced computing and artificial intelligence capabilities are concerned.

Naval Forces. The mission of the Soviet Navy is fundamentally different from that of the U.S. Navy. Whereas the United States must preserve its use of the sea to maintain its economy and to reinforce its military allies, the USSR's mission is primarily negative—to deny the West use of the sea-lanes. Only recently has a capability for Soviet naval power projection been developed, and this capability remains a limited one due to the size and quality of the force as well as operational constraints.

Consequently, submarines are the dominant force in the Soviet Navy. They accounted for about 43 percent of total naval tonnage produced by the USSR in recent years.[62] Offensive strategic operations by SSBNs are perhaps the highest priority mission of the Soviet Navy. This operation also encompasses tasks in support of SSBNs—namely, antisubmarine warfare. Antisubmarine warfare constitutes the mission of much of the submarine force, most surface combatants, and many sea- and land-based aircraft. Despite this emphasis, the Soviet Navy has a limited capability for open-ocean ASW search, and the submarine force is not without accidents. In May 1986, an Echo II-class Soviet submarine was spotted being towed in the Sea of Japan.

The ascendancy of the submarine was aided by the appointment of Admiral Vladimir Chernavin as commander in chief of the Soviet Navy in December 1985. Chernavin, who served in submarine operations for most of his distinguished career, characterized the submarine force as the main strike force of the Soviet Navy in the January 1986 issue of *Morskoi Sbornik*, the official Soviet Navy journal.

The Navy is charged with a strategic defense mission against enemy SSBNs and carriers. Preemptive attacks on land-based enemy nuclear forces or command and control also fit this category. The Soviet Navy supports ground force operations by providing mobility, fire support, and air support. Interdiction of sea lines of communication is accomplished through a variety of surface combatants and submarines, with an emphasis on mining. Finally, Soviet naval forces are used for diplomatic and political purposes to "carry the flag."

The Soviet Navy is hindered by geography, given its limited access to the open ocean. This hindrance is mitigated to some extent by use of overseas facilities. In difficult times, Soviet naval aircraft have operated for limited periods from Cuba, Guinea, Ethiopia, Angola, South Yemen, Libya, Syria, and Vietnam.[63] In addition, shore-based logistic and repair facilities have been provided by Syria, Cuba, Guinea, Angola, South Yemen, Ethiopia, and Vietnam.[64] For the most part, however, these facilities are not under Soviet control, and their disposition is subject to dramatic change.

In December 1985, the Soviet Navy launched its first conventional aircraft carrier at the Nikolaev shipyard. The nuclear-powered vessel—at 1,000 feet in length and displacing 65,000 tons—is considerably smaller than its U.S. modern counterparts. It is equipped with both a flight deck for conventional fixed-wing aircraft and a ramp for vertical short takeoff and landing (VTSOL) aircraft. Aircraft for the carrier are still under development. The carrier itself will not achieve operational status for another three to four years; in the meantime, a second carrier will be built, scheduled for launch in 1989.

Air Forces. Two new Soviet aircraft made their debut in 1986. The An-124 wide-body transport aircraft entered operational service under the auspices of Aeroflot, primarily for the purpose of heavy lift operations in Siberia. The aircraft, similar in size and configuration to the U.S. C-5, was shown at the Paris Air Show in June 1985. Four production models have been built so far. U.S. engineers who have examined the An-124 see many similarities between the Soviet aircraft and the Lockheed C-5. The general configuration is very similar, and observers noted that the design is cleaner than previous Soviet transports. The sweep of the wing and horizontal tail tips, the negative dihedral, the wing fuselage fairings, the control surfaces, and the aft door arrangement all mirror earlier models of the C-5.[65] The An-124 is the largest Soviet airlifter, with a maximum payload of 150 metric tons, and can accommodate oversized cargo such as the SS-20 transporter-erector-launcher, tanks, helicopters, and missiles.

The second new aircraft, the MiG-29 Fulcrum made its first appearance in the West in July 1986 when an aerobatic team of four MiG-29s visited Kuopio-Rissala Air Force Base in Finland. First deployed in 1984, some 100 Fulcrums are now in service in the USSR. The Fulcrum is reportedly the first Soviet fighter with a true look-down/shoot-down radar, and it is armed with up to six AA-10 active-radar homing medium-range air-to-air missiles. An export version is said to be imminent for India and Syria, armed with less capable AA-7 Apex and AA-8 Aphid missiles.[66] The Su-27 Flanker is being introduced in small numbers, after initial development delays.

The introduction of new aircraft carries with it the need to change operations, training, and (potentially) resource allocation. To take advantage of the latest generation of combat aircraft, for instance, the Soviets reportedly are beginning to adopt new tactics that place a greater emphasis on pilot initiative.

More expensive aircraft also force tough budgetary choices. There is no reason to believe that the Soviet Union has escaped the increasing unit costs for aircraft. Indeed, because skilled labor and quality materials are more scarce in the Soviet Union than in the United States, their true costs may be even greater. Manufacturing difficulties with new aircraft have also become evident. For example, the Su-27 and MiG-29 production lines were halted because of a lack of vital components (namely, Tumansky R-31 engines for the MiG-29s and long-range track-while-scan pulse Doppler radars for the Su-27s).[67] Such incidents suggest that the new technologies are stretching thin the ability of the Soviet military-industrial complex. Another possible indicator of rising costs is the slowdown in Soviet fighter aircraft procurement from 950 aircraft in 1983 to 700 in 1985.[68] Nonetheless, some U.S. analysts continue to believe that Soviet fighter production will return to its late 1970s peak of 1,200 aircraft a year as production of new models becomes established.[69]

Selected Regional Balances

The true test of military balance is war. In the absence of the ideal laboratory condition of East-West conflict, static measures of force levels and dynamic models, which estimate combat effectiveness, must serve as surrogates in judging the balance of power. For conventional conflict, data can indicate weapon lethality, mobility, and attrition based on test results and the experiences of recent wars. The tactics of each side are known to the other, and exercises are regularly conducted.

In principle, several conditions must be fulfilled in order to measure the military balance. First, the time of conflict must be specified, but with allowances made for mobilization and the addition of bonuses to account for the element of surprise. The quantities of manpower and weapons (i.e., the inputs for warfare) for each side must be known, including any allies that might be involved. Technical characteristics must be established for weapons, including maintenance and reliability indices. Tactics and operational methods should come into play, in addition to weighting factors for the quality of manpower, leadership, training, and morale. Finally, weather and geography must be considered crucial parts of the equation.

Unfortunately, neither adequate data nor convincing analytical frameworks exist to predict East-West conflict in a sophisticated fashion on paper or in a computer model. As a result, analysts too often end up "looking where the light is brightest," regardless of how incomplete the resulting analyses may be. For example, estimates of Soviet weapon performance have become enshrined in the Western literature without regard to their level of reliability. Although some weapons that have fallen into the hands of nations friendly with or allied with the United States have been tested extensively, other estimates are derived by far less precise means. Uncertainty increases when the "softer" areas of warfare—manpower, morale, and training—are addressed. Although the deficiencies of NATO forces have been openly discussed, the Warsaw Pact makes every attempt to conceal whatever weaknesses it may suffer. Some sketchy details on the effectiveness of Soviet troops have emerged from émigré and defector anecdotes, but they provide an insufficient foundation for Western force planning.

Even if the data were complete, measuring the military balance would be difficult. Warfare is the largest organized human activity, mobilizing the minds and resources of entire nations for years at a time. It is not easy to simplify the military balance into a scientific model or even to detail the factors of war along some metric of their importance.

NATO-Warsaw Pact. The most important contingency for the United States, short of strategic nuclear war, would be a Warsaw Pact attack on NATO. This threat is the primary determinant of the size and structure of U.S. general purpose forces.

It is artificial at best, and misleading at worst, to consider separately the NATO conventional and nuclear military balances or theater and strategic warfare. For the most part, these dichotomies have been adopted not for their meaning in strategy but for the sake of practicality and understanding in making comparisons of military forces.

Indeed, the distinction between conventional and nuclear warfare is artificial because weapons systems capable of delivering either nuclear, chemical, or conventional ordnance have become commonplace. In peacetime, it is difficult to arrive at ground rules for counting such dual-use systems as tactical aircraft and artillery. In the heat of battle, it would be even more difficult to determine when the nuclear firebreak is likely to be crossed, unless governments make their moves explicit, foresaking the tactical advantages of surprise and deception.

This is not to say that conventional forces are irrelevant. Rather, the goal of NATO's conventional forces is more limited than an ability to defeat Pact armies in a conventional conflict. Soviet operational art and tactics do not point to a "blitzkrieg" attack against NATO using strictly conventional forces. To do so, the Soviets would have to assume that NATO conventional forces could be defeated in a matter of days and that NATO, contrary to its declared doctrine, would refrain from using or be unable to use nuclear weapons as the Warsaw Pact swept through central Europe. Perhaps most problematic, the Soviets would have to believe that Britain and France would not use their own nuclear weapons when confronting total defeat.[70]

There is much that NATO could do to prevent the Warsaw Pact from contemplating the possibility of a conventional victory. NATO requires adequate forces to make a successful Warsaw Pact conventional offensive unlikely. NATO nuclear weapons should be made invulnerable to Soviet preemptive attacks utilizing conventional forces and, preferably, invulnerable to nuclear preemption as well. More survivable nuclear forces would create disincentives for Soviet escalation to nuclear weapons; they would also make the threat of NATO's nuclear use more plausible.

The United States' European allies have been reluctant to significantly improve conventional forces, and there is no evidence that this will change. The most obvious reasons for this reticence are political and economic: West European populations find the threats of war or Soviet coercion too remote to warrant significant growth in defense spending. In addition, each improvement in conventional forces, by raising the nuclear threshold, intensifies European fears that the U.S. nuclear guarantee—which the Europeans believe to be the true deterrent—may be withdrawn. The SDI fuels these concerns with its inherent appeal to isolationism.

Conventional forces complement the nuclear deterrent; they do not substitute for them. Indeed, raising the level of conventional forces without also improving the security of NATO nuclear forces deployed in Europe could lower the nuclear threshold, thereby tempting the Soviets to launch a preemptive strike against NATO's nuclear stockpiles. The present deployment arrangement, optimized for maintaining security against terrorists or other low-level threats, also makes nuclear weapons easy and lucrative targets. Collocating cruise missiles with NATO airfields presents a similar opportunity to a Soviet targeteer.

Figures 2.6, 2.7, and 2.8 provide updated information on NATO and Warsaw Pact force levels. In nearly every hardware and manpower category, NATO forces are outnumbered by those of the Warsaw Pact. A number of caveats must be attached to such side-by-side statistical comparisons, however.

Despite what the weapons numbers reveal, they also conceal many vital factors. The billions of dollars spent by NATO on less visible items such as maintenance, support, logistics, mobility, training, and C^3I are not reflected in the tables. Because these investments yield improvements in the strength of Western forces, they should be accounted for in weighing the balance.[71] In addition, weapons in inventory should not be counted with the same weight as weapons deployed in operational units. Statistics for actual deployment, however, are difficult to obtain, especially for the Warsaw Pact.

The most devastating scenario for NATO would be a Warsaw Pact attack with little or no strategic warning. Such a scenario, however, is a very expensive assumption to use as the basis for force planning, particularly if it is not a realistic contingency. In all likelihood, a period of extended political tension would precede any attack. NATO must make its mobilizable conventional forces strong enough to make the prospect of Warsaw Pact conventional victory a matter of weeks or months. This measure would not remove the specter of nuclear escalation from war in Europe, but it would diminish the political utility of a strong Soviet conventional force focused against Western Europe.

The greatest uncertainty for the Soviet Union is the reliability of Warsaw Pact allies. Not only might the potential effectiveness of Warsaw Pact troops be reduced by the lower capability of East European units,

FIGURE 2.6.

NATO-Warsaw Pact Combat Aircraft*

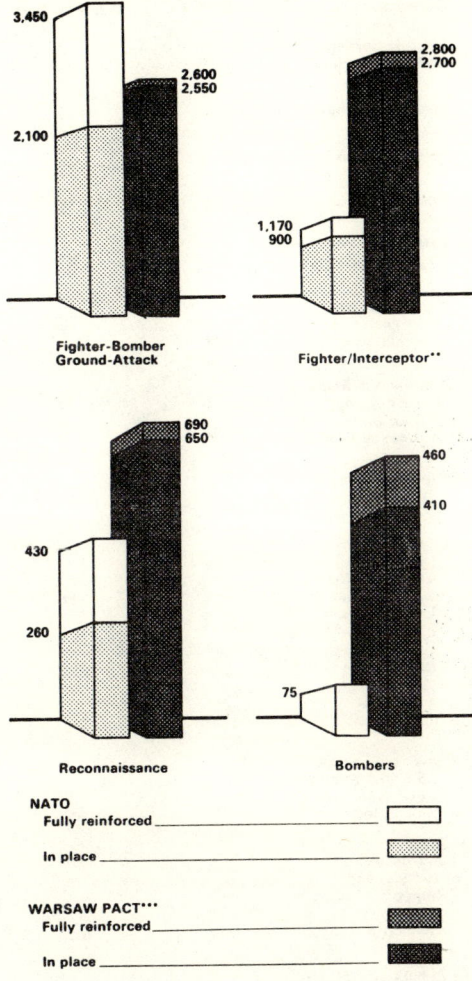

Excludes France and Spain.

* US estimate of 1986 NATO data.
** Excludes Soviet strategic interceptors.
*** An additional 4,000 trainers are available.

Source: *Soviet Military Power 1987* (Washington, D.C.: GPO, 1987), p. 92.

FIGURE 2.7.

NATO and Warsaw Pact Maritime Forces in the North Atlantic and Seas Bordering Europe 1986*

Category	NATO	Warsaw Pact
Aircraft Carriers VSTOL Carriers	11	—
KIEV-Class Ships	—	2
Helicopter Carriers	6	2
Cruisers	16	22
Destroyers, Frigates, Corvettes	310	201
Coastal Escorts and Fast Patrol Boats	267	586
Amphibious Ships		
- Ocean-going	57	24
- Other Ships/Coastal Craft	71	188
Mine Warfare Ships/Craft	270	330**
Total Submarines (All Types)	206	258
- Ballistic Missile Submarines	35	44
- Long-Range Attack Submarines	68	145
- Other Types	103	69
- % Submarines Nuclear Powered	50%	51%
Sea-based Tactical ASW and Support Aircraft Including Helicopters	832	205
Land-Based Tactical and Support Aircraft Including Helicopters	389	527
Land-Based Anti-Submarine Warfare Fixed-Wing Aircraft and Helicopters	462	209

   Excludes France and Spain
* US Estimate of 1986 NATO data
** Excludes minesweeping boats and drones

Source: *Soviet Military Power 1987* (Washington, D.C.: GPO, 1987), p. 92.

FIGURE 2.8.

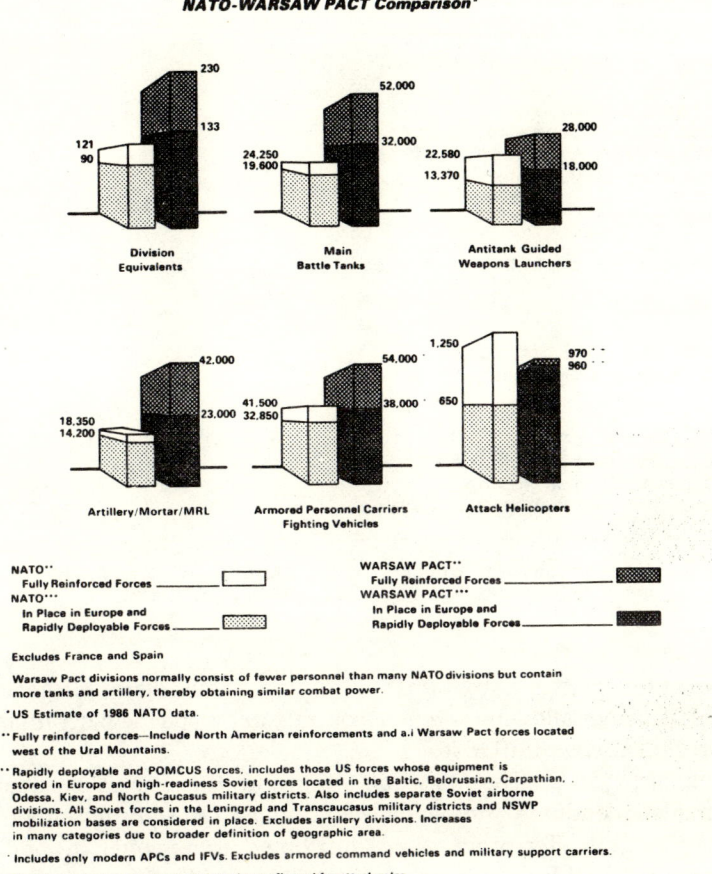

Source: *Soviet Military Power 1987* (Washington, D.C.: GPO, 1987), p. 93.

but Soviet forces may have to be diverted from fighting in order to control allied forces.

Just as the Warsaw Pact has a built-in weakness in its wartime alliance, NATO has hidden strengths. First, the morale and motivation of troops defending their own territory is inherently high. More important, the French armed forces—which are usually excluded from force comparisons because they do not participate in NATO joint planning—must be weighed on the side of the West. In 1986 France became more involved in NATO military planning, agreeing to hold joint maneuvers with

TABLE 2.10

Potential U.S. Forces in Southwest Asia

ARMY

1 airborne division
1 airmobile/air assault division
1 mechanized infantry division
2 infantry divisions

MARINE CORPS

1 1/3 Marine amphibious forces

AIR FORCE

7 tactical fighter wings
2 strategic bomber squadrons

NAVY

3 carrier battle groups
1 surface action group
5 maritime patrol air squadrons

Source: Organization of the Joint Chiefs of Staff, <u>Military Posture FY 1988</u> (Washington: GPO, 1987), p. 263.

German troops in West Germany, forming a joint staff college with the Germans, and allowing French contractors to participate in the U.S. Strategic Defense Initiative.

Southwest Asia. The Iran-Iraq War and the Soviet occupation of Afghanistan endured another year with no end in sight for either conflict as 1987 began. Terrorism also contributed to regional instability and raised the risk of U.S intervention. Iran occupied Iraqi territory in January 1987, and the campaign seemed headed for a costly war of attrition.

General Secretary Gorbachev announced that Soviet troop withdrawals from Afghanistan would take place in summer 1986. According to Western intelligence sources, these turned out to be illusory. The Soviet armed presence was not, in fact, cut. Nonetheless, Gorbachev has seemed more willing than his predecessors to enter into talks on Afghanistan.

The commander in chief of the Central Command (USCINCCENT) has responsibility for U.S. combat forces in Southwest Asia. Table 2.10 lists the assets at his disposal as of January 1987. Air Force and Navy mobility programs determine the ability of the United States to move forces to Southwest Asia. In 1980, only one division could be moved to the region in the first month of conflict. When planned mobility programs, including the C-17 heavy air lifter, are completed in the 1990s, the United States will have the capacity to transport seven divisions in the first month.[72]

Because of its geographical proximity to the region, the USSR has a much larger potential force in Southwest Asia. The southern theater of military operations, which covers Afghanistan, Iran, eastern Turkey, the Caucasus, and Turkestan, is made up of some 30 divisions. The number of divisions actually available, however, depends on the scenario.

First, many of the divisions in the southern TVD are Category II or Category III divisions, manned and equipped in peacetime at only a portion of their full combat strength. More important, most of the forces would need to be held in reserve for the contingency of a war with NATO. Any Soviet attack on Iran would clearly raise the prospect of U.S. involvement, and the USSR could hardly let down its guard on NATO's Southern Flank. According to a thorough analysis of the scenario, the Soviets could employ a maximum of 10 to 11 divisions in a war in Iran, provided that forces were built up in northern Iran for a drive to the oilfields in the south. In a direct drive from the USSR, some 7 divisions would reach Khuzestan.[73]

For a U.S.-Soviet conflict in Iran, the division counts may be less important than the harsh realities of geography. Soviet forces would have to cover around 1,200 kilometers of some of the least hospitable territory imaginable between their bases and the line of engagement in Khuzestan. There are only a dozen major rail or road arteries leading along the Soviet invasion route, each of which crosses mountain ranges and contains a number of choke points.

According to Epstein's analysis, a five-division U.S. force would be sufficient to make an overland advance seem quite risky to the Soviets. In the first phase of its defense, Western forces would delay the Soviet advance into northern Iran, chiefly with the use of air power, while setting up positions in Khuzestan. The second phase would be aimed at weakening the Soviet advance over the Zagros Mountains while building up for the main battle. The final phase would call for combined arms engagement of Soviet forces, using ground, air, and naval units.

East Asia. Increased tension along the Korean border and continued Soviet interest in the region were evident in 1986. In a speech in Vladivostok on July 29, 1986, General Secretary Gorbachev emphasized the importance of Asia to the Soviet Union. The speech reiterated his intention to improve relations with the People's Republic of China and hinted at troop reductions in Mongolia and Afghanistan. A year earlier, the Soviet Union made a more concrete gesture. In its OKEAN-85 exercise east of Japan, close to 75 percent of the Soviet Pacific Fleet simulated combat with one another.[74] According to a 1986 Japanese Defense Agency white paper, the Soviet Union currently deploys a quarter of its total military force in the Far East, including 162 SS-20 intermediate-range missiles and about 85 Tupolev Backfire bombers, along with 2,390 combat aircraft. Soviet forces also include two small V/STOL aircraft carriers—the Minsk and the Novorossisk, the battle cruiser Frunze, and destroyer and missile cruiser escorts. The Japanese estimate that 41 Soviet divisions in East Asia are equipped with T-72 tanks.[75]

China is continuing its path toward smaller and better trained and equipped armed forces. An important element of this program is the acquisition of advanced technology. In late 1986, the People's Republic of China signed an agreement to purchase $550 million worth of advanced U.S. radars and electronic equipment for their F-8 fighter aircraft, a Chinese version of the Soviet MiG-21. This is the largest Chinese military purchase since China became eligible under the U.S. Foreign Military Sales Act in 1984. Also under negotiation is the transfer of technology and production facilities for Mark 46 antisubmarine torpedoes. Secretary of Defense Caspar Weinberger visited China in early October 1986, followed by a port call by the USS Oldendorf, a Spruance-class destroyer, to Qingdao in November 1986.[76]

China has no real aspiration of meeting the force levels that the Soviets have deployed in Asia. Rather, the goals of the Chinese military have become intensive, particularly in their emphasis on nuclear capabilities and technology over quantity.

Japan has shown increased initiative toward its military responsibilities. In a compromise with the ministry of finance, Japan's Defense Agency agreed to a 6.3 percent increase in the FY 1987 defense budget, resulting for the first time in defense spending above 1 percent of GNP. The importance of this move is easily overestimated, however, as the amount over 1 percent is a small fraction of a percentage, much of which is devoted to officer pay raises. The new defense budget will not significantly change the Japanese force posture. According to a new white paper on defense, Japan will remain governed by the Defense Principle of 1976, limiting the air self-defense force to 10 fighter interceptor squadrons, 3 close support squadrons, a reconnaissance squadron, 3 transport squadrons, and an airborne early warning squadron with 28 air defense radar units. The maritime self-defense forces embody 16 land-based antisubmarine aircraft squadrons.[77]

North Korean military readiness was stepped up in 1986, apparently in preparation for a possible attack on South Korea. According to defector reports, civilians were stockpiling war provisions and working on an extensive network of underground tunnels near the demilitarized zone (DMZ).

Can the Soviets Compete in High-Technology Weapons?

The future military balance depends on the scientific investigation and engineering development being conducted today. Indeed, the long lead times of new weapon systems commonly stretch to a decade or more before initial deployment. Therefore, the technological competition is ultimately reflected in the arms competition between the East and the West.

For the past three years, the DoD has ranked relative U.S. and Soviet standing in basic military technologies (see Table 2.11). The United States remains ahead in fourteen of these categories, whereas the Soviet Union does not lead in any.

Although the standings indicated in Table 2.11 favor the West, technological trends may not. Despite a 56 percent increase in DoD research and development spending between FY 1981 and FY 1985, the relative U.S. standing in key technologies improved only in radar sensor technology, while declining in electro-optical sensors, microelectronic materials, and submarine detection.[78]

Technologies, like resources, merely indicate the potential for military power. It is potential that may be converted into fielded military forces. Although the Soviet Union continues to lag behind the West in many areas of technology, the gap in fielded military systems is narrowing. In many categories, Soviet weapons are the functional equivalents of their Western counterparts. Moreover, the Soviet Union has a good record for fielding large numbers of weapons using the best technology available at the time. According to Gerold Yonas, former chief scientist of the SDI program, the Soviets "get their equipment out in the field and learn by doing. In some cases they are able to deploy devices even before we do, even though we had the technology first."[79]

Some of the most interesting questions of Soviet military R&D involve the timing of decisions and their relation to outside factors, such as U.S. military programs. Unfortunately, the USSR does not reveal such dates in its open literature. Therefore, the impetus behind Soviet military programs cannot be explained satisfactorily with the available evidence.

Soviet aircraft design provides a number of case studies that illustrate overall weapons design practices, especially those for high-technology weaponry. A growing body of evidence indicates that Soviet aircraft-procurement practices have undergone significant changes in the past two decades. The conservatism that characterized Soviet designs up to the 1960s seems to have been abandoned in favor of an approach more like that of the West, taking greater technological risks and incorporating many new technologies in a single aircraft. The most tangible evidence

TABLE 2.11
Relative U.S./USSR Standing in the Twenty Most Important Basic Technology Areas*

Basic Technologies	U.S. Superior	U.S./USSR Equal	USSR Superior
1. Aerodynamics/Fluid Dynamics		X	
2. Computers and Software	←X		
3. Conventional Warheads (Including all Chemical Explosives)		X	
4. Directed Energy (Laser)		X	
5. Electro-Optical Sensor (Including Infrared)	X		
6. Guidance and Navigation	X		
7. Life Sciences (Human Factors/Biotechnology)	X		
8. Materials (Lightweight, High Strength, High Temperature)	X →		
9. Micro-Electronic Materials and Integrated Circuit Manufacturing	X		
10. Nuclear Warheads		X	
11. Optics		X	
12. Power Sources (Mobile) (Includes Energy Storage)		X	
13. Production/Manufacturing (Includes Automated Control)	X		
14. Propulsion (Aerospace and Ground Vehicles)	X →		
15. Radar Sensor	X →		
16. Robotics and Machine Intelligence	X		
17. Signal Processing	X		
18. Signature Reduction	X		
19. Submarine Detection	X →		
20. Telecommunications (Includes Fiber Optics)	X		

*1. The list is limited to 20 technologies, which were selected with the objective of providing a valid base for comparing overall U.S. and USSR basic technology. The list is in alphabetical order. These technologies are "on the shelf" and available for application. (The technologies are not intended to compare technology levels in currently deployed military systems.)

2. The technologies selected have the potential for significantly changing the military capability in the next 10 to 20 years. The technologies are not static; they are improving or have the potential for significant improvements; new technologies may appear on future lists.

3. The arrows denote that the relative technology level is changing significantly in the direction indicated.

4. Relative comparisons of technology levels shown depict overall average standing only; countries may be superior, equal or inferior in subcategories of a given technology.

5. These average assessments can incorporate a significant variance when the individual components of a technology are considered.

Source: Under Secretary of Defense, Research, and Engineering, *The FY 1987 Department of Defense Program for Research and Development* (Washington, D.C.: Department of Defense, 1987), p. II-11.

can be seen in the MiG-29, the Su-27, and the Su-25 fighters, as well as the An-124 heavy lifter. By the end of the 1960s, the Soviet Union was learning about the inadequacies of its aircraft from the war in Vietnam. Aircraft designers of the Stalinist generation were slowly fading from the scene. Artem Mikoyan and Mikhail Mil died in 1970, Andrei Tupolev in 1972, Pavel Sukhoi in 1975, and Mikhail Gurevich (the other half of the MiG name) in 1976.

Although it may have seemed that the USSR had foresaken quality for quantity in aircraft procurement, the Soviets want to have both high technology and large numbers of fielded weapons. The combat record of Soviet aircraft under Moscow's proxies must have awakened them to the lesson that quality counts in a sobering way. For instance, the poor showing of the MiG-21 and MiG-23 fighters of the Syrian air force against Israeli F-15s and F-16s did nothing to bolster the credibility of Soviet air power or, for that matter, the reputation of the USSR as an arms supplier.

As details of the new aircraft destined for the Soviet air forces emerge, U.S. understanding of the Soviet design process will grow clearer. The new aircraft are much more capable, more complex, and presumably more expensive than their predecessors.

After twenty-five years of simple and easily produced Soviet fighters—the MiG-15 and the Sukhoi Su-7 through Su-22 series—the MiG-23 that emerged in 1964 showed a noticeable Western design influence. Powered by the first Soviet afterburning turbofan (the Tumansky R-27), the MiG-23 featured a new variable geometry wing design and extensive avionics, including a pulse Doppler Highlark AI radar and laser ranger. This radar is comparable to the F-4Js AWG-10 radar and, overall, the Flogger seemed to emulate the F-4 Phantom, which had always dominated the MiGs in combat.[80]

The Su-24 Fencer that appeared in 1972 was more noticeably a Western design, and the surprising source for the Fencer was the F-111. The similarities between the Su-24 and the F-111 are more than physical. Both planes began as large fighters and ended as bombers. The addition of a weapons control officer to support the pilot, of all-weather capability, of terrain-following radar, and of extensive external load and internal fuel tank space were departures from previous Soviet designs.[81]

Improvements in the quality of Soviet military hardware carry important implications for procurement practices and economic planning. In some cases, sophisticated weapons not only raise costs but also increase the burden of training, maintenance, and support. In other cases, however, advanced technology leads to systems that are more reliable and easier to maintain. For example, manual flight controls in the latest generation of aircraft are being replaced by digital fly-by-wire or fly-by-light flight controls. These are much lighter than the manual controls that consist of actuator rods and servos that run the length of the aircraft. Fly-by-light and fly-by-wire also allow greater integration of controls with the flight computer, increasing maneuverability and decreasing pilot workload. Because the mission (and the life of the crew) depend on these flight controls, they must be reliable. Therefore, redundant systems are used for critical flight control functions. The least desirable state of military technology is to have mechanical systems as a backup to unreliable electronic controls. In such a case, one pays a design and maintenance penalty without the full benefit of the new technology.

New technology may run counter to traditional Soviet maintenance philosophy for combat aircraft. In many cases, weapons demand sophisticated diagnostic instrumentation. On the other hand, Soviet electronic systems are often merely replaced rather than repaired in the field, adapting well to Soviet depot maintenance practices. More sophisticated weapons also create new demands on training. These demands could be significant, considering the relatively low-skill levels of most soldiers in the Soviet army. Already, the Soviet military press is replete with complaints about the misuse of battlefield computers and other electronic devices.

Soviet Design Practice—A Balance Sheet

Design simplicity has its own advantages. Once a decision to produce is made, the production cycle is shorter for a system that requires minimum retooling and worker training. The result is a simple, sturdy, reliable, inexpensive, and easy-to-manufacture weapons system.[82] The USSR reduces R&D outlays by relying on foreign technology and uses foreign programs to allocate research funds and order investment policies. The Soviet procurement system, like those of Britain, France, and Germany, is superior to that of the United States in the first stages of a weapons program. System prime contractors are chosen quickly, usually without a costly and lengthy competition, and cost estimates approximate actual costs.[83] The ease with which prime contractors are chosen is due largely to the absence of intervention by legislatures.

Perhaps the most obvious advantage of Soviet design practices is cost. Simple, unsophisticated weapons can be produced cheaply. Standardization of subsystems allows for economies of scale otherwise impossible. Long production runs cut tooling cost as well as unit cost.

There is little reason to assume, however, that the Soviet Union will escape from rising procurement costs—the bane of the Western defense industry. Indeed, the cost of building comparable high-technology weapons in the Soviet Union may be higher due to the scarcity of high-quality inputs and skilled labor. It is not even clear that the simpler Soviet aircraft of the past cost less than their U.S. counterparts.[84] These problems may loom larger in the minds of the Soviet leadership if the opportunity costs are perceived to conflict with other goals, such as economic growth or the health of civilian industry.

Borrowing technology from another country is an approach with inherent limitations. First, only a country that is behind in an area of technology can gain by borrowing the work of another. Overreliance on foreign technology inhibits domestic innovation and ultimately weakens the nation's scientific base. The inferior performance of Soviet technology compared to that of the United States, in light of the fact that the USSR spends more on R&D than does the United States, testifies to the limits of this approach.[85]

There are also serious limits to the utility of incrementalism. For example, the Soviets have used electronic tubes in more applications and for a longer time than any other major electronic industry. Although the electron tube is fully capable of performing most electronic functions, tube technology has reached its limit in modern applications. Complex electron tubes are bulky, heavy, and have high power and cooling requirements. The prolonged use of such tubes has driven the Soviet aircraft designer to accept the weight penalty, find space to accommodate the larger devices, provide adequate electrical power to activate the tubes, and provide sufficient cooling to dissipate the generated heat.[86]

The USSR does not seem to be getting its money's worth from high R&D expenditures. Although the military market is one of the few markets in the Soviet Union in which the buyer prevails, products coming out of this sector have had difficulty competing commercially with Western products. This is most evident in the area of civil aircraft, where even Soviet Bloc countries would like to choose non-Soviet products. (Bloc countries find it difficult to choose non-Soviet products, however, because of export restrictions and foreign exchange problems.)[87] In addition, Soviet aircraft are at a disadvantage in the world market because of their poor record for maintenance and spare parts availability. In civil aviation, the cost of maintenance and operation is often more important over the lifespan of an aircraft than the acquisition cost. This maintenance and spare parts disadvantage is, to some extent, a deliberate result of military policies aimed at combat aircraft whose useful lifetime is much shorter than civilian aircraft.

One cause of the Soviet Union's relative technological backwardness appears to lie in the introduction and dissemination of technology. The centrally administered Soviet economy has no spontaneous mechanism that operates automatically to spur technological progress in the way that profit-seeking competition does in the West. On the contrary, the system contains automatic deterrents to innovation, in both the bureaucracy and the incentive structure.[88]

There seems to be an uncanny coincidence of Soviet aircraft development shortly after similar requirements are generated in the West. The difference is that the Soviet system shows greater inertia, developing and deploying even those weapons (e.g., the MiG-25) whose requirements have disappeared in the interim.

These obstacles can be overcome by the power and authority of the political leadership of the USSR, but such gains are not free of cost. As military equipment grows more complex, the insulation of weapon production from the deficiencies of the rest of the economy becomes increasingly difficult—even in the face of ministerial protectionism. Thus, at the 25th Party Congress, General Secretary Leonid Brezhnev insisted that planners and producers take greater cognizance of the interdependencies that exist among branches of the economy, and Major General M. Cherednichenko soon responded that the defense industries had heeded Brezhnev's order.[89] If high technology becomes the rule rather than the exception for military R&D in the Soviet Union, past practices will become increasingly inadequate to compete with the West.

The West depends on its technological edge to compensate for quantitative shortfalls in weaponry. The USSR is making a concerted effort, with at least some success, to close this gap, while at the same time taking into account the conditions that govern the manufacture and operation of these systems in the Soviet Union. Through borrowed Western technology and high-priority domestic efforts, the Soviet Union is fielding weapons that narrow the qualitative gap with the West.

Despite its progress, the Soviet leadership cannot be overly optimistic about the technology race. The USSR lacks a high-technology civilian sector essential for the rate of innovation enjoyed in the West. The computer industry is an example in which progress in defense technology in the West has been prompted by efforts to build civilian products such as office computers. In several key areas of military production, the USSR is being forced into a qualitative competition in which it is clearly at a disadvantage. The Soviet leadership faces a choice between high-quality production at high unit costs and low-quality production in greater numbers. Some key areas such as aviation and electronic warfare, however, will not tolerate the second approach.

Conclusion

The Reagan administration has succeeded in funding the largest peacetime defense buildup in U.S. history, spending roughly $1 trillion in the first Reagan five years. This buildup has reversed a relative decline in many U.S. military capabilities, improved the quality and morale of the armed services, and sent a strong signal to friends and enemies alike that the United States is serious about defense and will not let the growth of Soviet military power go unchallenged. This increase in spending, however, has not been sufficient to reverse negative trends for the United States in indices that measure quantities of military hardware.

Perceptions of the military balance have shifted to the West's advantage, regardless of these facts and statistics. The election of President Reagan instantly boosted perceptions of the strength of the United States and the morale of the U.S. armed forces. This was more the result of Reagan's rhetoric, which stressed the utility of force as an instrument in foreign policy, than the result of increased defense budgets, which were not significantly different from Carter's post-Afghanistan plans. Successful applications of U.S. military power in Grenada, in the *Achille Lauro* incident, and against Libya have heightened perceptions that U.S. military power has been enhanced.

Although these issues are related, the West should pay more attention to redressing the mismatches between its own requirements and capabilities than to keeping pace with growth in Warsaw Pact inventories. Neither the nuclear nor conventional forces of the West are presently sufficient for the stated strategies that would govern their use. In part, it is because these strategies were born of a combination of political exigency and wishful thinking. Another contributing factor is the propensity of the United States to issue doctrinal declarations long before the weapons to carry them out are available. In other cases, the U.S. force posture has never adequately responded to growth in the potential targets of its actions. The nuclear "countervailing" strategy, for example, has never been matched with sufficent survivable weapons capable of destroying hardened targets to meet its requirements. In peacetime, these mismatches may be tolerable, as long as forces are adequate to maintain deterrence. In wartime or crisis, however, these deficiencies would be extremely damaging to the West.

The democracies of the Western alliance do not judge their military requirements merely against military threats. Rather, the equation contains other key factors such as the economy, the state of international political relations, and domestic political concerns. Regardless of whether the military threat continues to grow, domestic requirements will curtail the share of the nation's resources devoted to defense. Barring some new and severe international crisis, it is hard to imagine a U.S. administration in 1988 able to create a new consensus for real growth in defense spending.

The Soviet Union, of course, will face its own problems. First, it is unclear how well the Soviet economy will perform in the next decade. Soviet General Secretary Mikhail Gorbachev has stressed repeatedly that the Soviet Union will maintain military technologies on a par with those of the United States. In order to improve the technological base of the Soviet economy, more must be invested in the USSR's scientific and industrial infrastructure, meaning less in either consumer goods or defense. Gorbachev's dilemma centers on the amount of technological development the USSR should pursue.

Already there are signs that the Soviet military-industrial complex has become overextended. The only way to produce the latest generation of weapons in numbers approximating those of previous generations is to increase defense spending. The question of how much the Soviet leadership is willing to spend to keep pace, especially in light of the investment needs of the rest of the economy, remains. Another dilemma the Soviets face is how to allocate defense rubles among procurement and R&D—that is, how much to spend on a possible war next year versus one that might occur in the next century.

Any Western policy that depends on Soviet incompetence or inefficiency, in tactics or in technology, is fundamentally unsound. The USSR has demonstrated its willingness to spend what is necessary to keep pace with improvements in the military forces of its adversaries. Although they may be conservative, the Soviets do not cling to outmoded hardware when it means defeat. The West should not only pay attention to the cost and effectiveness of military R&D programs in U.S. terms; the West should also tailor R&D to maximize the cost of Soviet responses. There is great potential in this area for effectively diverting Soviet resources toward areas of comparative Western advantage.

Notes

1. "Zero Growth Is 'Best Case' For FY '88 DoD Budget, Nunn Says," *Aerospace Daily* 140, no. 36 (November 21, 1986), p. 281.

2. "Washington Roundup," *Aviation Week and Space Technology* (July 28, 1986), p. 15.

3. John M. Collins, "What Have We Got For $1 Trillion?" *Washington Quarterly* 9, no. 2 (Spring 1986), pp. 47–54.

4. A. W. Marshall, *Long-Term Competition with the Soviets: A Framework for Strategic Analysis* R-862-PR (Santa Monica, Calif.: The RAND Corporation, April 1972), p. vii.

5. Richard Halloran, "Old Dispute on the MX Erupts Anew," *New York Times* (December 21, 1986), p. 4.

6. Caspar W. Weinberger, *Annual Report to the Congress, Fiscal Year 1988* (Washington, D.C.: GPO, 1987), p. 207.

7. Weinberger, *Annual Report to the Congress, Fiscal Year 1988*, p. 208.

8. David J. Lynch, "Air Force Favors MX on Trains," *Defense Week* 7, no. 45 (November 17, 1986), p. 1.

9. David J. Lynch, "Air Force in Quandry Over Two Missiles," *Defense Week* 7, no. 45 (November 17, 1986), p. 7.

10. David J. Lynch, "Air Force Readies Minutemen Decoys," *Defense Week* (August 11, 1986), p. 11.

11. James L. George, "START and the Navy," *U.S. Navy War College Proceedings* (April 1986), pp. 30–38.
12. Brent Scowcroft, John Deutch, and James Woolsey, "A Small, Survivable, Mobile ICBM," *Washington Post* (December 26, 1986), p. A23.
13. "B-1B Bombers Delivered to Operational Squadron," *Aviation Week and Space Technology* (October 27, 1986), p. 42.
14. Molly Moore, "Defects Found in B1 Bomber," *Washington Post* (December 4, 1986), p. A1.
15. David Evans, "The B1: A Flying Edsel For America's Defense?" *Washington Post* (January 4, 1987), p. C1.
16. Congressional Budget Office, *Modernizing U.S. Strategic Offensive Forces: The Administration's Program and Alternatives* (Washington, D.C.: GPO, May 1983), p. 3.
17. Caspar W. Weinberger, *Annual Report to the Congress, Fiscal Year 1987* (Washington, D.C.: GPO, 1986), p. 288.
18. Edgar Ulsamer, "Intelligence Update on Soviet Power," *Air Force Magazine* (December 1986), p. 91.
19. William T. Lee and Richard F. Staar, *Soviet Military Policy Since World War II* (Stanford, Calif.: Hoover Institution Press, 1986), p. 183.
20. International Institute for Strategic Studies, *The Military Balance 1986–1987* (London: International Institute for Strategic Studies, 1986), p. 31.
21. Ibid.
22. "Soviet Notebook," *International Defense Review* (November 1986), p. 1598.
23. Lee and Staar, *Soviet Military Posture Since World War II* p. 24.
24. Norman Polmar, "The Soviets Below," *Air Force Magazine* (September 1985), p. 102.
25. John Witherow, "Russia Boosts Its Bomber Force to Defeat Star Wars," *London Sunday Times* (August 24, 1986), p. 11.
26. Polmar, "The Soviets Below," p. 104.
27. Ibid., 105.
28. Lee and Staar, *Soviet Military Posture Since World War II* p. 33.
29. John Prados, Joel S. Wit, and Michael J. Zagurek, Jr., "The Strategic Nuclear Forces of Britain and France," *Scientific American* 255, no. 2 (August 1986), p. 36.
30. Lawrence Freedman, "British Nuclear Targeting," in Desmond Ball and Jeffrey Richelson (eds.), *Strategic Nuclear Targeting* (Ithaca, N.Y.: Cornell University Press, 1986) p. 124.
31. Peter Davenport, "Why Trident Might Never Be Scrapped," *London Times* (October 8, 1986), p. 16.
32. Prados, Wit, and Zagurek, "The Strategic Nuclear Forces of Britain and France," p. 35.
33. Stockholm International Peace Research Institute, *World Armaments and Disarmament: SIPRI Yearbook 1986* (New York: Oxford University Press, 1986), p. 63.
34. "China (PRC): Chinese Nuclear Capability," *Defense & Foreign Affairs Daily* 15, no. 9 (January 17, 1986), p. 2.

35. Barry M. Blechman and Victor A. Utgoff, *Economic and Fiscal Implications of Strategic Defense* (Boulder, Colo.: Westview Press, 1987).

36. Strategic Defense Initiative Office, *Report to the Congress on the Strategic Defense Initiative* (Washington, D.C.: Department of Defense, June 1986), p. IV-1.

37. Craig Cavault, "SDI Delta Space Vehicle Experiment to Aid Kill-Vehicle Design," *Aviation Week and Space Technology* (September 15, 1986), p. 18.

38. Weinberger, *Annual Report to the Congress Fiscal Year 1987*, p. 222.

39. Warren Strobel, "Kremlin Has Spent $150 Billion on its 'Star Wars,' CIA Estimates," *Washington Times* (November 26, 1986), p. 1.

40. Martin Sieff, "Soviets Fire New Booster into Space," *Washington Times* (August 22, 1986), p. 6.

41. "Soviet Laser Laboratory Destroyed," *International Defense Review* (August 1986), p. 1023.

42. Department of Defense and Department of State, *Soviet Strategic Defense Programs* (Washington, D.C.: GPO, 1985), p. 17.

43. Warren Strobel, "Pact to Scuttle Mid-Range Missiles Would Hurt NATO, Rogers Warns," *Washington Times* (December 11, 1986), p. 3.

44. Organization of the Joint Chiefs of Staff, *Military Posture FY 1987* (Washington, D.C.: GPO, 1986), p. 24.

45. A. W. Marshall, "A Program to Improve Analytic Methods Related to Strategic Forces," *Policy Sciences* 15 (1982), p. 48.

46. Stephen M. Meyer, "Soviet Nuclear Operations," *Signal* (December 1986), p. 47.

47. "Army Modernization Slows: Aircraft Programs Hardest Hit," *Aviation Week and Space Technology* (January 12, 1987), p. 29.

48. Ibid., p. 30.

49. Robert R. Ropelewski, "Army Revises LHX Schedule, Advances Operational Capability to 1995," *Aviation Week and Space Technology* (November 24, 1986), p. 21.

50. David M. North, "Defense Department Approves First Phase of Army Air Defense Modernization," *Aviation Week and Space Technology* 125, no. 8 (August 25, 1986), p. 28.

51. Under Secretary of Defense, Research, and Engineering, *The FY 1987 Department of Defense Program for Research and Development* (Washington, D.C.: DoD, 1986), p. IV-37.

52. Office of Technology Assessment, *Technologies for NATO's Follow-On Forces Attack Concept—Special Report*, OTA-ISC-312 (Washington, D.C.: GPO, July 1986).

53. Department of Defense, *Soviet Military Power* 5 ed. (Washington, D.C.: GPO, March 1986), p. 60.

54. Ibid., p. 67.

55. Yu Boyiko, "Light Helicopters," *Krasnaya Zvesda* (June 5, 1985), p. 3.

56. Robert L. McDaniel, "Mi-26 Halo: Star of Farnborough. Is Halo Flawed? Odin Chort Znaet," *Armed Forces Journal International* (October 1984), p. 45.

57. Graham H. Turbiville, Jr., "The Attack Helicopter's Growing Role in Russian Combat Doctrine," *Army* (December 1977), p. 30.

58. Ibid., p. 28.
59. "Military Aircraft of the World: Soviet Union," *Flight International* (August 3, 1985), p. 70.
60. Tom Donnelly, "Next Generation of Soviet Attack Helos Pose Serious Threat, Warns Dickerson," *Defense News* (October 21, 1985), p. 8.
61. North, "Defense Department Approves First Phase of Army Air Defense Modernization," p. 28.
62. James T. Westwood, "The Soviet Navy: What Will Its Meticulous Planning Lead to Tomorrow?" *The Almanac of Seapower, 1986*, (Arlington, Va.: Navy League of the United States, 1986), p. 38.
63. Office of the Chief of Naval Operations, *Understanding Soviet Naval Developments* (Washington, D.C.: GPO, April 1985), p. 31.
64. Ibid., p. 32.
65. "An-124 Called 'Remarkable Copy of C-5,'" *Aerospace Daily* 133, no. 27 (June 7, 1985), p. 209.
66. "Fulcrum in Finland," *Flight International* (July 12, 1986), p. 3.
67. Jim Bussert, "Can the USSR Build and Support High Technology Fighters?" *Defense Electronics* 17, no. 4 (April 1985), p. 124.
68. Organization of the Joint Chiefs of Staff, *Military Posture FY 1987*, p. 52; Department of Defense, *Soviet Military Power*, p. 120.
69. Bill Sweetman, "New Soviet Aircraft: Quality with Quantity?" *International Defense Review* 17, no. 1 (January 1984), p. 35.
70. Stephen J. Cimbala, "Soviet 'Blitzkrieg' in Europe: The Abiding Nuclear Dimension," *Strategic Review* 14, no. 3 (Summer 1986), p. 69.
71. Joshua M. Epstein, "Assessing the Military Balance: Defense Analysis and the Defense Debate," *The Brookings Review* 3, no. 3 (Spring 1985), p. 17.
72. Weinberger, *Annual Report to the Congress Fiscal Year 1987*, p. 52.
73. Joshua M. Epstein, *Strategy and Force Planning: The Case of the Persian Gulf* (Washington, D.C.: The Brookings Institution, 1986), p. 71.
74. Westwood, "The Soviet Navy: What Will Its Meticulous Planning Lead to Tomorrow?" p. 37.
75. "Japan Plans to Increase Defense Spending 6.3% Over Current Year," *Aviation Week and Space Technology* 125, no. 7 (August 18, 1986), p. 26.
76. Daniel Southerland, "U.S. Navy Call at Chinese Port Symbolizes Growing Military Relationship," *Washington Post* (November 5, 1986), p. 23.
77. "Japan Plans to Increase Defense Spending 6.3% Over Current Year," p. 26.
78. Anthony H. Cordesman, "Theater Forces," in Joseph Kruzel (ed.), *American Defense Annual 1986–1987* (Lexington, Mass.: Lexington Books, 1986), p. 110.
79. William J. Broad, "Experts Say Soviet Union Has Conducted Space Tests on Anti-Missile Weapons," *New York Times* (October 15, 1986), p. 14.
80. Bussert, "Can the USSR Build and Support High Technology Fighters?" p. 121.
81. Ibid., p. 122.
82. Clyde Autio, "Soviet Aircraft Design," in Paul J. Murphy, (ed.) *The Soviet Air Forces* (Jefferson, N.C.: McFarland and Co., 1984), p. 78.

83. Robert A. Magnun, "In Search of the End Game: A Comparison of U.S. and Foreign Weapons Acquisition Systems," a study conducted under the DCI Exceptional Intelligence Analyst Program, 1985, p. 98.

84. Rebecca V. Strode, "Soviet Design Policy and Its Implications for U.S. Combat Aircraft Procurement," *Air University Review* 35, no. 2, (January-February 1984), p. 49.

85. Ibid., p. 52.

86. Autio, "Soviet Aircraft Design," p. 79.

87. Arthur J. Alexander, *Armor Development in the Soviet Union and the United States* (Santa Monica, Calif.: The RAND Corporation, September 1976), p. 52.

88. Gertrude E. Schroeder, "Soviet Technology: System Vs. Progress," *Problems of Communism* 5 (1970), p. 21.

89. Strode, "Soviet Design Policy and Its Implications for U.S. Combat Aircraft Procurement," p. 54.

3
The International Economy with a National Security Perspective

*Gary C. Hufbauer
and Kimberly Ann Elliott*

**The International Economy and
National Security: Where Do They Meet?**

What does the international economy have to do with national security? The premise of this essay is "a great deal." In the early Middle Ages, the small city-state of Venice exercised great influence across the Mediterranean through its role as trader and banker. By the time of Queen Victoria's Diamond Jubilee in 1897, England had acquired power over much of Africa, the Far East, and Oceania through commerce, finance, and investment. Since World War II, a multilateral system of trade and finance has reinforced the national security of the United States. On a day-to-day basis, the United States exerts far more global influence through the magic of the market than through the might of the military. Market forces display the wares of capitalism; they put U.S. citizens in daily contact with foreign nationals; and they give foreign countries a very practical stake in cordial relations with the United States.

There is general agreement on the broad congruence between a smoothly functioning international economy and the security interests of the United States. But the broad congruence of interests has not turned the United States into a giant free-trade zone. In many contexts, the United States has questioned whether the laissez-faire model best serves its own security needs. The economic questions that regularly come up on the national security agenda include the following:

1. High-technology export controls. What high-technology exports should be controlled, for how long, and to which destinations?

Should the controls be applied "extraterritorially" to limit shipments by foreign subsidiaries of U.S. firms?[1]
2. Broad economic relations with the Soviet bloc. Can better economic relations improve the political atmosphere and help divert the Soviet Union from its military buildup? Or do Western technology and finance abet that buildup? Should the Soviet Union be allowed to join the General Agreement on Tariffs and Trade (GATT), the World Bank, and the International Monetary Fund (IMF)?
3. Economic sanctions. Can economic sanctions be used effectively to carry out U.S. foreign policy? Or do failed sanctions exact too high a price both in economic and political terms?[2]
4. U.S. industrial base. Should the United States restrain imports when foreigners, even if they are allies, supply a significant and growing portion of basic defense-related products, such as steel, machine tools, and semiconductors? Should the United States prevent the takeover of high-technology firms by foreign interests?[3]

In addition to specific economic transactions and industrial policy issues that directly affect the national security, broader security issues arise in the conduct of international economic policy. Two examples may be cited. First, the trade deficit, the budget deficit, and the Pentagon budget are related. Correction of the huge U.S. trade deficit probably requires a substantial reduction in the budget deficit. And any cut in the budget deficit will further curb the Pentagon budget, with obvious implications for weapons procurement, arms control, and NATO. Second, economic policy disputes may begin to spill over into the political sphere. When international disputes over commercial and financial policies cannot be harmoniously resolved, tension rises within the Western bloc, undermining the sense of shared interests that underpins the alliance. Repercussions may be felt on issues such as burden-sharing of defense expenditure, deployment of advanced weapon systems, and arms control policy.

In the sections that follow, we first provide a broad overview of international economic developments during 1985 and 1986. Next, we turn to trade policy, focusing initially on U.S. trade policy and then on the Uruguay Round of multilateral negotiations under the auspices of the General Agreement on Tariffs and Trade. We then look at the ongoing debt crisis. Finally, we examine the dominant financial issues in the world economy—in particular, the overvalued dollar, efforts to deal with the resulting trade imbalances, and the consequences for defense spending and the alliance.

An Overview of 1985 and 1986

The years 1985 and 1986 found U.S. officials groping for improved balance, both at the international level and within the U.S. economy. The Group of Five (G-5) initiative of September 1985 succeeded in bursting the speculative bubble in the foreign-exchange markets and bringing the dollar down 35 percent from its peak by early 1987.[4] Still, the 1986 U.S. merchandise trade deficit came in at $166 billion and could well exceed $150 billion in 1987. Meanwhile, the U.S. budget deficit for fiscal year (FY) 1986 was $220 billion and threatened to reach $180 billion in FY 1987, well above the Gramm-Rudman target of $144 billion. U.S. growth remained sluggish and Japanese expansion sank toward a postwar low. Only West Germany enjoyed reasonable growth, but even it continued to experience painfully high unemployment in many regions.

In 1986, the developing country debt crisis reemerged as a threat to the world financial system when the Mexican economy faltered. It remains to be seen whether the current policy approach—which combines debt rescheduling with policy reform—will provide a lasting answer.

On the trade policy front, there were two noteworthy events: Congress adjourned at the end of 1986 without passing major protectionist legislation, and the Uruguay Round of multilateral trade negotiations was inaugurated in September. But the president found himself taking incremental protectionist steps—on lumber products, machine tools, textiles, and semiconductors—to head off more severe restraints threatened by Congress. In the early weeks of 1987, "competitiveness" promised to serve as an umbrella theme for U.S. concerns about both the overall trade deficit and the performance of individual industries.

U.S. Trade Policy

Trade expanded rapidly in the postwar period. From 1950 to 1981, world trade grew an average 10.1 percent annually in nominal terms. Over that same period, U.S. dependence on trade doubled from 8.4 percent of GNP to 16.9 percent of GNP. In 1982, at the beginning of the recession, however, world trade dropped 7 percent and increased an average of only 1 percent in each of the next three years, despite the recovery.[5]

Prosperity in the immediate postwar decades was built on rapid productivity gains, buoyant markets, and a shared commitment to an open trading system. In the post-1980 world of slow growth, however, economic disputes among trading partners became more serious, and trade was increasingly viewed as a "zero-sum game." The frictions now threaten to affect the political sphere, worsening tensions within the Western alliance over defense spending, arms control, and East-West relations.

Between 1983 and 1986, unprecedented U.S. trade deficits severely undermined the United States' commitment to free trade. The virtues of a liberal trade regime are questioned by those who see U.S. access to foreign markets blocked by a range of government measures, by those who doubt the ability of macroeconomic policies to correct the U.S. trade deficit, and by those who see trade in "strategic terms"—as a world chess game for leadership in high-tech industries.

The Reagan administration responded to the new mood by adopting a more aggressive stance against unfair trade practices abroad, subsidizing agricultural exports, and moving to correct the overvalued dollar. It concluded a trade agreement with Israel, opened bilateral negotiations on a free-trade area with Canada, and succeeded in launching the Uruguay Round of multilateral trade negotiations.

Reagan attempted to head off Congressional pressure on trade by using the tactics developed in his first administration. In September 1985, he directed U.S. Trade Representative Clayton Yeutter to initiate Section 301 cases against several countries for their alleged unfair trade practices.[6] He also expressed sympathy for stronger legislation against unfair trade and foreign counterfeiting, and he endorsed a $300 million "war chest" for the Export-Import Bank to promote U.S. exports. Congress, unimpressed, moved ahead with hearings on the Bentsen-Gephardt-Rostenkowski surcharge bill, which targeted countries with large bilateral surpluses for retaliation (the countries fitting the criteria at that time were Japan, Korea, Brazil, and Taiwan). Other congressional committees approved bills on telecommunications and textiles trade. Reagan responded with a one-two punch on September 22–23, 1985.

The G-5 initiative on the dollar was revealed on September 22. The president followed the next day with a major speech on trade policy. He pledged to attack unfair trading practices abroad, to promote U.S. exports, to retaliate against foreign import barriers, and to open multilateral negotiations as quickly as possible. He restated his opposition to protectionist legislation that would "harm economic growth, cause loss of jobs, and diminish international trade."[7]

These initiatives only temporarily cooled the congressional fever. The House of Representatives was the first to move on trade in 1986. Speaker Tip O'Neill gave HR 4800, an omnibus trade bill, legislative priority and it was overwhelmingly approved by the full house on May 22, with a vote of 295 to 115. HR 4800 included planks on industries injured by imports, reciprocity in telecommunications trade, export promotion, exchange rates, international debt, foreign labor rights and U.S. labor retraining, agricultural trade, and foreign corrupt practices. A revised Gephardt amendment to identify and reduce "excess" bilateral surpluses was also included, but with greater discretion for presidential action. The bill also extended until January 3, 1991 the president's tariff-cutting authority and the "fast-track" provisions for congressional implementation of nontariff agreements—authorities the president will need to complete the Uruguay Round of trade talks.[8]

President Reagan attacked the bill as "kamikaze" legislation, and resurrected the familiar tactic of diffusing pockets of political pressure with tailored doses of special protection. On May 20, 1986, he acted on a three-year-old import relief case brought by the machine tool industry on national security grounds, announcing that "voluntary" restraint agreements would be negotiated with major suppliers to limit their exports. A week later he approved a U.S. International Trade Commission recommendation to provide temporary relief to the cedar shakes and shingles industry in the form of a 35 percent tariff, which principally limited imports from Canada.

In early August 1986, the administration returned from Geneva with a more restrictive Multi-Fiber Arrangement and with new agreements from three major textile and apparel suppliers (Korea, Hong Kong, and Taiwan), limiting their growth in shipments to the United States to less than 1 percent per year (Japan later signed a similar agreement). In late October, the president prepared to retaliate against Taiwanese exports if Taiwan failed to respond to the Section 301 complaint on its trade barriers to U.S. exports of beer, wine, and tobacco.[9] In November, he announced an agreement by Japan to roll back machine tool exports to their 1981 level. A similar agreement was later reached with Taiwan; meanwhile, West Germany and Switzerland were threatened with unilateral quotas if they failed to respect suggested limits on their machine tool exports to the United States. The administration also warned seven smaller suppliers that they would be subjected to restraints if they attempted to increase their market shares. At the end of 1986, President Reagan sent a New Year's message of trade retaliation to the European Community, in response to the loss of U.S. corn and sorghum markets in Spain, resulting from Spanish membership in the enlarged EEC.[10] The two trading partners reached agreement on compensation just before the January 30, 1987 deadline and the United States withdrew its plan to impose 200 percent retaliatory tariffs on selected European goods. In late December 1986, the administration also concluded an agreement with Canada that requires a 15 percent Canadian export tax on softwood lumber exports shipped to the United States, in order to avoid the imposition of a countervailing duty by the United States. In the spring of 1987, the United States and Japan could not resolve a dispute over implementation of an earlier agreement on semiconductors and President Reagan retaliated against Japan for the first time since World War II, imposing 100 percent tariffs on $300 million of imports from Japan.

Thus, six years into his presidency, free trader Reagan had a distinctly mixed record. He had restricted imports of carbon steel, autos, textiles and apparel, sugar, machine tools, and lumber through "voluntary" agreements and statutory quotas. He provided import relief under the escape clause to the motorcycle, specialty steel, and cedar shakes and shingles industries, but he denied relief to the copper and footwear producers. At the same time, the president successfully opened markets to U.S. goods and services in Japan, Korea, and Taiwan. The Reagan administration concluded a one-way free-trade arrangement, on selected products, with the Caribbean Basin nations, and a reciprocal free-trade-area agreement with Israel. Further, the administration successfully launched the Uruguay Round of multilateral trade negotiations and is negotiating a free-trade agreement with Canada.

Despite the president's offensives on both the trade and macroeconomic fronts, Congress remained hawkish on trade, with competitiveness" promises providing the umbrella for the hot trade issues in 1987. A Congressional Caucus on Competitiveness has been formed, and the administration, reversing its 1986 strategy, submitted trade legislation centered on the competitiveness theme. Trade legislation introduced in both houses of Congress attacked the competitiveness issue from two directions. The Gephardt amendment to the House bill and the Danforth amendment to the Senate bill both require "mandatory" retaliation against unfair trading practices. Both provisions actually leave the president wide latitude as to whether and what actions to take. Senate-proposed section 201 reforms bring adjustment explicitly into the escape clause process, although the language unfortunately emphasizes revitalization over the more realistic outcome of downsizing.

In the debate, disturbing questions are being asked. Can the United States still compete on world markets, even after exchange rates are ironed out and the playing field is leveled? Are U.S. business leaders beset with "corpocracy"—complacency and inefficiency—as Deputy Secretary of the Treasury Richard Darman has charged? The challenge facing the 100th Congress is to ensure that the competitiveness debate generates new answers for opening foreign markets and accelerating the pace of adjustment within the United States, rather than becoming a packaging label for new forms of protection against foreign goods.

The Uruguay Round of Multilateral Trade Negotiations

Trade ministers from the GATT member countries met in Punta del Este, Uruguay the week of September 15, 1986 to lay the groundwork for a new round of multilateral trade negotiations, the first since the Tokyo Round ended in 1979. The United States succeeded in getting its top priorities—agriculture and services—on the agenda. In addition, the agenda was replete with "old" issues: for example, subsidies on traded goods, temporary safeguards for industries injured by imports, and protection of intellectual property.

At Punta del Este, the United States took a middle position between a group of fourteen agricultural exporting nations—including Australia, New Zealand, Argentina, and Uruguay—that wanted accelerated negotiations on eliminating agricultural subsidies, and the European Community, pushed by France, which did not want to discuss agriculture at all. The outcome is that all agricultural policies affecting trade, including the European Community Common Agricultural Policy (CAP), are up for discussion—but not on an accelerated basis.

Are the economic giants prepared to reform their glut-producing agricultural policies? Is the United States willing to abandon price supports and import quotas?[11] Is Japan prepared to phase out high-cost rice production? Is Europe willing to dismantle the CAP? Unfortunately, in recent years the economic giants have responded to agricultural surpluses and plummeting prices with yet more subsidies.

But there is a glimmer of hope. The CAP threatens to bankrupt the European Community; U.S. agricultural subsidies add significantly to U.S. budgetary woes; and Japanese city dwellers want rice land for home construction. In other words, the situation is getting so bad that it could get better. Conceivably, the leaders of the Economic Summit countries could strike at the heart of subsidized trade by issuing a declaration of principles to guide agricultural production and trade, limit domestic subsidies, and devote funds to retiring agricultural land rather than maintaining farm prices.[12]

Inclusion of services trade in the Uruguay Round was the other major U.S. objective. The U.S. goal is to liberalize trade in services and to forestall the erection of new barriers; but countries such as Brazil and India want to apply generous doses of infant industry protection in the years ahead to nourish their nascent banking, insurance, and telecommunications industries. GATT negotiations on services were thus resolutely opposed by several developing nations. In the end, a compromise was found through the establishment of a parallel negotiating track for services. Negotiations will not be officially held under GATT auspices, but "GATT procedures and practices shall apply" and "GATT secretariat support will be provided."[13] Results will be reported to the GATT Trade Negotiations Committee (TNC), where implicit trade-offs will be made between the goods and services sectors.[14]

One of the most important old issues returning to haunt negotiators will be safeguards. Since the 1940s, trade liberalization has been accompanied by safeguards for injured industries. A safeguards action provides temporary relief from imports; during the relief period, the industry is supposed to adjust to new competitive conditions in world markets. This usually means downsizing the troubled industry, with labor and firms moving into more promising sectors. However, neither Article XIX of the GATT nor parallel "escape clause" laws in national legislation provide adequate incentives for meaningful adjustment. Partly as a result, Article XIX and escape clause legislation have been little used in recent years. Instead, countries have increasingly resorted to "voluntary" restraints and other extra-GATT measures, such as the Multi-Fiber Arrangement, which often create incentives for their own perpetuation. A new safeguards code should restrict the use of extra-GATT methods and should reemphasize adjustment. Revenue for costly but necessary adjustment programs could be obtained by converting existing quotas to tariffs or by auctioning the quotas to the highest bidder.[15]

A time limit of four years was set for the Uruguay Round of negotiations. That may prove too short to reach agreement on difficult issues such as agriculture and services. In the meantime, negotiating momentum and political support could be maintained by concluding early agreements on easier subjects, such as a code against counterfeit merchandise.

Dealing with Third World Debt

Contrary to expectations, the debt crisis lingers on. Debtor nations have not collapsed, but they have not recovered either.[16] The debt saga of recent years is illustrated by the fluctuating fortunes of the two largest debtors, Mexico and Brazil. These countries have traded the status of "model debtor" back and forth since 1982.

Mexico triggered the debt crisis by announcing in August 1982 that it could no longer pay its external debt. A rescue plan was devised, with the U.S. government, private banks, and the Mexican government all playing roles. As its contribution, Mexico slashed public spending and devalued the peso. In 1983 and 1984, the situation improved and Mexico was able to meet its interest payments. But the oil price collapse in late 1985 deprived Mexico of both tax revenues and foreign exchange.

Mexico then adopted the austerity program prescribed by the International Monetary Fund (IMF), cutting subsidies and devaluing the exchange rate to improve its trade balance. Despite these measures, in 1986 Mexico once again informed its creditors that it could not meet its obligations without additional funds.

In 1985 and 1986, Brazil was viewed as the "model debtor," owing to strong growth and good export performance. Brazil's economy was growing at an annual rate in excess of 7 percent, with average monthly trade surpluses of $800 million, but the economic picture worsened at the end of the year. The price freeze imposed in February 1986 as part of President Jose Sarney's Cruzado anti-inflation plan ignited consumer demand and devastated the trade surplus, which fell to about $200 million in October, the lowest level in three years. In response, the government imposed an austerity program that raised taxes and increased prices. A public demonstration turned into the first violent rioting in Brasilia's twenty-six-year history. In this charged atmosphere, Brazil sought a concessional rescheduling agreement with its private bank lenders. Otherwise, Brazilians warned, "the political pressure for a moratorium, or some unilateral limitation of our payments, could become overwhelming."[17]

In the midst of the long-playing debt crisis, the Washington prescription was set forth by Secretary of the Treasury James Baker at the joint World Bank and International Monetary Fund meetings in Seoul in October 1985. Baker called on commerical banks to lend an additional $20 billion to Third World nations over three years, with the international lending agencies and finance authorities of the industrialized countries contributing another $9 billion. In exchange, fifteen identified debtor countries were supposed to adopt more open market-oriented policies, reduce trade barriers, and sell state-owned enterprises.

In 1986, Mexico became the first patient in Secretary Baker's debt clinic. It barely survived. It took two months after Mexico reached agreement with the IMF to secure consent of the private Bank Advisory Group, and another two months after that to persuade 90 percent of the affected private banks to subscribe. The agreement provides for about $12.5 billion in external financing for Mexico: $6.0 billion in new loans from the banks, $1.6 billion from the IMF, and another $5.0 billion from other international lending institutions and the financial agencies of industrialized countries. In addition, $1.7 billion in contingency funds will be made available if oil prices fall further or if Mexican economic growth does not reach a specified target. Moreover, maturities on new and existing public-sector loans were stretched to twenty years, with an interest margin of only thirteen-sixteenths percent over LIBOR.[18]

Senator Bill Bradley (D-NJ) criticized the Baker plan for simply piling new debt on top of old. In a speech at the second Bradley-Kemp meeting[19] in Zurich in June 1986, he proposed a form of debt relief. The Bradley plan calls on the banks to forgo 3 percentage points of interest a year for three years and to write off 3 percent a year of principal. In return, debtor nations are expected to adopt economic reforms to promote growth and stem capital flight. Bradley estimated the relief provided by his plan, and the parallel cost to the banks, at $42 billion, compared to only $29 billion in new resources provided under the Baker plan. Bradley argued that more relief was necessary to get indebted countries back on a growth and development path, which in turn would expand market opportunities for U.S. exports.

Several objections to the Bradley plan were lodged: first, that there was no mechanism for persuading the banks to accept the contemplated losses; second, that forced implementation of the plan would make banks unwilling to lend to developing countries in the future; and, finally, that the plan would provide relief to some countries not really in need.[20]

With the financial establishment, the administration, and the Federal Reserve all arrayed against the Bradley plan,[21] the stage is set for continuation of the case-by-case approach to the problems of debtor countries. So long as the world economy remains buoyant, the Baker approach promises a continuation of the status quo: no dramatic collapse, but no quick recovery either.

Monetary and Financial Issues

The Reagan administration entered office in 1981 promising to slow inflation, lower taxes, strengthen defense, and balance the federal budget. Rapid progress toward the first three goals quickly put the fourth out of reach. Enthusiastic "supply siders" preached that fast economic growth would lead to a balanced budget despite lower tax rates and price disinflation. But economic growth remained at a level far under the administration's hopes and aspirations, and public spending on domestic programs simply could not be slashed enough to offset burgeoning defense spending. The deficit dilemma worsened as political positions hardened—Reagan against tax increases, Congress against additional cuts in domestic spending, and no one willing to slash the defense buildup (see Table 3.1).

If the U.S. economy were closed off from world trade and financial markets, the superexpansionary Reagan administration budgets year after year might well have triggered a domestic boom, with high profits, high employment, and renewed inflation. But in the open economy of

FIGURE 3.1. U.S. Fiscal and Trade Deficits

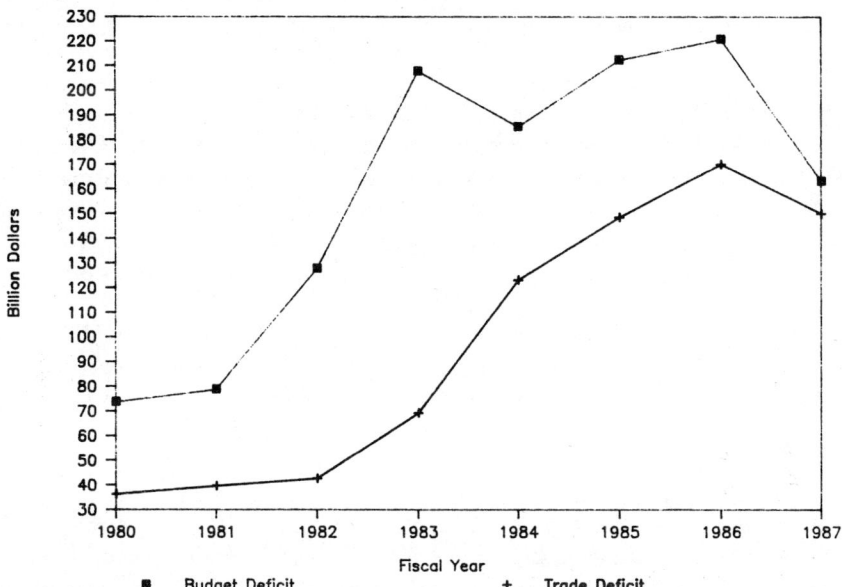

Source: Office of Management and Budget, *Economic Report of the President* (Washington: Office of Management and Budget, 1987); Office of Management and Budget, *Budget of the United States, Fiscal Year 1988: The Budget in Brief* (Washington: Office of Management and Budget, 1987).

the 1980s, the economic response was quite different. In the first instance, the budget deficit raised interest rates. At the same time, the 1981 Economic Recovery Tax Act raised after-tax profits on business investment. The combination of higher U.S. interest rates and lower corporate tax rates attracted large capital flows from abroad. Capital flows were further encouraged by restrictive budget policies in the United Kingdom, West Germany, and Japan.[22] To overstate the matter, public profligacy in the United States was offset by public parsimony in the rest of the OECD area.

This seemingly complementary state of affairs required huge U.S. trade deficits as the counterpart to budget deficits (see Figure 3.1). On the financial side of the international accounts, every billion dollars of trade deficit was necessarily accompanied by a billion dollars of foreign capital flowing into the United States. In order to accomplish the massive transfer of goods and money, the dollar appreciated by an astounding 70 percent against a basket of foreign currencies from its trough in the third quarter of 1980 to its peak in February of 1985. As a result, by early 1985 the dollar was 40 percent overvalued relative to its "fundamental equilibrium" level.[23]

The overvalued dollar was the single largest cause of the ballooning U.S. trade deficit. In addition, the quicker and much stronger U.S. recovery from the deep recession of 1982–1983 created a "growth gap" between the United States and its major trading partners. Because of the growth gap, Americans bought more imports while the Europeans and Japanese barely increased their purchases of U.S. exports. The Third World debt crisis made its own contribution to the deteriorating U.S. trade balance: Many developing nations were forced to strictly limit their imports and promote their exports. For example, the bilateral U.S. trade balance with Latin America shifted from a surplus of $4.8 billion in 1980 to a deficit of $19.1 billion in 1986.[24]

To the consternation of many observers, the dollar continued to rise in the face of the deteriorating trade position. In 1984, a speculative bubble developed. Foreign investors ignored the trade figures and bought dollars simply because the dollar has risen against other currencies so persistently.[25]

Ascending protectionist pressures in the face of record trade deficits finally forced the Reagan administration to concede that the strong U.S. dollar was creating problems for U.S. industry and agriculture. On September 22, 1985, Secretary of the Treasury James Baker, accompanied by Chairman of the Federal Reserve Paul Volcker, met with counterparts and the central bankers from the G-5 countries at the Plaza Hotel in New York to discuss remedies for the growing imbalances in the world economy. The markets responded immediately to the change in policy stance. The dollar dropped 5 percent against other major currencies on the first day after the meeting.

By fall 1986, the dollar had fallen 30 percent on a trade-weighted basis from its February 1985 peak against currencies of the major industrialized countries.[26] Nevertheless, the 1986 merchandise trade deficit hit a record $166 billion. According to "J-curve" analysis, the price effects of an exchange-rate depreciation will make a trade deficit worse before it gets better.[27] This explanation received most of the blame for the poor trade figures in 1986 and early 1987. According to most accounts, the deficit should decline by at least $20 billion annually in 1987 and 1988 after the J-curve effect has worked through.

In 1986, senior U.S. officials devoted considerable effort to persuading West Germany and Japan to boost their own home demand by cutting taxes and lowering interest rates. There was a coordinated interest rate reduction in March 1986. This was followed by additional cuts in U.S. and Japanese discount rates later in 1986. But U.S. efforts to sell fiscal expansion to West Germany and Japan met with little success. At the Tokyo Economic Summit in May 1986, Secretary Baker did, however, get agreement on a set of economic "indicators" that are to be monitored as a first step in coordinating economic policies among the major powers. The indicators include inflation, interest rates, growth, unemployment, budget deficits, current accounts, monetary growth, and exchange rates. When the indicators suggest a problem, the major powers will supposedly discuss coordinated remedies.

The first test of the indicator system occurred in late September 1986, when the G-5, followed by the G-7 (the G-5 plus Canada and Italy), met on the eve of the Bank/Fund meetings in Washington. At this meeting, the cooperative spirit of the Plaza Hotel seemed to have vanished. The United States argued that reduction of the U.S. budget and trade deficits, if not accompanied by expansionary policies abroad, would lead to world recession. But West Germany was unconvinced, more afraid of inflation than unemployment, and refused to stimulate domestic demand.

When no consensus could be reached, the United States turned to a G-2 initiative with Japan in November 1986. The United States agreed on yen-dollar stability in return for Japanese commitments to expand domestic demand. As a first step, Japan reduced its discount rate yet again, pledged to accelerate an earlier announced 3.6-trillion-yen (about $23 billion) fiscal-stimulus package, and promised to lower tax rates. The United States repeated the need to reduce its budget deficit and promised to work against protectionist legislation. The G-2 announcement established implicit upper and lower bounds for the yen-dollar rate.

Preliminary signs for the success of the G-2 initiative are not promising. The United States seems unlikely to meet its 1987 budget targets, much less the targets for 1988 or beyond,[28] and the Japanese stimulus package actually amounts to less than 1 percent of GNP. Further, the Japanese tax reform will be revenue neutral.[29] West Germany also refused to play, ruling out a cut in the discount rate or other expansionary steps, at least until after the January 25 national election.

At the end of December, the monthly trade numbers were released, showing an unexpectedly large deficit of $19 billion for November (30 percent above the October figure), and sending the dollar into a steep slide. The dollar decline was abetted by Reagan administration officials who despaired of getting significant cooperation from Japan and West Germany and therefore decided to "talk the dollar down." Both the West German and Japanese central banks intervened in the currency markets, buying up dollars in an attempt to halt the slide, but without U.S. support their intervention efforts had little effect.

The December trade deficit of $10 billion, announced at the end of January, was much smaller than that in November and helped slow the dollar's slide.[30] Moreover, in late January, Japanese Finance Minister Kiichi Miyazawa visited Washington to remind Secretary Baker of the earlier G-2 commitment to stabilize the yen-dollar rate. And, just two days before the January 25 election, West Germany cut its discount rate to 3 percent. But these assorted events did nothing more than arrest the dollar slide. Overall, the dollar dropped nearly 10 percent against the major currencies in the month of January.[31]

Failure to achieve a much higher degree of fiscal cooperation among West Germany, Japan, and the United States will mean continued reliance on exchange-rate adjustments to reach external balance. If foreign investors lose confidence and begin pulling money out of the United States, the dollar could plunge in a free-falling fashion. This situation could reignite inflation, raise interest rates, and hinder growth. Or the United States could pass unilateral legislation to attack the trade deficit by restraining imports. Either scenario—violent exchange-rate movements or import restraints—could reduce total trade, slow world growth, and risk a world recession. Such a chain of events would badly damage the Western alliance.

The Economy, Defense, and the Alliance

A country's economy provides the resource base for its military forces. The larger the economy and the faster it grows, the more resources are potentially available for defense needs. Conversely, the proportion of limited resources devoted to defense partly determines what is left over for investment in new plant and equipment and, hence, in the rate of economic growth.

Defense spending also plays a leading role in determining the budget deficit and, indirectly, the trade deficit. Efforts to reduce the U.S. budget deficit have already slowed the planned defense buildup. Constraints on U.S. defense spending highlight the burden-sharing problem that has plagued the Western alliance ever since Europe and Japan regained their economic strength in the late 1950s.

The administration's economic policies have inadvertently provided a temporary solution to the burden-sharing problems of the alliance. In essence, major U.S. allies, while resisting increases in defense spending at home, have helped finance the U.S. buildup with their capital outflows. The capital inflow into the United States of approximately $400 billion from 1982 to 1986 "roughly equals the cumulative increase in U.S. military spending over the same period."[32] This solution, however, is unsustainable.

The budget deficit results from the pursuit of incompatible goals: lower tax rates, lower inflation, and substantially increased defense spending. President Reagan remains adamantly opposed to tax increases, and Congress refuses to slash nondefense spending. By 1984, Congress

TABLE 3.1

Growth of the U.S. Budget Deficit (in billions of dollars)

Fiscal Year	Outlays			Total Outlays	Total Revenues	Deficit
	Defense	Nondefense	Net Interest			
1982	185.3	560.4	85.0	745.7	617.8	127.9
1983	209.9	598.4	89.8	808.3	600.6	207.8
1984	227.4	624.4	111.1	851.8	666.5	185.3
1985	252.7	693.6	129.4	946.3	734.1	212.3
1986	273.4	716.4	136.0	989.8	769.1	220.7
1987*	282.2	733.3	137.5	1,015.6	842.4	173.2

* estimate

Source: Office of Management and Budget, The United States Budget in Brief, Fiscal Year 1988 (Washington: GPO, 1987), p. 98.

had concluded that cutting defense was politically the least painful way to trim the budget deficit.

Despite a consensus that 3 percent real growth in defense spending authority was justified on its merits, defense appropriations were virtually frozen for fiscal years 1985–1987. Yet the Defense Department continued to plan using unrealistic assumptions about its budgets. In 1985, the Pentagon called for real growth of 5.9 percent in FY 1986 and more than 8 percent in FY 1987 and FY 1988. In 1986, even after three no-growth years, the administration requested and presumably planned on 3 percent real growth in FY 1987 and beyond. Though credited as being more realistic, the FY 1988 budget is still likely to be trimmed by Congress (see Table 3.1).[33]

The consequences of the Pentagon's overly optimistic planning have been severe. Some category of defense spending must suffer as budget authority is squeezed. One response has been to stretch out purchases of hardware. Recent estimates, however, revealed that this default response—which stems from Pentagon and congressional unwillingness to slash entire programs—could result in significant price *increases:* for example, $93,000 more for a single Sidewinder air-to-air missile, and $24 million more for just one EA6B electronic warfare plane.[34] From 1980 to 1985, while procurement spending rose slightly more than 100 percent, spending on personnel and operations and maintenance rose only 13 percent and 37 percent, respectively.[35] Inasmuch as hardware

FIGURE 3.2. Relative Defense Expenditures

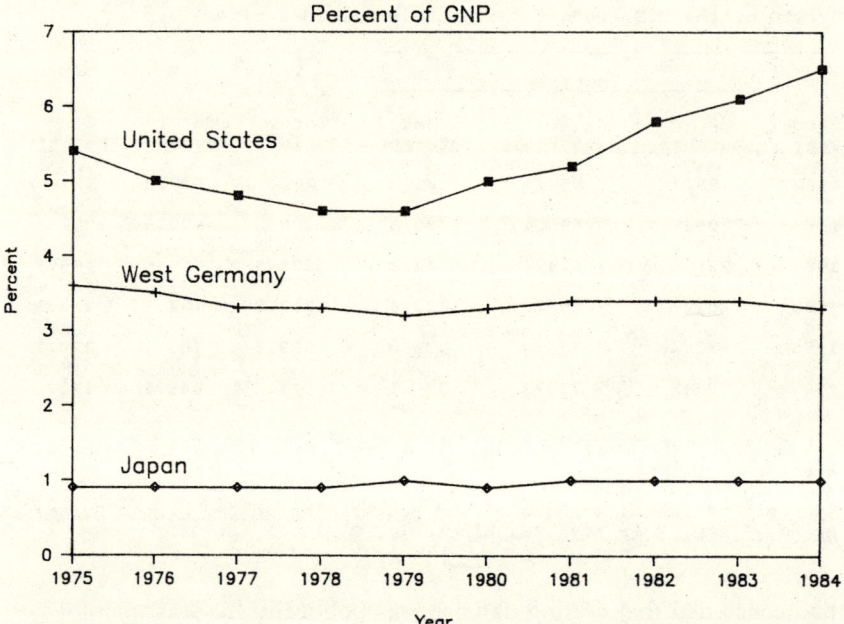

Source: Directorate of Intelligence, Handbook of Economic Statistics (Washington: Central Intelligence Agency, 1986).

and R&D contracts represent long-term commitments, the deescalation of defense spending put extra pressure on the personnel and operations and maintenance accounts. As a result of budgetary pressures, the United States could end up with "a military establishment rich in powerful, complicated, expensive weapons but poor in spare parts for them, short of the funds to exercise and maintain these armaments, and, because of insufficient pay scales, without skilled personnel to operate them."[36]

Is there a connection between defense spending and international competitiveness? U.S. defense spending is alleged to have eroded U.S. productivity by depriving the economy of badly needed capital investment and skilled labor. Thus, it is said, a central reason for declining U.S. economic performance relative to Japan and West Germany is found in the disparate levels of defense expenditures.[37] Since World War II, Japan has spent an average of less than 1 percent of GNP on defense.[38] West Germany has spent somewhat more, between 3 and 4 percent, but still much less than the United States. During the Reagan buildup, the United States has spent an average of 6.2 percent of GNP on military needs (see Figure 3.2). Faced with large budget and trade deficits and sluggish growth, American willingness to bear the lion's share of the defense burden could evaporate as some of its partners become relatively richer, enjoy large trade surpluses, and refuse to cooperate on macroeconomic policies. This willingness will be tested in the years ahead, now that West Germany has surpassed the United States as the world's leading exporter, and now that Japanese per capita income at prevailing exchange rates has reached the U.S. level.[39] Regardless of whether high defense spending contributes to low economic performance, these statistics are bound to highlight the burden-sharing question.[40]

In the early 1970s, under trying economic circumstances, Senator Mike Mansfield (D-MT) proposed removing U.S. troops from the front line in Europe. In recent years, Senator Sam Nunn (D-GA), the new chairman of the Senate Armed Services Committee, revived the idea of bringing U.S. troops home. This idea has been rationalized as a means both of improving the trade balance (though only marginally so) and of forcing the allies to spend more on their own defense. With these arguments in the wind, it is questionable whether the United States will still be supporting large armies in Europe and the Far East by the year 2000.[41]

In the end, whether economic constraints will unravel the Western alliance depends on whether a sense of common purpose can be maintained. Throughout the postwar period, the Soviet threat has provided the foundation stone for the alliance. Assessments about that threat will ultimately determine whether economic frictions lead to dealignment. If the Soviet threat is perceived as continuing and serious, the allies will pull together and pool their resources, despite economic differences. If the threat appears to diminish, however, economic disputes will acquire greater strategic significance. Agricultural disputes with the European Community, unilateral initiatives by the United States on the arms control front, and a sustained public relations blitz by General Secretary Gorbachev could weaken conservative European governments and improve the prospects of leftist parties with weaker commitments to the alliance. In Japan, protectionist actions by the United States could threaten Prime Minister Yasuhiro Nakasone's position and persuade his successors to become less willing to accommodate U.S. political and economic needs.

The United States might unwisely choose to count on inept Soviet policies to sustain the alliance. Otherwise, the United States will need to renew emphasis on the diplomatic three Cs: consultation, cooperation, and coordination among members of the Western alliance. On the political front, this agenda would mean prior consultation on arms control and economic sanctions initiatives, not after-the-fact notification. It would mean avoiding situations like the Iran imbroglio, in which the administration publicly pressured the allies to follow one policy while privately pursuing the opposite policy. In the international economic arena, this agenda would require major efforts to breathe life into the Uruguay

Round negotiations; it will also call for the political courage to resist import protection and a willingness at very high levels to coordinate macroeconomic policies in a way that promotes vigorous world growth.

Notes

1. For a historical survey of export controls, see Gunnar Adler-Karlsson, *Western Economic Warfare 1947–1967* (Stockholm: Almquist and Wikssell, 1968). For a more recent analysis, see Office of Technology Assessment, *Technology and East-West Trade* (Washington, 1983); Dean L. Overman, "Reauthorization of the Export Administration Act: Balancing Trade Policy with National Security," *Law and Policy in International Business*, vol. 17 (1985), pp. 325–393; and the National Academy of Sciences report released early in 1987.

2. For analysis of the role of sanctions in foreign policy and details on 103 case studies, see Gary C. Hufbauer, Jeffrey J. Schott, and Kimberly Ann Elliott, *Economic Sactions Reconsidered* (Washington: Institute for International Economics, 1985).

3. At the end of 1986, a Japanese company, Fujitsu, attempted to buy 80 percent of Fairchild Semiconductor Corporation, a major supplier of computer chips to the Pentagon. An American company had offered to buy the defense-related sections of Fairchild, but the owner was reluctant to break up the company. The Reagan administration was reviewing the case on both security and antitrust grounds when Fairchild pulled out of the deal (*Washington Post*, January 10, 1987).

4. The Group of Five consists of France, Germany, Japan, the United Kingdom, and the United States. In recent monetary talks, the G-5 has been enlarged to the G-7 by the inclusion of Canada and Italy.

5. International Monetary Fund, *International Financial Statistics*, 1979 yearbook and monthly issues.

6. Section 301 of the Trade Act of 1974 grants the president broad authority to take action, either in response to an industry petition or as self-initiated by the administration, against a variety of unfair trade practices that negatively affect U.S. exports.

7. Ronald Reagan, "Remarks of the President to Business Leaders and Members of the President's Export Council and Advisory Committee for Trade Negotiations," Washington, September 23, 1985, p. 4.

8. The "fast-track" provisions require an up or down congressional vote, without amendments, within sixty days after submission of implementing legislation by the president.

9. In December, Taiwan succumbed to the pressure and agreed on specific measures to open its market. U.S. exports are expected to increase $150 million in the first year (*New York Times*, December 9, 1986).

10. *Washington Post*, January 30, 1987.

11. Section 22 of the Agricultural Adjustment Act of 1933 (1935 amendment) authorizes the use of import quotas or fees to protect domestic price-support

programs. Quotas currently restrict imports of cheese, peanuts, and sugar (the last under authority of Headnote 2 of the Tariff Schedules of the United States).

12. Gary C. Hufbauer and Jeffrey J. Schott, "A Strategy for U.S. Trade Policy: 1986–1990," Paper for the CSIS Quadrangular Forum, Washington, October 1, 1986, p. 10.

13. *GATT Focus*, October 1986, p. 5.

14. Jeffrey J. Schott, "Punta del Este: A Postmortem," Address to the World Trade Forum, Washington, October 3, 1986.

15. On adjustment, see Gary C. Hufbauer and Howard F. Rosen, *Trade Policy for Troubled Industries*, Policy Analyses in International Economics 15, Institute for International Economics, Washington, 1986; for details on auction quotas, see C. Fred Bergsten, Kimberly Ann Elliott, Jeffrey J. Schott, and Wendy Takacs, *Auction Quotas and United States Trade Policy*, Institute for International Economics, Washington, forthcoming.

16. Third World debt problems are addressed only briefly here; for more analysis see Chapter 7, on Latin America.

17. *Wall Street Journal*, December 1, 1986.

18. LIBOR stands for London Inter-Bank Offer Rate. See *Financial Times*, December 1, 1986; *IMF Survey*, October 20, 1986, p. 1. In an effort to avoid a "most-favored-borrower" stampede, the banks warned that these concessions should not be viewed as precedents for other rescheduling arrangements. The Philippines immediately requested, however, that negotiations on its debt be reopened, and the Philippines finance minister stated that it would be politically unacceptable to agree to terms any more stringent than those granted Mexico. See *Journal of Commerce*, December 1, 1986; *Washington Post*, January 13, 1987. In January, Argentina reached an agreement with the IMF that, while not including an automatic trigger, "stresses the possibility of reassessing the package if the nation does not achieve an economic growth rate of 4 percent."

19. This meeting was the second of three conferences focusing on monetary issues sponsored by Senator Bill Bradley (D-NJ) and Congressman Jack Kemp (R-NY).

20. See William R. Cline, "Bradley's Debt Plan Won't Work," *Washington Post*, July 15, 1986. See also Richard N. Cooper, "The Lingering Problem of LDC Debt," *The Marcus Wallenberg Papers on International Finance*, vol. 1, no. 5 (1986).

21. See *Washington Post*, January 20, 1987.

22. For a detailed analysis of the events and policies leading to the current imbalances, see Stephen Marris, *Deficits and the Dollar: The World Economy at Risk*, Policy Analyses in International Economics 14 (Washington: Institute for International Economics, 1985).

23. The fundamental equilibrium exchange rate for a country is the exchange rate that would lead to a current account balance plus or minus a sustainable level of long-term capital flows for that country. See John Williamson, *The Exchange Rate System*, 2d edition, revised, Policy Analyses in International Economics 5, (Washington: Institute for International Economics, 1985).

24. Morgan Guaranty Trust Company, "The Dollar's Decline: Mission Accomplished?" *World Financial Markets* (New York, October/November 1986), p. 4.

25. See Jeffrey A. Frankel and Kenneth A. Froot, "The Dollar as an International Speculative Bubble," *The Marcus Wallenberg Papers on International Finance*, vol. 1, no. 1 (1986).

26. Debate flared about the actual extent of the dollar decline. Estimates differ depending on which currencies are included in the basket, how they are weighted, and whether they are adjusted for inflation. See *Washington Post*, November 23, 1986; and Morgan Guaranty Trust Company, "Dollar Index Confusion," *World Financial Markets* (New York, October/November 1986), pp. 14–15.

27. According to J-curve analysis, as the dollar depreciates it takes more dollars to buy the same volume of imported foreign goods. Meanwhile, in the short run, the value and volume of exports remain unchanged. Hence, the trade deficit expressed in dollars gets worse. Eventually, however, the currency changes are reflected in purchasing patterns—a smaller volume of imports and a larger volume of exports. Then the deficit improves. See C. Fred Bergsten, "Crisis and Reform of the International Monetary System," The Ernest Sturc Memorial Lecture, presented at the Johns Hopkins School of Advanced International Studies, Washington, November 13, 1986, pp. 7–8.

28. At the end of 1986, the President's Council of Economic Advisers lowered its growth prediction for 1987 from 4.2 percent to 3.2 percent; most private estimates were even lower. Lower growth means reduced revenues and increased expenditures on unemployment and other assistance programs.

29. In Japan, cuts in personal and corporate tax rates are expected to be largely offset by a 5 percent national sales tax (*Washington Post*, January 11, 1986).

30. The January data also showed a revised trade-deficit figure of $15 billion for November.

31. *Wall Street Journal*, January 26, 1987.

32. Sherle R. Schwenninger and Jerry W. Sanders, "The Democrats and a New Grand Strategy," *World Policy Journal* (Summer 1986), p. 376; Kenneth A. Oye, "Constrained Confidence and the Evolution of Reagan Foreign Policy," in *Eagle Resurgent*, edited by Kenneth A. Oye, Robert J. Lieber, and Donala Rothchild (Boston: Little, Brown, and Co., 1987).

33. William W. Kaufmann, *A Reasonable Defense* (Washington: The Brookings Institution, 1986), p. 85; *Washington Post*, November 13, 1986 and January 6, 1987.

34. *Washington Post*, January 9, 1987.

35. Kaufmann, *A Reasonable Defense*, pp. 26–27. The procurement binge has meant that congressional control over actual outlays, as opposed to budget authority, has become increasingly difficult to exercise. As the portion of the budget allocated to procurement has grown, so has the buildup of unspent obligational authority. Expenditures of funds allocated for long-term projects often occur years after they are authorized. The proportion of prior-year authority

outlays to total outlays grew from 27 percent in 1980 to 36 percent in 1985 and is still rising. The implication is that well over a third of defense spending each year is uncontrollable without explicit congressional recision.

36. See Michael Mandelbaum, "The Luck of the President," *Foreign Affairs*, vol. 64, no. 3 (1985), pp. 393–412. See also Kaufmann's recommendations for a more "reasonable defense" at a lower cost, in Kaufmann, *A Reasonable Defense*.

37. See Schwenninger and Sanders, "The Democrats." See also Hobart Rowen, "Japan's Rising Economic Power," *Washington Post*, August 24, 1986.

38. The 1 percent ceiling grew out of constitutional limits on Japanese armed forces. In a decision of symbolic importance taken in December 1986, Japan decided to break the 1 percent threshhold.

39. Calculations of per capita income at prevailing exchange rates do not, however, accurately reflect living standards. By most accounts, U.S. living standards are well ahead of Japanese living standards.

40. A supporting argument holds that the "productivity gap" will widen further as the Strategic Defense Initiative and other military technology becomes increasingly complex, with limited peaceful applications. Schwenninger and Sanders, "The Democrats," p. 379; Congressional Budget Office, *Defense Spending and the Economy* (Washington, February 1983), pp. 38–39.

41. Expenditures on defense and troop commitments will obviously depend on what, if any, arms control agreements are signed. Substantial cuts in nuclear weapons would require significantly more reliance on conventional defenses. In fact, just as this book was going to press, interest in the burdensharing issue on Capitol Hill was intensifying, though with a different twist. Many members reportedly recognize that a withdrawal of U.S. troops from Europe simultaneous with the elimination of medium-range missiles would not be an appropriate strategy. Instead, the proposals being circulated focused on financial compensation, perhaps by levying a fee on imports, to offset the "greater financial burden" shouldered by the United States in the defense area. Thus, the economic and political pressures on the alliance seem to be building even more quickly than anticipated (*Wall Street Journal*, 30 June 1987, p. 1).

4
The Soviet Economy: In Search of Reform

Herbert S. Levine

The Soviet economy in the mid-1980s is an economy in transition. From a past in which growth was based primarily on the supply of increasing amounts of capital and labor to the economy, in particular to the major growth-inducing sectors, Soviet leaders are struggling to shift to a future wherein growth will be based primarily on increasing factor productivity. The realization that such a shift was desirable dates back to the 1960s, but Soviet leaders did not realize that this shift had become a pressing political necessity until a sharp deterioration in rates of growth set in at the end of the 1970s.

From the end of World War II to the middle of the 1970s, Soviet economic growth had been trending downward. Although the centrally planned Soviet economy differs in many ways from market economies, it is not of an altogether different species. The downward growth trend of a maturing industrial economy was not unusual, nor should it have been unexpected. The sharp deceleration in growth after 1975, however, was a different matter. Although some slowing occurred in the growth of labor and capital inputs, the primary cause of the deceleration in output growth was a sharp drop in the growth of factor productivity.

The essence of the growth strategy of the past (referred to by the Soviets as the "extensive" growth strategy) was that by maintaining a high level of growth of inputs (especially capital) into the economy, proportional and even greater-than-proportional increases in production would be derived. The deterioration of productivity growth in the 1970s destroyed the confidence of the Soviet leaders in this approach and convinced them that a new growth strategy that would reverse the slowdown in growth productivity was essential. Therefore, in order to understand what is happening in the Soviet economy today, it is necessary to have an understanding of what took place in the Soviet economy in the period 1976–1982.

TABLE 4.1

Soviet Growth of Output and Productivity, 1961-1982
(Average Annual Rates of Growth, in Percentages)[1]

	1961-65	1966-70	1971-75	1976-80	1981-82
I. Official Soviet Data					
A. National Income, Produced[2]	6.5	7.8	5.7	4.4	3.6
Labor Productivity	5.5	6.8	4.3	3.2	2.9
[Total Factor Productivity][3]	1.6	3.3	1.1	0.7	0.3
B. Industrial Output	8.6	8.5	7.4	4.4	3.2
Labor Productivity	4.6	5.8	6.0	3.2	2.5
[Total Factor Productivity]	0.8	2.1	1.7	-0.6	-1.2
II. Western Calculations					
A. Gross National Product[4]	4.7	5.0	3.0	2.3	2.0
Total Factor Input[5]	4.8	4.4	4.5	3.7	3.3
[Total Factor Productivity]	-0.1	0.6	-1.4	-1.4	-1.3
B. Industrial Output	6.4	6.2	5.4	2.6	1.0
Total Factor Input[6]	7.7	6.3	5.6	5.0	4.5
[Total Factor Productivity]	-1.2	-0.1	-0.2	-2.3	-3.3

1. For the calculation of average annual rates of growth, the base year is the year previous to the stated period.
2. Based on the Soviet concept of material product, omitting most services.
3. Computed by relating the Western calculation of total factor input growth (in section II of table) to the official Soviet data on output growth.
4. Based on indexes of GNP (in 1982 rubles), by sector of origin, at factor cost.
5. Combined inputs of labor-hours, capital, and land, weighted at factor shares.
6. Combined inputs of labor-hours and capital, weighted at factor shares.

Source: Official Soviet data: Statistical Yearbook, *Narodnoe khoziaistvo SSSR,* 1975 and 1983 volumes; Western calculations: CIA, *Handbook of Economic Statistics,* 1986, CPAS 86-10002 (1986), p. 70.

The data in Table 4.1 present a record of what occurred. In the upper part of the table, official Soviet data are presented. The assumption is that Soviet leaders base their policy decisions on their own data. It is also known, however, that Soviet economists and advisers look at Western recalculations of Soviet data and take them into account in their analyses. An example of such data is presented in the lower part of the table. These data are based on Western statistical concepts and methods.

The deterioration in Soviet output and productivity growth in the period 1976–1982 is clearly seen in both the Soviet and the Western data. It is particularly sharp in industry, where the rate of growth of output in 1976–1982 was markedly lower than in the previous periods.[1] The sharpness of the deterioration in aggregate economic activity is not as clearly seen because 1975 was a bad year for Soviet agriculture, and agriculture in the Soviet Union accounts for 15 to 20 percent of GNP, thus pulling down the growth of national product and of factor productivity.[2]

What were the causes of this growth slowdown? It is not simply a question of the Soviet economic system qua system. The growth slowdown was a result of a number of different types of causes. To understand the current economic situation in the Soviet Union, we must identify these causes and determine both the extent to which they are transient and the extent to which they are structural. The structural problems will require basic changes in economic management and mechanisms.

The causes can be grouped into three categories: (1) exogenous factors, (2) policy decisions, and (3) systemic elements. Each is discussed below.

Exogenous Factors

This category consists of those factors that are outside of the control of Soviet leaders and of the direct influence of the Soviet economy. Whether they are transient depends on their own pattern and causes.

One such factor is weather, which during the seven-year period from 1976 to 1982 was particularly harsh. There were four bad weather years that led to poor harvests. As indicated above, low food production was directly reflected in the national product, but it also had indirect effects. It increased the time Soviet workers spent searching for food—time that increasingly came out of the hours during which workers were officially recorded as being at work. Low food supply also contributed to poor worker morale, low confidence in the system, and weak incentives to work. Finally, bad weather had an effect on the economy outside of agriculture. In 1979 and 1982, the weather was so cold during the first quarter that it caused significant reductions in transportation activity. This, in turn, had a substantial impact on industrial activity through disruptions in the supply system. During the rest of the year, the economy had a very difficult time recovering from weather conditions in the first quarter. In fact, in both 1979 and 1982, railroad freight turnover for the entire year was below that of the previous year.

Another exogenous factor worth noting is the state of world economic conditions. There were both negative and positive elements in this connection. On the negative side, the recession in the West reduced the demand for Soviet exports, thus limiting the Soviet ability to import Western machinery. On the positive side, the rapid run-up of oil and gold prices provided the Soviet Union with a major windfall in its hard currency earnings, counteracting the negative effects of the recession in the West.[3]

Policy Decisions

This category involves policy decisions made by Soviet leaders that show evidence of having contributed to the growth slowdown. Such decisions were made on the basis of an evaluation of their expected effects and, therefore, if Soviet leaders perceived that these expectations were not fulfilled, the policies could have been altered. Clearly, because any specific policy decision is made in the context of an interrelated set of policies involving the interests of different groups within the society, and more particularly within the decisionmaking elite, policy reversals are not easily altered. Nevertheless, the essential characteristic of policy decisions is that they fall under the control of Soviet leaders, more so than the elements of the other causal categories.

The key elements in this category are Soviet policy decisions on defense and investment expenditures. The Soviets devote a significant share of their society's final demand to defense. According to Western calculations, the share of defense expenditures in Soviet GNP in the late 1970s and early 1980s was approximately 15 percent. Moreover, a high proportion of machinery production consisted of military machinery, probably in the range of 30 to 40 percent.[4] These represent a substantial drain of resources away from growth-producing uses. This quantitative dimension, however, is only part of the burden of defense. Even more important in its impact on the growth of output and productivity is its qualitative dimensions. A very high share of the best quality human and material resources have been committed to the needs of the military, thus depriving the civilian sector of resources critical to the maintenance of growth.

The second important element in this category was the decision taken by Soviet leaders to cut the rate of growth of investment in the five-year plan period of 1976–1980 to half of what it was in the previous plan period and to devote an increasing share of investment to machinery and equipment rather than to construction (the latter policy actually began before the mid-1970s). This investment strategy was retained in the subsequent five-year plan for 1981–1985, and it engendered a fair amount of controversy. Defenders of the policy argued that too rapid growth in investment in the past had led to a proliferation of investment projects, long gestation periods delaying the commissioning of new capital stock, and the excessive growth of unfinished construction.[5] What was necessary to improve the situation, they argued, was slower growth of investment—focusing on fewer projects but completing them, thus increasing the growth of the commissioning of new capital—and greater emphasis on the renovation and modernization of the machinery stock at existing enterprises.[6]

Opponents of the new investment policy argued that, although in theory the policy had its merits, its timing was bad.[7] The crux of their position, and what turned out to be one of the fundamental factors in the growth slowdown, was that production in the Soviet economy in the first half of the 1970s had grown faster than productive capacity. Thus, by the middle of the decade, capacity utilization levels were very high; that is, the economy was taut and prone to bottlenecks. What was needed to break these bottlenecks was substantial investment growth, not its reduction. Capacity constraints were particularly tight in the early stages of production chains. For example, in the ferrous metals sector, the capacity constraint was most severe in iron ore mining, which then affected the entire chain through the production of crude and rolled steel. There was sufficient capacity to produce rolled steel, but insufficient material through-put to employ that capacity. The same pattern of early-stage capacity constraint was evident on an interindustry scale. Because of the low investment growth policy, it was argued, economic planners were prevented from reducing the critical bottlenecks owing to a lack of sufficient investment resources.

Systemic Effects

That the Soviet system of economic organization, planning, and management has led to low efficiency and low factor productivity has long been argued in both Soviet and Western literature. These systemic effects on efficiency have existed for a long time, but what specific role did they play in the post-1975 growth slowdown?

First of all, there were interactive effects. Because of its strong and stiff centralization, the Soviet system responded in a ponderous and inflexible manner to the other factors that have been identified as having contributed to the growth slowdown.

Second, with the maturing of the Soviet economy, several systemic factors have become increasing constraints on economic growth. As an economy matures, there is a tendency for natural resources to be depleted. We have just discussed an example of this phenomenon with regard to Soviet iron ore in the 1970s. It can also be seen in the depletion of coal and oil resources. Although this development is a natural one, effective investment planning can ameliorate its impact. Soviet investment planning, however, has failed to take sufficient account of the depletion of existing sources of iron ore, coal, and oil and to begin in an adequate way the development of new sources of these mineral resources.

The observed inefficiency of investment planning in the Soviet centralized economy runs counter to the putative advantages that centralized investment planning is supposed to obtain from its theoretical ability to internalize in its decisionmaking information, which is external to decisionmakers in market economies. The low quality of Soviet investment planning results basically from the difficulty of moving meaningful and reliable information effectively from the periphery to the center. This difficulty is a consequence of the number of hierarchical levels through which the information must pass and of the fact that in the Soviet administrative system, the economy is partitioned into industrial branch hierarchies (ministries), each concerned with its own needs and objectives. As a result, the center's ability to identify and evaluate investment requirements is severely constrained. Furthermore, the center's ability to respond to the identified investment needs is hindered by the slowness and intractability of the large planning bureaucracy.

Another particularly important aspect of the maturing of an industrial economy is the growth and aging of its capital stock. If the growth of capital is more rapid then that of labor, the capital-labor ratio increases. If, in this process, additions to capital easily substitute for labor (high elasticity of substitution), then, although the growth of factor productivity may be decreasing, it will remain substantial nevertheless. In the Soviet economy, however, owing to a number of systemic characteristics, the elasticity of capital for labor substitution has been low.

As the economy matured and the capital stock expanded, this low elasticity became a constraint on growth of major importance. For example, there is little effective pressure on machine producers in the Soviet economy to change the assortment, quality, and technological level of the machines they produce. This situation results primarily from the dominant position of suppliers in the pervasive seller's market that exists in the Soviet economy. It also results from an incentive system that makes managerial rewards and penalties a function of enterprise performance relative to explicit, quantitative targets, as well as from the absence of interenterprise competition and the threat of bankruptcy. In such an environment, Soviet managers can avoid the risks of change while enjoying security in their managerial status (with its attendant perquisites and privileges) in addition to a satisfactory level of monetary income. Thus, when new machines are added to the capital stock, they tend to be little different from the previous machines; therefore, their contribution to improved productivity is limited. In fact, in Soviet practice, each machine is designed to be manned by a given number of workers. Consequently, the addition of new machines only increases the number of "work places" and in this way adds to the appearance of labor shortages in the Soviet economy. This situation in turn has led to the transfer of workers from evening and night shifts to day shifts and, thus, to the decreased utilization of the capital stock as that stock has grown relative to the labor force.

The situation is further worsened by a very low rate of capital retirement. For the Soviet economy as a whole in the 1960s and 1970s, the rate of retirement was about 1.5 percent (capital retired during a year as a percentage of the capital stock at the beginning of the year); in industry, it was a little below 2 percent. In the United States, the comparable figures were more than twice that level—3.7 and 4.2 percent, respectively.[8] The low Soviet rate of retirement is the result of an earlier policy of retaining capital stock for long periods of time, a policy that is reflected in very low amortization rates for fixed capital in Soviet accounting practice. But it is also a consequence of systemic elements reflected in Soviet managerial behavior. Given that the primary criterion for the evaluation of managerial performance (and thus for job security and monetary bonuses) is the meeting of quantitative production targets, Soviet managers try to avoid any actions that may jeopardize their chances of meeting those targets. Therefore, even in those situations in which they are supplied with new, technologically advanced and more productive machines, Soviet managers prefer to keep working with their old, familiar and reliable machines, rather than run the risks entailed in breaking in new equipment. This practice is a powerful force that keeps the rate of retirements low, even though Soviet planners have recently called for an increase in the rate of capital retirement.

The Soviet capital stock, as it has grown, has "aged" more rapidly than has been true in market economies because of the limited technological improvement in newly produced machines and because of the high retention rate of old machines. The capital stock thus has aged both technically and physically. One important consequence of the latter is the substantial commitment of resources to capital repair that is required to keep the physically aged stock in operating condition. One Soviet economist has estimated that as much as 40 percent of the stock of machine tools has to be used for the repair of old capital.[9] This strain on capital repair facilities is a major contributor to the high proportion of machine "down-time" observable in the Soviet economy.

Another important systemic element among the causes of the Soviet growth slowdown was that, in addition to the increasing importance of technical change as a source of growth in a maturing economy, the nature of this technological change involves an expanding scope of relationships among industrial branches. Technological changes in one branch or ministry depend more and more on related technological changes in one or more other branches. The Soviet system of branch ministerial organizations, each pursuing its own targets and objectives, stressed vertical communication and resisted horizontal coordination, thus adding yet another constraint on technical progress in the Soviet economy.

A final, general systemic element in the Soviet growth slowdown derives from the fact that as the Soviet economy grew in size and, to some extent, in sophistication, the number of interactions to be planned and controlled grew disproportionately and the requirements for technical precision became more demanding, making the basic tasks of centralized planning increasingly more difficult. Moreover, the centralized system of supply within the Soviet economy intensified the impact of these difficulties by constraining the ability of agents at the periphery to respond flexibly to errors and imbalances in the economy.

Three additional causal factors of the growth slowdown, while themselves not integral elements of the Soviet economic system, had significant effects on the way in which the system performed. The first of these was the decline of discipline in the economy that was apparent from the mid-1970s as then-General Secretary Leonid Brezhnev's health and strength weakened. This decline of discipline applied not only to labor in terms of quality of work, effort put forth, and absenteeism, but also to management, particularly with regard to the "discipline of the plan." That is, the influence of the central economic plan on enterprise activity weakened. One aspect of this situation was the increased adjustment of plans to correspond to performance, rather than the reverse. In an economic system dealing with the institutions of centralized planning, weakness at the center and low levels of discipline lead not to useful decentralization but rather to sloth and inertia. For effective decentralization to take place, it is important that peripheral agents be in a position to make decisions; but they also have to have the resources, information, and incentives to make economically effective decisions.

A second element was the increase in private economic activity. This increase had a number of possible effects, real and statistical, direct and indirect, on output and productivity growth in the official Soviet economy. A basic effect was its deflection of effort and materials from this official economy, reducing the growth of output and productivity there. But to some extent this effect is statistical rather than real. For although reported output was reduced, reported inputs were not, thus leading to a statistical understatement of productivity. If the output of the private economy were recorded in official statistics, output (particularly of consumer goods) and productivity would have been higher. One can speculate about the possible indirect effects of the private economy on overall economic activity. On the one hand, the growing supply of desirable, good-quality consumer goods and services available in the private economy should tend to increase people's incentive to earn money in the official economy to finance purchases in the second economy. And this would lead to an increase of labor effort in the official economy. On the other hand, the growth of a private economy in an officially centralized system tends to undermine respect for government and for its laws and regulations, leading to a decrease of labor effort and productivity.

This brings us to the final element among the causes of the Soviet growth slowdown: the deepening disillusionment with the system that was discernible in the Soviet Union in the 1970s and early 1980s.[10] This is an ephemeral factor with which to deal, in terms of both its sources and its effects. To some extent it was probably a consequence of the disappointment of the very heady expectations raised from those who were entering their working ages during the Khrushchev years, at the end of the 1950s and early 1960s. This disappointment was intensified by the growing feeling of stagnation and the increased corruption and official privilege that was evident in the last half-dozen or so years of Brezhnev's rule. The resulting aura of disillusionment and pessimism in Soviet society contributed to the increase in alcoholism, morbidity, and mortality rates (particularly of working-age males), which in turn contributed to the decline in labor discipline and productivity growth.[11]

Both the poor performance of the Soviet economy and, for the most part, the underlying reasons for these problems have been well understood by Soviet economists and leaders for quite some time. Efforts to remedy the situation were initiated by Yuri Andropov when he succeeded Brezhnev in 1982. Far more ambitious reforms are now being tried by Mikhail Gorbachev, formally in power since 1985. The extent to which these reforms will be successfully implemented, however, as well as their consequences for Soviet economic performance, remain to be seen. The remainder of this chapter summarizes the reforms in the Soviet economy initiated during the 1980s, assesses the actual record of the economy between 1983 and 1986, and examines the prospects for change in the future.

Efforts to Reform the Soviet Economy:
1982–1987

When Yuri Andropov came to power after the death of Brezhnev in November 1982, there was great hope and excitement that he would bring new ideas, efficient management, and energy to the running of the nation. Andropov was highly regarded for the effectiveness of his fifteen years of leadership of the Soviet secret police (KGB), during which time he turned the organization into an efficiently run and respected—if also feared—organ of the government. Serious health problems quickly overtook Andropov, however, limiting what could be accomplished during his short fifteen months in power. He was followed by the aged and infirm Constantine Chernenko, whose reign was even shorter, lasting only a year before he died in March 1985.

Nevertheless, some changes were initiated during this period by Andropov that were more or less maintained under Chernenko. The first was a vigorous, well-publicized campaign to restore discipline in the society. With his KGB background, Andropov was in a good position to conduct such a campaign. It was rather quickly reestablished that workers and managers were to be at their workplaces during working hours, rather than in the stores and bathhouses. Several prominent cases of corruption were prosecuted.

Along with the discipline campaign, Andropov emphasized the importance of the interrelationships among the growth in labor productivity, money wages, and the supply of consumer goods. The issue concerned both incentives and the macro-balance between money incomes and the supply of consumer goods and services. A program was introduced to advance the development of labor brigades in industry and agriculture, a labor brigade being a subunit of the work force engaged in an identifiable and measurable production activity. The program involved setting incentive payment schemes related to the performance of the brigade, in the hope of establishing a close relationship between labor effort and reward thus stimulating higher labor productivity. Emphasis was to be put on the organizing of brigades that would be involved in a production process from start to finish, with its pay based on the final results of its activity rather than on the fulfillment of plan assignments for intermediary stages of production, as is customary in Soviet planning practice.

With regard to macro-balance, stress was placed on convincing workers of the necessity of tying wage increases to productivity increases. In fact, the policy was to set the growth of wages considerably below that of productivity. Second, stress was placed on the need to validate the incentive effect of increases in money wages through both the increased supply of food along with nonfood consumer goods and services and an improvement in their quality with assortment corresponding to consumer demand.

A third significant program initiated under Andropov involved the issue of decentralization. In his first speech as party leader at the end of 1982, Andropov stressed the need for greater managerial independence and for managerial responsibility to grow with increased independence. But he also criticized the practice of issuing reform decrees with insufficient care in their preparation and effort in their implementation. Changes in the economic mechanism should not be rushed into, he said; carefully worked out experiments should be tried first. One such experiment was undertaken beginning in January 1984. It involved the extension of managerial independence and decisionmaking rights in five industrial ministries: two in heavy industry, two in consumer goods on a regional level, and one in local, small-scale industry. Neither Andropov nor his successor, Chernenko, lived long enough to see concrete results from this experiment or from the other modest reforms instituted during this period. When Gorbachev took office in March 1985, the scope and intensity of the reform movement changed drastically.

It is impossible to do justice to the changes brought to the Soviet scene by Gorbachev within the framework of this chapter. At best, it is possible to provide an impressionistic picture. An important aspect of that picture is the man himself and characteristics he conveys: intelligence, vigor, confidence, strong leadership ability, the conviction of a need for change, and the commitment to bringing it about. Gorbachev has not only launched a broad set of economic changes; he has also altered the very tone of the discussion of economic matters in the Soviet Union. Certain matters rarely discussed before, even in the recent past, are now being openly mentioned and written about. And as is well known and well chronicled in the West, this is true also of a wide range of political and social issues, not only of economic matters.

There are several components of the Gorbachev economic program. One is his policy on economic growth. Among his first pronouncements on the economy after he assumed power was a ringing call for growth acceleration, a renewal of economic dynamism coupled with modernization, and an improvement in the quality of output. It might seem that the policy objective of returning to the high rates of growth enjoyed in the Soviet economy in the past was natural and expected. However, that was not entirely the case. For there were some Soviet economists and Western analysts (the present writer included) who believed that an environment of moderate growth with reduced pressure from the center on economic ministers and managers was a better environment for addressing some of the basic problems of the Soviet economy, such as the poor quality of output, the barriers to innovation and technical change, the low retirement rate of old and obsolete capital, and the need to alter the structure of investment so as to achieve a better balance in productive capacity. The pressure for accelerated growth will make it difficult to achieve these objectives. For example, Soviet managers operating under the pressure of meeting high output targets are not likely to alter their past patterns of behavior and begin to give increased attention to the quality of output. They know that, as before, they will be judged primarily by their ability to meet their quantitative output targets; and although their quality targets will now get somewhat more attention, quality of output is hard to measure and harder to monitor.

It is of interest to note that in the spring of 1985 the Gosplan drafts of the forthcoming 12th five-year plan (FYP), covering the years 1986–1990, were not consistent with Gorbachev's growth acceleration policy and that several revisions were required before the publication of the Plan Guidelines in November. The Guidelines were discussed at the 27th Congress of the Communist party in February–March 1986, and some further upward revisions were made in the version of the 12th FYP published in June 1986.[12]

Why did Gorbachev opt for immediate growth acceleration? Probably for two major reasons. First, he apparently felt a need for a quick expansion in resources (1) to support his modernization program (which in addition to changes in the Soviet economic mechanism will require substantial increases in investment, especially in the machine-building sector), (2) to support increases in consumption for worker incentives, and, at the same time, (3) to support the military sector at an acceptable level. Second, it would appear that Gorbachev chose a policy of immediate growth acceleration for its psychological impact on the Soviet people. There was a clear need to restore the confidence of the people in the system, to counteract the malaise and disillusionment that had developed. The reversal of the growth slowdown and the return of higher rates of economic growth could give a feeling of success that would contribute to the restoration of confidence and faith in the basic principles of the system.

Another component of the Gorbachev program is his "people program," which emphasizes the human factor. This program involves a continued stress on discipline and the work ethic; it involves the highly publicized anti-alcohol campaign, which has led in a very short time to a dramatic drop in the level of alcohol consumption in the Soviet Union. Above all, it involves a massive change in the personnel of the political and economic leadership of the country. People have been removed because of advanced age, incompetence, and corruption, and they have been replaced by younger, more energetic people who have demonstrated high administrative and leadership abilities, including many who have espoused creative ideas and approaches to problems. Not since the 1930s has there been so sweeping a turnover of the political and administrative elite in so short a time. By the time the Party Congress had convened in the year after Gorbachev's assumption of power, a majority of the highest party and administrative leadership cadre had been changed; 60 percent of the department heads in the Party Central Committee and 40 percent of the members of the Council of Ministers had been replaced; new heads were named for the two main planning bodies, the State Planning Committee and the State Committee on Supply.[13]

Another aspect of the "people component" of Gorbachev's approach is the dramatic increase in the provision of information to the Soviet people associated with the policy of "openness." A historically unprecedented change has occurred in the attitude of the government toward making information public, and censorship of the arts—literature, theater, and cinema—has begun to loosen. It would appear that the new Soviet leaders are operating on the belief that to run an effective modern economy and society, effort and initiative must come from below and people must be held responsible for their actions; and for this ethic to take hold, people must be given full and accurate information about the economic and social situations with which they have to deal.

The third component of the Gorbachev economic program concerns changes in the economic mechanism itself. One obvious characteristic of this component is the fact that the present Soviet leaders and economists recognize the nature of the problems they face. They understand that the economy is a complex set of interrelationships and thus changes in one part of the system will lead to the need to make appropriate changes in other parts of the system. At the beginning of his campaign to improve the economic mechanism, Gorbachev used the term "restructuring." He now frequently uses the term "reform" and "radical reform." Put within a Marxist framework, the argument is that the economy has outgrown its old institutional superstructure, which is now constraining its continued growth. The institutional structure must undergo radical change to be consistent with the now-advanced level of the economy, so as to promote its further development.

The need for basic reform appears to be accepted by the leadership, but the means by which to accomplish this end remain to be worked out and agreed upon. Thus far, the changes that have been announced officially have clear objectives, but they do not form a coherent, well-constructed program of economic reform. The core elements of the reform program are the increase in independence and flexibility of enterprises and the development of real incentives in the system that could lead people, both workers and managers, to work harder, more efficiently, and more honestly.

The five-ministry experiment initiated by Andropov, which was aimed at increasing enterprise independence, is to be spread throughout industry. Soviet leaders recognize that to make it possible for enterprises to operate with greater independence and flexibility, the existing systems of supply, finance, credit, and price formation will have to undergo reform. With regard to the centralized system of supply, which involves the central planning and distribution of thousands of input materials, an experimental introduction of wholesale trade in a very limited sector of the economy was announced to begin in January 1987. In addition, the dominance of suppliers over purchasers has been identified as a fundamental cause of inefficiency in the Soviet economy. Now recognized is the importance attached to giving purchasers access to alternative suppliers—hence the corresponding need for an element of competition in the system.

Enterprises are also being given more freedom in the use of their own financial resources. Such freedom will lead to an increase in decentralized investment, as reflected in the 12th FYP: Decentralized investment is to account for one-half of all investment in 1990, the last year of the plan. In addition, there is widespread discussion of making enterprises responsible for their own financial integrity—the Soviet equivalent of "meeting one's own payroll"—as opposed to having the assurance that one will be bailed out by the state in the event of financial trouble (what the Hungarian economist Kornai has referred to as the "soft budget"). Thus, the issue of bankruptcy is beginning to be discussed as well. There are arguments heard that the state should not maintain enterprises that are losing money. They should be put under new management, merged with other enterprises, or simply closed and their workforces and transferable assets moved elsewhere.

A major source of flexibility and increased economic efficiency is to come from expansion in the rights of enterprises in the setting of prices. A reform of the price system is being planned for the end of the 1980s. Its shape and the significance of the reform itself are not yet clear, but proposals range from a simple revision of relative prices to a radical change in the basic price-setting mechanism, in which the state would regulate the prices of only major products and the others would be set by contract negotiation between buyers and sellers (under certain constraints such as "no excessive profits").[14]

Another element of the systemic reform component of Gorbachev's program pertains to the restructuring of certain planning and administrative institutions. There has been a lively discussion in recent years about the need to reduce the power of ministries that are seen as interfering excessively with managerial decisionmaking and as inhibiting intersectoral cooperation so crucial to the effective functioning of the economy in general and innovation in technology in particular. Suggestions have been made to replace the approximately fifty economic ministries with a small number of "super-ministries" whose primary function would be to guide a complex of related branches of the economy. So far, one organization of this nature and two partial organizations have been set up.[15] What constitutes their functions is not yet clear, however. The first of these new organizations, the one resembling a super-ministry, is the State Agro-Industrial Committee, which has replaced six former ministries that supervised specific activities in agriculture and food processing. The second is the Machine-Building Bureau, which was set up to coordinate the activities of eleven civilian machine-building and metal-working ministries that continue to exist. There are indications that some support also exists for combining these eleven ministries into one super-ministry, but opposition forced a compromise that established the coordinating bureau. The third organization is the Fuel-Energy Bureau, set up to supervise the five ministries responsible for fuel and energy production.

A further organizational change was made in the administration of foreign trade. Again the problem was excessive centralization on the part of the Ministry of Foreign Trade and its network of branch-based foreign trade organizations. The old arrangement limited the role played by the enterprises that were the ultimate users of imports (particularly of machinery) and the producers of exports. Under a new arrangement announced in the summer of 1986, production ministries and a number of important enterprises have the right to play a more direct role in foreign trade negotiations. Moreover, a new commission was created to administer the activities of all the organizations engaged in foreign trade, including the activities of the Foreign Trade Bank. In addition, a new decree promoting joint ventures with foreign companies on Soviet soil was published in 1986. These organizational changes aim to improve the ability of Soviet decisionmakers to identify, acquire, and assimilate advanced technology from the outside world.

Indeed, the goal of improving the ways in which the system creates and introduces new technology and of modernizing the system and the economy pervades the reform activity. In addition to changes in the economic system, some direct measures were introduced to increase the production of new, technically better machinery and to speed up the retirement of obsolete capital. One measure to stimulate the production of new machinery was the definition of a "new" machine as one whose productivity is at least 50 percent greater than the machine it replaces, twice as reliable, and 70 percent lower metals cost per ruble of output. The production of new machines is to be further encouraged by progressively decreasing the prices of old machines, thereby lowering the profitability of the enterprise and its bonuses. The price reductions are scheduled to begin at 5 percent in 1987 and are planned to rise to 20 percent in 1990, at which time old machines could be produced only with special permission. With regard to speeding up the retirement of obsolete capital, targets for capital retirement are to rise substantially during the 12th FYP. The annual rate of retirement of industrial capital is to rise from 2.2 percent to 5 percent; in the machinery sector itself, it is to rise from 4 percent to 13 percent. Half of the stock of machinery and equipment in the machine-building and metal-working sectors is to be scrapped in the five-year period of the 12th FYP.

Before we leave this brief and incomplete sketch of the systemic reform component of Gorbachev's economic program, some changes regarding private activity should be mentioned. In June 1986, a rather harsh edict attacking unearned incomes was published. It appeared to some that the Gorbachev administration was launching a strong attack against the private economy. Others argued that Gorbachev was laying the groundwork for an expansion of private activity, but in a controlled way. In the fall, a decree was published supporting the usefulness to the socialist economy of certain types of private activity. The decree listed more than twenty types of such activity that were to become legal. Among these were handicraft production of clothing and shoes; repair of buildings, automobiles, and other consumer durables; and the provision of private transport. Licenses to engage in private activity will be issued, and the income earned will be subject to taxation. The decree went into effect in May 1987.

The Performance Record, 1983–1986

The data presented in Table 4.2, both the official Soviet and the Western recalculations, show a clear improvement in economic performance in 1983, the year of Andropov, compared to 1981–1982 (see Table 4.1). The main reasons for this improvement most likely included the fresh air brought in by Andropov coupled with his discipline campaign and the good weather enjoyed that year by the Soviet economy.

The picture after that is not as clear. The official Soviet data show that the rates of growth for the national product in 1984 and 1985 were somewhat lower than those in 1983 but more or less on a par with 1981–1982, whereas the CIA's data show GNP growth in 1984 and 1985 to be lower than that in both 1983 and 1981–1982.[16] On the other hand, both sets of data indicate that industry grew at equal yearly rates during 1983–1985 and well above the 1981–1982 rates.

Focusing on the Gorbachev years, we find that the performance of the economy in 1985 does not, at first glance, look very impressive. But when we take into account the fact that the weather in the first two months was extremely bad, Gorbachev's accomplishments in his first year look much better. In contrast to the devastating consequences of bad weather in the first months of 1979 and 1982, the economy in 1985 quickly recovered and turned in an annual growth performance equal to that in the previous year. Gorbachev's energetic leadership, his discipline campaign, and extensive changes of administrative personnel probably were the main factors in this rapid recovery.

TABLE 4.2

Soviet Growth of Output and Productivity, 1983-1986

	1983	1984	1985	1986
I. Official Soviet Data				
A. National Income, Produced[1]	4.2	3.2	3.5	4.1
Labor Productivity	3.7	3.0	3.2	3.8
[Total Factor Productivity][2]	1.0	0.0	0.5	N.A
B. Industrial Output	4.2	4.1	3.9	4.9
Labor Productivity	3.6	3.7	3.4	4.6
[Total Factor Productivity]	0.1	0.2	0.1	N.A
II. Western Calculations				
A. Gross National Product[3]	3.4	1.4	1.2	4.2
Total Factor Input[4]	3.2	3.2	3.0	N.A
[Total Factor Productivity]	0.2	-1.7	-1.8	N.A
B. Industrial Output	2.6	2.5	2.8	3.6
Total Factor Input[5]	4.1	3.9	3.8	N.A
[Total Factor Productivity]	1.5	-1.3	-0.9	N.A

1. Based on Soviet concept of material product, omitting most services.
2. Computed by relating the Western calculation of total factor input growth (in section II of table) to the official Soviet data on output growth.
3. Based on indexes of GNP (in 1982 rubles), by sector of origin, at factor cost.
4. Combined inputs of labor-hours, capital, and land, weighted at factor shares.
5. Combined inputs of labor-hours and capital, weighted at factor shares.

Sources: Official Soviet data: Statistical Yearbook, Narodnoe khoziaistvo SSSR, 1983, 1984, and 1985 and Pravda, January 18, 1987; Western calculations: CIA, Handbook of Economic Statistics, 1986, CPAS 86-10002 (1986), p. 70 and CIA, Gorbachev's Modernization Program: A Status Report (Washington: CIA, March 19, 1987).

The data for 1986 have only recently been published. On the basis of initial analysis, the performance of the economy appears to have been fairly strong, although there were some important weak spots.[17]

In the first instance, the good performance included national product and industry: Both exceeded the planned levels for the first year of the 12th FYP. Industrial growth was particularly impressive, attaining a level not reached since the mid-1970s. The growth rate of steel output, at 4 percent, was the highest it has been since 1973. Energy and fuels also did particularly well.[18] Oil output, which had decreased in 1984 and again in 1985, increased by 3.4 percent to a level of 615 million metric tons (mmt) or 12.300 million barrels per day (mbd)—falling just short of its 1983 peak of 616.3 mmt (12.326 mbd). Another notable success was the 3.4 percent increase in coal production to a record level of 751 mmt. This was the most rapid growth of coal output since 1965.

In the production of electric power, the Soviets were able to counterbalance a 3 percent decrease in nuclear power (the impact of the Chernobyl accident) and a 2 percent decrease in hydroelectric power (the result of drought in certain regions of the Soviet Union) by running their thermal power stations full blast and achieving a growth of thermal power estimated at 5.6 percent, for a growth of total electric power of 3.6 percent. Altogether, aggregate energy output (in standard fuel units) grew by 4 percent, the highest since 1978. It is interesting to note that given the growth of apparent energy consumption at a level of 3.6 percent, an increase in 1986 of net energy exports of 6.6 percent can be estimated, with net exports to socialist countries estimated to have increased by 3.3 percent and those to nonsocialist countries by 11.5 percent.[19]

Other strong performances included a 6 percent growth of machinery output (although the plan fulfillment report states that the meeting of contractual delivery obligations decreased from the previous year). Grain output rose to 210.1 mmt, up from 191.7 mmt in 1985 and at an average of 177.5 mmt in 1981–1984. Transport freight turnover increased by 4.8 percent and labor productivity in transport by 7.5 percent, implying a rather substantial shifting of labor out of the transport sector. Most consumption indicators showed a healthy increase, but perhaps the most important contribution to consumer well-being was the 37 percent decrease reported in sales of alcoholic beverages.

On the negative side, one development affecting the core of the modernization program was the introduction of new, technically advanced capital into the economy. The plan report states that "basic changes in the investment process did not take place; the dispersion of investment projects continues."[20] Although investment grew at the very high rate of 8 percent, barely missing its planned level of 8.4 percent, the commissioning of new capital grew only 6 percent, less than half of its planned growth of 14.1 percent. And in the critical machine-building sector, although the commissioning of new capital increased by 5 percent, it was 23 percent below plan. Furthermore, the plan report reveals that the introduction of technologically advanced machinery, equipment, and instruments had been insufficient.

The value of Soviet foreign trade turnover decreased by 8 percent in 1986, but when calculated in constant prices, the turnover increased by 2 percent. In recent years, the terms of trade have turned against the Soviet Union, decreasing their gains from trade and straining their ability to import advanced technology from the West.[21] The Soviet hard-currency trade balance, which showed a surplus of over $3 billion in 1983 and 1984, turned negative in 1985 with a deficit of a little under $1 billion and a current account deficit of $1.1 billion. This deficit led to an increase in Soviet indebtedness to the West in 1985 of $5 billion, bringing the Soviet net hard-currency debt to almost $16 billion (and the gross hard-currency debt to almost $29 billion). Full data for 1986 are not in yet, but the nine-month data[22] indicate that although the value of Soviet exports to the developed West decreased by 13.5 percent, they managed to maintain their expenditures on imports from the developed West, actually increasing them by 1 percent. However, because the prices the Soviets had to pay increased by 6 percent, the quantity of imports decreased by about 5 percent. The Soviet hard-currency trade deficit with the developed West surged from $1.2 billion in the first nine months of 1985 to $3.5 billion in the first nine months of 1986.

One final note on the 1986 nine-month trade data. The strength of Soviet arms sales to the Middle East is surprising, at a time of collapse in the price of oil. These sales apparently increased in the first two quarters of 1986 (compared to 1985) by 29 percent and then rose in the third quarter by 56 percent in nominal dollar terms. The sales were made primarily to Iraq, Libya, and Syria and were most likely financed by Soviet long-term credits.

The Prospects for Growth in the Soviet Economy and Their Implications for Western Security

The analysis in this section is based upon a model of the Soviet economy that was developed at PlanEcon, Inc.[23] In Table 4.3, data are presented from several model projections over the period of the 12th FYP. The data in column (a), which were taken from the final (June 1986) version of the plan, indicate the planned rates of growth over the five years from 1986 to 1990.

In the first trend scenario, the model's parameters—labor productivity, capital-output ratios, and unit energy and materials requirements—are projected at their time trends in the period 1960–1985, and the annual rate of growth of defense machinery (weapons) production is set at its 1976–1985 average annual rate of 8.5 percent. The sectoral investment shares, however, are adjusted to reflect the investment priorities incorporated in the 12th FYP.

The data from this scenario are presented in Table 4.3, column (b). The last three entries in this column indicate that with the output levels calculated, there would be low to negligible excess demand for labor and no excess demand for energy, but moderate excess demand for materials. In fact, in all the scenarios, labor and energy constraints are not significant, by contrast to materials constraints. The calculations indicate that during the 12th FYP period and, indeed, increasingly so in the 1990s, the Soviets will be forced to focus on the problem of

TABLE 4.3

Growth Rates of Selected Economic Indicators for the
12th Five-Year Plan Period, 1986-1990
(in percentages)

	Plan	Trend Scenarios With Defense Machinery Annual Growth at:			Plan-Compatible Scenarios With Defense Machinery Annual Growth at:		
		8.5%	4%	10%	8.5%	4%	12%
	(a)	(b)	(c)	(d)	(e)	(f)	(g)
National Income, Utilized	22.1	15.0	24.9	11.4	22.4	32.5	13.6
National Income, Produced	24.9[4]	20.7	24.4	19.4	24.8	28.6	21.6
Labor Productivity	23.0	16.5	16.5	16.5	23.0	23.0	23.0
Investment[1]							
- Total	23.6	14.5	35.7	6.8	22.2	43.4	3.8
- In Machinery Sector	80.0	67.5	99.7	55.9	79.3	111.5	51.3
- In Energy Sector	35.0	25.5	48.9	17.1	34.0	57.5	13.7
Machinery Output	43.0	42.6	48.4	40.5	50.6	56.7	45.4
Consumer Goods Output[2]	26.9	21.9	25.1	20.7	26.8	30.0	24.0
Excess Demand (Shortage)[3]							
- Labor		Low	Low	Low	No	Low	No
- Energy		No	No	No	No	Low	No
- Materials		Mod	Mod	Mod	Mod	High	Mod

1. Sum of investment, 1986-1990 divided by sum of investment 1981-1985.
2. In plan: Industry Group B output; In model: aggregation of nonfood consumer goods and food processing output.
3. "Mod" signifies "moderate."
4. Implied in plan.

Source: Column (a): *Pravda*, June 19, 1987 and June 20, 1987; Columns (b)-(g): Herbert S. Levine and Bryan Roberts, "Soviet Economic Prospects and Their National Security Implications," paper presented at NATO Workshop, Brussels, November 6-7, 1986.

materials, to increase their output, and, even more important, to improve the efficiency of their use in the economy.

Comparing column (b) to column (a), we find that if there is no change in capital productivity trends, the Soviet economy will fall far short of the 12th FYP targets—even given the plan's sectoral investment priorities, which have been built into the scenario. "National-income-utilized" will grow only 15 percent (or 2.8 percent per annum) instead of the planned 22.1 percent (4.1 percent per annum). "Industrially-produced-consumer-goods-output" will also fall short of the plan, but not by as much as "national-income-utilized."

The trend scenario reveals a substantial effect on total investment. The increase in total investment during the years 1986–1990 will be only 4.5 percent of the total investment during the period 1981–1985. This is barely 60 percent of the total called for in the 12th FYP. But owing to the priority allocation of investment to machine building and energy in the model, the growth of investment in those sectors comes closer to the plan.

In the second set of scenarios, shown in columns (e), (f), and (g), the aim was to see what changes might be made in the model's parameters, consistent with Soviet intentions, that would bring the Soviet economy to levels of growth approximate to those called for in the 12th FYP. It was found that this objective could be achieved by raising the growth of labor productivity from the trend 16.5 percent (3.1 percent per annum) to the plan level of 23 percent (4.2 percent per annum) and by significantly improving upon the trended path of capital productivity in the machinery and nonfood consumer goods sectors. In machinery, the average annual rate of growth of capital productivity was raised from -0.55 percent to $+0.25$ percent; and in nonfood consumer goods, it was raised from -2.71 percent to -1.38 percent. These changes led to the data shown in column (e) of Table 4.3. As can be seen, these growth levels are quite close to those in the plan.

One projection not shown in the table is that the Soviet gross debt will grow to a level of $50 billion and net debt to a level of $35 billion by 1990. It is felt, however, that with their high creditworthiness, lenders will be available and the Soviets will be able to handle such debt. Whether they will be willing to take it on is another matter.

The major question in the plan-compatible scenario concerns the feasibility of the projected improvement in capital productivity. The critical element in this scenario is the projected turnaround in the growth of capital productivity in machine-building. To accomplish this, the Soviets would have to be highly successful in many of the programs and policies they have been discussing. (1) Management style in the machinery sector would have to improve dramatically. In this respect, economic reform figures into the issue: increased rights and incentives of enterprise managers, the role of the machine-building bureau, and Gorbachev's personnel and discipline policies. (2) The technological level of new equipment added to the machinery-sector capital stock would have to be significantly raised. Relevant here are the policies being introduced to encourage the production of new, more productive machines and to discourage the production of old, obsolete machines. In addition, the rate of retirement of old capital will have to increase. Also relevant are the recent changes in foreign trade management and the reinstitution of the legal right to set up joint ventures with Western companies on Soviet soil.

Although Soviet efforts are being directed specifically toward greater productivity in the machinery sector, it is unlikely that they will be sufficiently successful in the short period of the next five years. Hence the plausibility of the plan-compatible scenario cannot be considered to be very high. In the longer run, the success of Gorbachev's reforms will depend to a significant extent on his staying power. Reform is a process, not an event, and fundamental reform is a long process. Gorbachev is already running up against substantial resistance. Basically, if the reforms are to be successful, the Soviet managers and workers must give up some of their security and stability in order to bring more efficiency and dynamism to the system. Toward that end, Gorbachev must demonstrate concrete benefits of his programs, not just promises of what will come in the future. He is therefore in a very difficult bind. Successful reform will require a great deal of time, but maintenance of the process of reform will call for some immediate success and benefits along the way. It is a difficult task. With its explicitly machinery-investment balance, the model is also well-suited to an examination of the implications of Soviet growth prospects for national security considerations, specifically the production of military equipment. Pursuing this issue, scenarios envisioning decreased and increased growth of defense machinery output were run for both the trend scenario and the plan-compatible scenario. The results of these defense scenarios are shown in columns (c), (d), (f), and (g) of Table 4.3.

It can readily be seen from the defense scenarios that variations in the growth of defense machinery output in the model have dramatic effects on the growth of "national-income-utilized" and "total-gross-investment." In fact, in both scenarios envisioning high growth in defense machinery, the increase in total gross investment is practically wiped out.

Of particular interest is the result that a decrease in the growth of defense machinery output from 8.5 to 4 percent, even in the absence of any improvement in productivity growth over past trends, would allow the Soviet economy to approximate the growth levels in the 12th FYP. With the assumptions of substantial improvements in productivity in the plan-compatible scenario, the model indicates that the economy could meet the plan's growth targets while maintaining the 8.5 percent trend growth of defense machinery output; however, it could not raise the growth of defense machinery output to 12 percent and come close to meeting the 12th FYP growth levels.

It should be observed, nevertheless, that in order to achieve the substantial increases in productivity assumed in the plan-compatible scenario, high-quality personnel, equipment, and materials will have to be moved from defense machinery production to civilian machinery production. In a recent study,[24] U.S. intelligence analysts argued that the Soviets already have the productive capacity to manufacture the military hardware that will be in production into the early 1990s. But the competition for resources between civilian and military users relates to Gorbachev's drive for modernization. It is for the purpose of this modernization drive that civilian machinery producers will need to draw away some of the skilled engineers and machinists, systems analysts, microprocessors and microelectronic components, and high-quality specialty steel products currently being employed in the production of military machinery. Therefore, the plan-compatible scenario is not, in fact, achievable with the trend 8.5 percent growth in defense machinery output; instead, a lower growth of defense production is required. The need for high-quality resources in the civilian sector to achieve the growth acceleration targets is a major reason for the great concern of Soviet leaders with the United States' Strategic Defense Initiative. If they conclude that they will have to match the U.S. initiative, the modernization of the Soviet economy—the core of Gorbachev's program—would be critically threatened and the process of reform endangered.

Notes

1. In the 1960–1965 period, the very high rate of growth of total factor input in industry and the consequent negative rate of growth of total factor productivity were the results of an extremely high capital stock growth of 11.4 percent per annum. This figure dropped to 8.8 percent per annum in the subsequent five-year period.

2. According to Soviet data, the rate of growth of aggregate labor productivity in the period 1970–1974 was 5.9 percent per annum, compared to the 4.3 percent per annum, in the full five year period of 1970–1975.

3. See Ed A. Hewett, "The Foreign Sector in the Soviet Economy," in A. Bergson and H. S. Levine (eds.), *The Soviet Economy Toward the Year 2000* (London: Allen & Unwin, 1983).

4. See the estimates in Bonnie K. Matosich, "Estimating Soviet Military Hardware Purchases: The Residual Approach," in the Joint Economic Committee, *Gorbachev's Economic Plans* (Washington: Government Printing Office, forthcoming).

5. See, for example, D. Chernikov, "Intersifikatsiya i sbalansirovannost," *Ekonomicheskaya gazeta*, no. 10 (March 1981), p. 10; and A. F. Andreev, "Investitsionnaya politika i sbalansirovannost' narodnogo khozyaystvo," *Ekonomika i matimaticheskie metody* no. 5 (1982), pp. 776–783.

6. For a strongly critical analysis of the renovation and modernization program, see Boris Rumer, "Soviet Investment Policy: Unresolved Problems," *Problems of Communism* (September/October 1982), pp. 53–68.

7. See, for example, K. K. Val'tukh, "Investitsionnyy kompleks i intensifikatsiya proizvodstva," *Ekonomika i organizatsiya promyshlenogo proizvodstva (EKO)* no. 3 (March 1982), pp. 4–31; and N. N. Baryshnikov and B. L. Lavrovskiy, "Moshchnosti i reservy," *EKO* no. 3 (March 1982), pp. 31–50.

8. CIA, *Soviet Statistics on Capital Formation* (Washington, August 1982), p. 10.

9. V. Trapeznikov, article in *Pravda*, May 7, 1981, pp. 2–3. For a translation, see *Current Digest of the Soviet Press* 34, no. 18 (June 2, 1982), pp. 1–4.

10. See John Bushnell, "The New Soviet Man Turns Pessimist," *Survey* 24, no. 2 (Spring 1979), pp. 1–18.

11. See, for example, Murray Feshbach, "Population and Labor Force," in Bergson and Levine, *The Soviet Economy*.

12. A compilation of some data comparing the Guidelines and the five-year plan can be found in *Narodnoe khoziaistvo v 1985g* (Moscow: Finansy i Statistika, 1986), pp. 61–62.

13. See Thane Gustafson and Dawn Mann, "Gorbachev's First Year: Building Power and Authority," *Problems of Communism* (May/June 1986), pp. 1–19.

14. See the comments of academician A. Aganbegyan at the 11th Annual Symposium of SRI International and the Institute for World Economics and International Relations, Moscow, July 1, 1986.

15. See Ed A. Hewett, "Reform or Rhetoric: Gorbachev and the Soviet Economy," *Brookings Review* (Fall 1986), p. 17.

16. There are some inconsistencies in the Soviet national income data for the years 1984 and 1985 that Western analysts have not yet figured out. For example, national income produced in constant prices grew by 3.5 percent in 1985 over 1984; but in current prices the increase was only 1.4 percent, implying a decrease in prices of 2.1 percent, which was not very likely. For a discussion of this issue see Jan Vanous (ed.), *PlanEcon Report* (Washington, August 14, 1986, February 4, 1987, and February 13, 1987); and Philip Hanson, "Puzzles in the 1985 Statistics," *Radio Liberty Research Bulletin*, RL 439/86 (November 20, 1986).

17. See the plan fulfillment report in *Pravda*, January 18, 1987.

18. See the discussion of Soviet energy in *PlanEcon Report*, January 21, 1987.

19. Ibid., p. 1.

20. *Pravda*, January 18, 1987, p. 3.

21. *PlanEcon Trade and Finance Review: The Soviet Union* (Washington, Summer 1986).

22. See *PlanEcon Report*, January 7, 1987.

23. For a description of this model, see Herbert S. Levine and Bryan Roberts, "Soviet Economic Prospects and Their National Security Implications," in Murray Feshbach (ed.) *National Security Issues After the 27th Party Congress of the USSR* (Brussels: NATO, forthcoming). The material in this section draws heavily upon this article. Bryan Roberts is the principal architect of the model.

24. CIA and DIA, *The Soviet Economy Under a New Leader* (Washington, March 19, 1986).

5
Southern Africa: Descent into Chaos?

Michael W. Clough

Between the fall of 1984 and the end of 1986, the security situation in southern Africa was transformed. In mid-1984, South Africa's white minority government appeared to be on the verge of accomplishing many long-sought goals. A November 1983 whites-only referendum had endorsed decisively a new "reform" constitution that significantly increased the executive powers of then prime minister, P. W. Botha (and upgraded his title to state president); it also established a tricameral parliament with separate houses for whites, Coloureds, and Indians. South Africa signed separate security agreements with Angola (the Lusaka Accord) in February 1984 and Mozambique (the Nkomati Accord) in March 1984 that appeared to stabilize a deteriorating security situation in the region and to affirm Pretoria's claims to regional superpower status. These developments paved the way for a major European trip by Prime Minister Botha in May. Botha's so-called total strategy of domestic reform and regional aggressiveness seemed to be succeeding.

Within three years, however, South Africa's "reform" program had been largely discredited. Widespread and sustained unrest had gripped the country for twenty-eight months, leaving over 2,200 people dead. A draconian national state of emergency was put into effect. The Botha government's "diplomatic" successes of early 1984 had faded from memory. Instead of abating, conflicts in Angola and Mozambique escalated. Moreover, passage of increasingly stringent economic sanctions by the EEC, the Commonwealth, and the U.S. Congress left South Africa more isolated than ever before.

The major cause of the sharp deterioration of the situation in South Africa was Pretoria's continuing failure to address the underlying political demands of the country's black majority. So long as apartheid and white rule are preserved, South Africa will remain unstable and, because of the high degree of interdependence between Pretoria and its neighbors, so will the region.

Regional Interdependence:
The Gordian Knot

Nowhere else in the world is the fate of a region more closely and inextricably linked to the fate of a single country than in southern Africa. Developments in South Africa now largely determine the prospects for political stability and economic development in five countries—Botswana, Lesotho, Mozambique, Swaziland, and Zimbabwe—and one territory—Namibia; and they significantly influence those prospects in four other countries—Angola, Malawi, Zaire, and Zambia.

The increasingly asymmetrical pattern of regional interdependence in southern Africa is a product of economics, geography, internal conflicts in Angola and Mozambique, and the regional policies of the South African government.

In contrast with its neighbors, South Africa has a comparatively developed, semi-industrial economy (see Table 5.1). The South African economy exerts a strong influence on the regional economy. But the degree of dependence of neighboring states on South Africa varies considerably (see Table 5.2).

South Africa serves as a source of employment for perhaps as many as 1 million legal and illegal workers from neighboring states. In 1983–1984, migrant workers legally employed in South Africa represented approximately 74 percent of the wage labor force for Lesotho, 20 percent for Botswana and Mozambique, 18 percent for Swaziland, 8 percent for Malawi, and 2 percent for Zimbabwe.[1]

A substantial proportion of foreign investment in southern Africa also originates from South Africa. For example, about 60 percent of Botswana's mining sector, 90 percent of Zimbabwe's mining sector and 60 percent of its manufacturing sector, and 25 percent of total foreign investment in Swaziland is controlled by South African interests.[2]

The most critical area of regional dependence on South Africa, however, is the transportation sector. In 1981, 50 percent of the extraregional trade of the five land-locked members of the nine-nation Southern African Development Coordination Conference (SADCC) organization flowed through South Africa. Despite the priority the SADCC has given to reducing this dependence, by 1985 this figure had increased to 85 percent. The data in Table 5.3 shows the trends for Zambia and Zimbabwe since 1981.[3]

A major cause of the SADCC's increased dependence on South African railways and ports has been the deteriorating security situation in Angola

TABLE 5.1

Basic Economic Data

Country	Area (1000 sq km)	Pop. (millions)	GNP (per capita 1984 $)	GDP 1984 ($ millions)
Angola	1,247	9.9	--	--
Botswana	600	1.0	960	990
Lesotho	30	1.5	530	360
Malawi	118	6.8	180	1,090
Mozambique	802	13.4	--	--
Swaziland	--	--	--	--
Tanzania	945	21.5	210	4,410
Zambia	753	6.4	470	2,640
Zimbabwe	391	8.1	760	4,580
South Africa	1,221	31.6	2,340	73,390
Zaire	2,345	29.7	140	4,700

(Table continues)

and Mozambique. The Benguela railroad running roughly east-west through the center of Angola, which formerly carried approximately 50 percent of Zambia's exports, has been closed since 1975. Railways from Zimbabwe to Mozambican ports at Beira and Maputo, which in 1974 carried 2,703,000 metric tons of what was then Rhodesia's exports, now have a capacity of less than 300,000 metric tons. In cooperation with international donors, the SADCC has begun a major effort to rehabilitate the rail and road network that connects Zimbabwe with the port at Beira. The success of the "Beira corridor" project will depend, however, on the ability of Mozambique and its supporters to find ways to protect transport links from attack by antigovernment guerrilla forces of the Resistencia Nacional Mocambicana (MNR).

TABLE 5.1 (continued)

Country	GDP growth 1973-84 (%)	Gross domestic investment 1973-84 (annual average growth)	Value added in manufacturing 1970 ($ millions, 1980$)	Value added in manufacturing 1983 ($ millions, 1980$)
Angola	--	--	--	--
Botswana	10.7	1.4	11	55
Lesotho	5.0	--	3	--
Malawi	3.3	-2.6	72	136
Mozambique	--	--	--	--
Swaziland	--	--	--	--
Tanzania	2.6	--	336	--
Zambia	0.4	-13.7	524	720
Zimbabwe	1.7	--	798	1,326
South Africa	2.7	--	9,747	--
Zaire	-1.0	--	213	168

Source: World Bank, World Development Report 1986 (New York: Oxford University Press, 1987).

South Africa's economic dominance of the region is important for several reasons. First, it provides Pretoria with leverage over neighboring states that can be used to extract political concessions. A dramatic example of the use of this leverage was a January 20, 1986 coup in Lesotho, which was largely precipitated by South African economic pressure. On other occasions Pretoria has used its ability to slow the regional flow of goods and services to force neighboring states to meet with South African officials, to moderate anti-South African rhetoric, and to expel South African refugees. More generally, the economic realities of the region have served to limit neighboring states' practical support for sanctions against South Africa. For example, Zambia and Zimbabwe have balked at implementing sanctions agreed upon at an August 1986 Commonwealth mini-summit, even though they were among

TABLE 5.2

Economic Dependence on South Africa (in millions of U.S. dollars)

	Exports to South Africa	% of Total	Imports to South Africa	% of Total	Index of Economic Vulnerability*
Angola	0	0	0	0	Low
Botswana	59	9	552	78	High
Lesotho	8	33	370	74	Absolute
Malawi	23	7	109	40	Moderate
Mozambique	8	4	64	12	High
Swaziland	100	37	315	90	High
Tanzania	0	0	0	0	None
Zambia	5	1	129	21	High
Zimbabwe	212	18	184	19	High

* These assessments are based on the author's judgments of a number of key factors such as transportation alternatives, existing trade patterns, ability to absorb economic losses, and strategic location. Given the paucity of reliable data and the difficulty of integrating them into a single matrix, I am forced to rely on rough measures.

Source: Canadian International Development Agency, "The Impact of Economic Sanctions Against South Africa on the SADCC States" (February 1986).

the leaders in pushing for their adoption. The Botha government has also sought to use threats to shift the costs of sanctions onto the economies of neighboring states to deter the United States and other Western powers from imposing anti-apartheid sanctions. In the short run this strategy has not worked. Over the long run, however, it remains to be seen whether the international community will be willing to commit the resources that will be necessary if the SADCC countries are to survive extended economic warfare with Pretoria. South Africa's ability to influence developments in neighboring states is also a function of its position as the region's dominant military power (see Table 5.4).

South Africa's military edge over its neighbors is greater than the figures in Table 5.4 suggest. In addition to its regular forces, Pretoria can call on a trained reserve force of 317,000. Moreover, the educational and technological skill levels of South African soldiers are far higher

TABLE 5.3

External Trade of Zambia and Zimbabwe that Moves Through South Africa (in percentages of total)

Year	Zambia	Zimbabwe
1981	36	67
1982	33	63
1983	70 (imports) 40 (exports)	76
1985	65 (imports) 35-40 (exports)	85*

* estimate

Source: Canadian International Development Agency, "The Impact of Economic Sanctions Against South Africa on the SADCC States" (February 1986)

than those of their counterparts in the region. In addition, a decade of combat experience in Angola and Namibia has allowed the South African Defense Force (SADF) to test and adapt its equipment and techniques to the regional terrain. Only Zimbabwe and, to a lesser extent, Angola can field a military force with equivalent experience.

In response to the 1963 United Nations arms embargo, which was made mandatory by the UN Security Council in 1977, South Africa has developed its own arms industry. ARMSCOR, the state-owned armaments corporation, which produces more than 8,000 defense items and now supplies more than 90 percent of South Africa's military equipment needs, is the third largest industrial group in the country. Its arsenal includes armored vehicles, rocket and missile systems, coastal patrol boats, tanks, radar systems, and more than 200 types of ammunition. In 1986 ARMSCOR unveiled a new attack helicopter (Alpha-XH1) and the Cheetah—an upgraded Mirage III fighter aircraft.

South Africa is also widely believed to possess or be on the verge of developing a nuclear capability. According to informed estimates, it has had the ability since 1981 to produce approximately 50 kilograms of highly enriched uranium annually, which would give Pretoria a potential nuclear arsenal of 11 to 18 weapons of approximately the size used on Hiroshima in World War II. In the past, most analysts have assumed that concerns about the probable adverse reactions of Western powers would deter the South African government from conducting a nuclear test. Writing in early 1987, Leonard Spector, a senior fellow at the Carnegie Endowment for International Peace, suggested that this

TABLE 5.4

The Military Balance in Southern Africa

Country	Total (millions of dollars)	Total Armed Forces (1985)	Combat Aircraft (1985)	Tanks (1985)	Index of Military Vulnerability*
Angola	984	50,000	--	--	Moderate
Botswana	8 (86-87)	3,000	5	0	High
Lesotho	--	--	--	--	Absolute
Malawi	21	5,250	0	0	Low
Mozambique	239	15,800	--	--	High
South Africa	2,012	106,400	372	250	--
Swaziland	--	--	--	--	Absolute
Tanzania	103	40,350	29	30	Low
Zambia	--	16,200	43	30	High
Zimbabwe	250	42,000	49	8	High

* These assessments are based on the author's judgments of a number of key factors such as transportation alternatives, existing trade patterns, ability to absorb economic losses, and strategic location. Given the paucity of reliable data and the difficulty of integrating them into a single matrix, I am forced to rely on rough measures.

Source: International Institute of Strategic Studies, *The Military Balance 1986*.

assumption might no longer be valid. "With South Africa's Western ties already under strain because of [President] Botha's unwillingness to share power with the nation's black majority," he warned, "the added diplomatic costs of a test—which would give a boost to white morale—may not loom as large in Botha's calculations as they once did."[4]

Over the last decade, the SADF has steadily become an increasingly important instrument of South African regional policy. Until the resounding defeat of its favored candidate, Bishop Abel Muzorewa, in the 1980 independence elections in Zimbabwe, the Botha government had hoped to create a "constellation of states" linking "moderate, pro-Western" governments in the region to South Africa through cooperation in economic and other functional areas. Once it became clear that this scheme was politically infeasible, Pretoria began to place greater emphasis on the military strand of its regional strategy. Efforts to destabilize the government of Angola through economic pressure, support for the antigovernment National Union for the Total Independence of Angola (UNITA) guerrillas of Jonas Savimbi and for direct military intervention had been a part of South African policy toward Angola since the Vorster government's abortive intervention in late 1975. In 1980–1981, destabilization was extended to other states. Between 1980 and 1985, SADF forces attacked the alleged facilities of the African National Congress (ANC) in Mozambique and Lesotho twice and Botswana once. In addition, Pretoria provided varying degrees of support to antigovernment forces in Mozambique, Lesotho, and Zimbabwe. Until 1986, however, a struggle raged within the South African government between those such as Foreign Minister Roloef "Pik" Botha, who viewed military action as a supplement to diplomatic maneuver, and the "hawks," including most of the military establishment, who placed little faith in diplomatic accommodations with neighboring leaders. A dramatic May 1986 combined raid on the alleged offices of the ANC in Botswana, Zambia, and Zimbabwe appears to have resolved this struggle in favor of the hawks.

Has the strategy of destabilization worked? Tactically, it produced several successes. In addition to the 1984 pacts with Angola and Mozambique, Pretoria has imposed formal and/or informal security agreements on Swaziland, Lesotho, Botswana, and Zimbabwe. As a result of South African pressure, supporters of the exiled ANC have been expelled from neighboring states. For example, hundreds of refugees were airlifted out of Lesotho in January 1986, and in December 1986 Mozambique's newly installed President Joaquím Chissano expelled six ANC officials. The interventions in Angola have slowed infiltration by Southwest African People's Organization (SWAPO) guerrillas into Namibia. Moreover, by strengthening the military position of UNITA, South Africa has made it less likely that the Angolan government will find it possible to agree to send home the Cuban troops that have been present in the country, at Luanda's request, for over a decade.

In more fundamental terms, however, the Botha government's destabilization strategy has been a clear failure. Regional successes have not resolved the internal tensions that lay at the heart of South Africa's problems. Paradoxically, the white regime's foreign policy victories only served to more deeply embitter disenfranchised blacks at home. Over the long run, destabilization may also prove to be counterproductive militarily. For example, despite—or perhaps because of—ten years of South African intervention, Angola now has one of the most experienced, best-trained, and best-equipped military forces in Africa. Moreover, as became evident in 1984–1985, as long as apartheid remains, public opinion will exert a powerful constraining influence on the ability of

TABLE 5.5

Racial Composition of the South African Population, 1985

Race	Number	Proportion
African	21,197,253	72.0%
Asian	801,758	2.7%
Coloured	2,853,964	9.7%
White	4,590,639	15.6%
Total	29,443,614	100.0%

Source: South African Institute for Race Relations, *Survey of Race Relations 1985*.

conservative administrations in the United States and other Western nations to normalize relations with South Africa.

South Africa: The Internal Crisis

The central problem in South Africa is the existence of a system of enforced white domination that deprives the black majority of all political rights at the national level. (See Table 5.5 for a breakdown of the racial composition of South Africa.)

Over the past decade, South African leaders have sought to implement a series of "reforms" that would narrow the range of legally entrenched social and economic discrimination, expand economic opportunities in the modern sectors of the economy, and create alternative structures of political representation. Changes have come in three waves. In 1979–1981, the government extended official recognition to independent black trade unions and eliminated laws restricting many skilled and supervisory jobs to whites. This first wave of reform opened the way for the emergence of a powerful black trade-union movement. The second wave came in 1983–1984 with the adoption of the tricameral constitution and the establishment of a new system of black township councils.

A third wave of reform crested in 1985–1986 with the adoption of wide-ranging changes in laws governing the social relations and economic movement of blacks. Among the legislative actions taken during this period were (1) the repeal of laws preventing mixed marriages and interracial sexual relationships, (2) the repeal of laws enforcing segregation of hotels and restauraunts, (3) the amendment of the Black Communities Development Act to allow blacks to acquire property in urban areas, and (4) the repeal of prohibitions on racially mixed political parties. Action in these areas was overshadowed, however, by controversy surrounding two other 1986 "reforms."

In April 1986 the Parliament passed the Restoration of South African Citizenship Bill that made possible the granting of South African citizenship, but only upon application, to black men who permanently work and reside in the townships with their wives and families. According to South African government estimates, out of the appproximately 9 million blacks who lost their citizenship when four "homelands" (Transkei, Bophuthatswana, Venda, and Ciskei) were granted "independence," only 1.75 million will be eligible to obtain citizenship under the new law.

In early 1986 Parliament also passed the Abolition of Influx Control Act of 1986, which abolished the hated passbook and replaced it with a uniform identity document for both whites and blacks. This measure, along with the repeal of influx-control regulations governing black employment under the Black Labor Act of 1964 and the Black (Urban Areas) Consolidation Act of 1945, will ease restrictions on movement within the country for blacks categorized as citizens of the republic. Although widely hailed as significant and long overdue, these changes were seriously limited in their impact in several respects. They do not apply to the more than 7 million blacks, including some 2 million residing in "white" South Africa, who do not qualify for citizenship. Moreover, although arrests for influx-control violations were halted on April 18, a growing number of blacks who previously would have been prosecuted for pass-law violations began to be prosecuted under trespass laws and local ordinances prohibiting squatting.

Through early 1986, assessments of Pretoria's "reform" program varied widely. At the center of this debate were differing assessments of President Botha's ultimate goals. Some observers—especially Assistant Secretary of State Chester Crocker—have long argued that Botha was a committed reformer whose policies would lead inevitably, albeit gradually, to the abandonment of apartheid. In this view, the ambiguous and often circumlocutory language used by South African officials to describe the reform process was part of a calculated strategy to deflect conservative opposition to change. In the view of most analysts, however, such language was intended to disguise the real limits of Pretoria's commitment to change. By mid-1986 this debate had ended with a near consensus that, in the words of the January 1987 report of the Secretary of State's Advisory Committee on South Africa, "reforms such as those which have enhanced the status of black trade unions are significant, but they have done little to alter the basic structure of apartheid."[5] Within South Africa itself, leading voices in the white political community, including a growing number of National party supporters, began to criticize openly the Botha government's backtracking on issues such as abolition of the Group Areas Act and to suggest that a change of leadership might be necessary before certain fundamental issues could be addressed.

A watershed in the "reform" process occurred in December 1983 with the adoption of the tricameral constitution. Through a complex arrangement based on a distinction between "own" and "general" affairs, the new constitution extended national political rights to the Coloured and Indian segments of the population without threatening the Afrikaner-based National party's control over the government. Despite its clear limitations, most whites viewed the change as a significant step toward a more inclusive political system. But for blacks, who were not even mentioned in the new constitution, the change served only to dramatize the limited character of the "reforms" being dispensed by the Botha government.

National elections scheduled for August 1984 to select Coloured and Indian members of the new Parliament became the focus of a nationwide boycott campaign. Two new organizations—the United Democratic Front (UDF) and the National Forum (NF)—were formed to mobilize opposition to the new constitution. Black resentment was fueled further by the establishment of a new system of local township councils. In an attempt to make these councils financially self-sufficient, township rents were raised, imposing an additional hardship on impoverished black residents. As the September elections were taking place, national and local grievances combined to spark township protests.

Events then followed a pattern similar to the one that had unfolded in South Africa in 1960 and 1976. Harsh attempts by the police to suppress the protests created highly publicized incidents, which in turn fueled protests elsewhere. But the challenge to white rule that began in the fall of 1984 has proven to be far more serious than earlier challenges.

Between September 1984 and January 1987, more than 2,200 people were killed in incidents related to the unrest in the black community, the majority of them at the hands of the police, security forces, or progovernment vigilantes. A partial state of emergency was put into effect in July 1985. It was suspended in March 1986, only to be reimposed on a national basis three months later.

The current phase of the struggle against apartheid differs from earlier phases in several respects, the most important of which are these:

- the extent, depth, and militance of community-based opposition to apartheid;
- the growth of an increasingly powerful and politically sophisticated independent black trade-union movement; and
- the destruction of Pretoria's ability to govern many black townships without an armed presence.

These developments changed the character of the South African conflict. By early 1986, Pretoria was on the defensive. The collapse of governmental authority in the townships, best measured by the success of school, rent, and consumer boycotts, had created openings for the emergence of alternative institutions. Civic associations, youth committees, and parents' crisis committees began to assume responsibility for organizing local communities, providing public services, and negotiating with white business people. This widely publicized trend reinforced the growing impression that the political balance was shifting, perhaps irreversibly, against white rule. Speaking to the March 1986 meeting of the National Education Crisis Committee, Zwelakhe Sisulu, editor of the *New Nation*, a leading opposition newspaper, assessed the new situation:

> We stand at a crossroads in our struggle for national liberation. When we say that we have reached a decisive historical moment, this is based on a careful assessment of our current reality. In any struggle it is extremely important to recognize the critical moment, the time when decisive action can propel that struggle into a new phase. It is also important to understand that this moment doesn't last forever, that if we fail to take action that moment will be lost.
>
> This moment has a number of important features: (1) The state has lost the initiative to the people. It is no longer in control of events. (2) The masses themselves recognize that the moment is decisive, and are calling for action. (3) The people are united around a set of fundamental demands, and are prepared to take action on these demands.
>
> Having said this, I want to strike a note of caution. It is important that we don't misrecognize this moment, or understand it to be something which it is not. We are not poised for the immediate transfer of power to the people. The belief that this is so could lead to serious errors and defeats. We are, however, poised to enter a phase which can lead to a transfer of power. What we are seeking to do is to decisively shift the balance of forces in our favor.[6]

Another factor reinforcing the impression that the political tide was running against the government was evidence that the African National Congress (ANC) was gaining strength inside the country. Formed in

TABLE 5.6

Explosive Devices Incidents, Annual Numbers

1981-1982	70
1982-1983	54
1983-1984	76
1984-1985	76
1985-1986	158

Source: Michael Morris and Thian Combrinck, <u>S.A. Bomb Summary: Use of Explosive Devices in Sabotage and Terrorism in South Africa 1981-1986</u> (Cape Town, 1986).

1912, the ANC is the oldest nationalist movement in sub-Saharan Africa. After more than a decade of nonviolent protest against apartheid and the outbreak of nationwide unrest in March 1960, the ANC and its major nationalist rival, the Pan-Africanist Congress (PAC), were banned. During its long exile, the ANC has gained considerable international recognition and support. Until recently, however, its support inside South Africa was more uncertain.

The protests and unrest that began in September 1984 were neither initiated nor controlled by the ANC; but the new climate of resistance benefitted the movement tremendously. Funerals for victims of police shootings were marked by the open display of ANC banners and flags and by the expression of pro-ANC loyalties. A proliferation of opinion polls followed, showing the ANC's jailed life president, Nelson Mandela, as the nation's most respected black leader and the ANC as its most widely supported opposition party. Most important, the UDF—and its 600 plus affiliates—clearly, albeit carefully, identified itself with the ANC tradition by selecting as patrons several leading ANC figures (including Nelson Mandela) and endorsed the 1956 "Freedom Charter," which still stands as the basic statement of the ANC's vision for a postapartheid South Africa.

When it was banned in 1960 the ANC formed a military wing—Umkhonto we Sizwe ("Spear of the Nation"). In the first two decades of its existence, Umkhonto made little headway with its tactics of "armed propoganda." In the early 1980s, however, it successfully carried out several symbolically important attacks on highly visible targets in South Africa, including the Koeberg nuclear power reactor and the SASOL coal-to-oil facilities. Following the expulsion of Umkhonto's operatives from Mozambique at the time of the Nkomati Accord, many observers predicted that its military activities would be sharply curtailed. As Table 5.6 shows, however, this has not proven to be the case.

From the South African government's perspective, one of the most worrisome developments was the steady stream of delegations that began to make the trip to Lusaka to consult with the ANC's leadership. Visits by leading white business people, opposition politicians, a homeland chief minister, the head of the National African Chamber of Commerce, and others conferred a new legitimacy on the ANC; and more and more whites began to call for negotiations with "real," "genuine," "legitimate," or "credible" black leaders—all widely interpreted as synonyms for the ANC.

On the international front, the most important indicators of growing acceptance of the ANC were the decision of the United States and United Kingdom to begin high-level consultations with the ANC's exiled leadership. This shift, which was pushed along by the efforts of the Commonwealth Eminent Persons Group (EPG) and the U.S. Secretary of State's Advisory Committee on South Africa, began in mid-1986 with contacts between senior British and U.S. officials and ANC leaders. It culminated in a January 28, 1987 meeting between Secretary of State George Shultz and ANC President Oliver Tambo in Washington.

The emergence of increasingly visible "alternative" leaders inside the country and the growing legitimacy of the ANC seriously undermined a central element in Pretoria's reform program: The attempt to create a system of "power sharing" linking together existing "homeland" structures with new local and regional bodies run by compliant and dependent black officials. As evidence of widespread support for opposition leaders increased, it became more and more difficult for the government to discount those leaders' total rejection of government plans. In fact, opposition to the government's plans became the litmus test of the credibility of black leaders, putting Pretoria in a paradoxical situation: The only way it could legitimize its "reform" program was to gain the support of leaders whose own legitimacy was based on their opposition to the government.

The changes inside South Africa also had a major impact on external attitudes and policies. Media coverage of South African events increased public awareness of the injustice of apartheid. At the same time, the extent and duration of unrest caused Western officials and business people to doubt the Botha government's ability to carry out its "reform" program successfully. Together, these developments caused a major shift in Western policy.

In 1985, the rhetoric emanating from Washington, London, and other Western capitals changed substantially: General statements abhorring apartheid and urging a quickening pace of reform were replaced by increasingly specific demands for steps leading to the initiation of open-ended negotiations. The first important concrete result of this change came on September 9, 1985 when President Ronald Reagan, under pressure from Congress, issued an executive order that imposed a series of limited sanctions on South Africa and created an Advisory Committee to make recommendations for a new U.S. policy.[7] In November 1985, the Commonwealth appointed the EPG "to encourage through all practicable ways the evolution of [a] necessary process of political dialogue."

The EPG initiative was in many respects the most important single event of 1986 for southern Africa. By May of that year, the group appeared to have made remarkable progress in defining a basis for the beginning of a process of negotiation. But then, on May 19, the SADF launched coordinated attacks on alleged ANC targets in Botswana, Zambia, and Zimbabwe, sending a thinly veiled signal to the EPG and the rest of the world that it was unwilling to proceed any further down the negotiating path. In its final report, the EPG concluded:

> Our mandate was to foster a process of negotiation across lines of colour, politics and religion, with a view to establishing a non-racial and representative government. It is our considered view that, despite appearances and statements to the contrary, the South African Government is not yet ready to negotiate such a future—except on its own terms. Those terms, both in regard to objectives and modalities, fall far short of reasonable black expectations and well accepted democratic norms and principles. . . .
> While we are not determining the nature or extent of any measures which might be adopted, or their effectiveness, we point to the fact that the Government of South Africa has itself used economic measures against its neighbors and that such measures are patently instruments of its own national policy. We are convinced that the South African Government is concerned about the adoption of effective economic measures against it. If it comes to the conclusion that it would always remain protected from such measures, the process of change in South Africa is unlikely to increase momentum and the descent into violence would be accelerated. In these circumstances, the cost in lives may have to be counted in the millions.
> From the point of view of the black leadership, the course now taken by the world community will have the greatest significance. That leadership has already come to the view that diplomatic persuasion has not and will not move the South African Government sufficiently. If it also comes to believe that the world community will never exercise sufficient effective pressure through other measures in support of their cause, they will have only one option remaining: that of ever-increasing violence. Once decisions involving greater violence are made on both sides, they carry an inevitability of their own and are difficult, if not impossible, to reverse, except as a result of exhaustion through prolonged conflict.

The question in front of the Heads of Government is in our view clear. It is not whether such measures will compel change; it is already the case that their absence and Pretoria's belief that they need not be feared, defers change. Is the Commonwealth to stand by and allow the cycle of violence to spiral? Or will it take concerted action of an effective kind? Such action may offer the last opportunity to avert what could be the worst bloodbath since the Second World War.[8]

The failure of the EPG initiative and a subsequent last-ditch effort by British Foreign Secretary Sir Geoffrey Howe made passage of new international sanctions inevitable. By the end of 1986, stronger sanctions—including bars against new investment and new bank loans, trade restrictions, and travel restrictions—had been put into effect by the United States, the European Economic Community, the Commonwealth, and others.

Sustained internal unrest and growing international pressure forced Pretoria to choose between starting down a path leading to genuine negotiations and power sharing, and resorting to increased repression. The Botha government chose the latter course. Efforts to win international sympathy through internal "reform" and regional diplomacy have been largely abandoned. A new, harsher, and more defiant strategy appears to be emerging.

Imposition of the June 12, 1986 national state of emergency signaled the beginning of a determined effort by the police and security forces to destroy the leadership of alternative community institutions and to reassert government control in the townships. Since the declaration of the state of emergency, more than 25,000 people have been detained. The major targets of the crackdown have been leaders of UDF-affiliated organizations and bodies, such as the National Education Crisis Committee, that are in the forefront of creating community-based alternatives to government-backed structures. In October 1986, the government declared the UDF an "affected" organization, thus preventing it from receiving foreign funds. The imposition of tighter restrictions on township students and prohibitions against the teaching of "alternative" curricula provided further indications of the government's tougher stance. The campaign against internal opposition was accompanied by a stepped-up propaganda attack on the ANC.

As part of its assault on opposition organizations, the state authorities began to rely increasingly on conservative black groups to challenge and attack militants in the townships and rural areas.[9] For example, in July 1986, government-backed vigilantes destroyed a large area of Crossroads, a squatter camp outside of Cape Town that had become an important symbol of black resistance to apartheid. In the KwaNdebele "homeland," clashes between a vigilante group aligned with homeland authorities and the residents who opposed a decision by those leaders to accept "independence" from Pretoria resulted in more than 100 deaths in 1986. Similar conflicts occurred in a number of areas across the country.

A far-reaching crackdown on the media was also put into effect in 1985–1986. The government has had wide-ranging authority to censor news since passage of the Suppression of Communism Act of 1950 (the main provisions of which were incorporated into the Internal Security Act of 1982). Until 1985, the press was relatively free to report on political events inside the country. Over the past two years, however, press restrictions have been progressively tightened. In 1985, the main targets of media restrictions were foreign television crews. In 1986, Pretoria directed its attention against the press, both foreign and domestic. As part of the June state of emergency, reporters were prohibited from being "within sight of" any unrest, restricted gathering, or security action. In December, the government broadened the restrictions to prohibit publication of "subversive statements," which were defined so as to cover virtually any statement seen as opposing government security efforts. These restrictions were accompanied by direct action against several journalists. For example, in December, Zwelakhe Sisulu was detained; then *the New York Times* South African correspondent was expelled, and his proposed successor was denied a visa.

Pretoria has responded to the sanctions with a series of threats and actions against neighboring states intended to prove that those states, rather than South Africa, will suffer the most from international sanctions. In the latter half of 1986, the flow of goods into Zambia and Zimbabwe was slowed by the imposition of new customs requirements and higher fees. In October, a halt to employment of Mozambican workers in South Africa was announced. But there are limits to how far Pretoria can go in this area. Paradoxically, as international sanctions close off some European and U.S. markets, it becomes more important than ever that South Africa retain profitable markets in neighboring countries.

President Botha has also tried to use sanctions and international pressure as a rallying cry to quiet dissident white voices. One of the early themes in the elections for the white chamber of Parliament held in May 1987 was the need to stand up against "hypocritical" and "self-serving" foreign "meddling." So far, however, the predictions of some observers that sanctions would cause whites to join ranks behind Botha have not been borne out. Instead, in early 1987 two National party supporters—M. P. Weynaud Malan and Ambassador to the United Kingdom Dennis Worrall—resigned their posts and announced their intention to run in the May elections on antigovernment platforms.

The shift in government strategy is in part both a cause and a consequence of the growing influence of the military and military thinking in South African politics. The uniformed military's political influence has increased steadily since P. W. Botha took office. Botha, who served for twelve years as minister of defense prior to becoming prime minister in 1978, shares the military's hardline views on regional and international issues. Among the hardliners' most fundamental premises are (1) that the threat to South Africa is closely linked to a more global "communist" threat emanating from Moscow, and (2) that compromise and accommodation in the face of threats will serve only to increase pressure. At the same time, President Botha and the military share the view that the most important black grievances are socioeconomic. Their solution to the nation's ills, therefore, is a strategy of managed "reform" that will expand economic opportunities for blacks while at the same time maintaining order—and preserving white control.

Two institutional developments have markedly increased the ability of President Botha and the security establishment to dominate the policymaking process. One was passage of the 1983 constitution, which created a strong executive presidency. The other was the introduction in 1979 of a National Security Management System (NSMS) that established a vast network of committees, effectively controlled by the military and police. This network—which parallels the normal structure of national, regional, and local institutions—assumed increasing informal authority when the June state of emergency was put into effect. At the national level, the key body in the NSMS is the State Security Council (SSC), which meets twice a week and makes recommendations on national "total strategy" to the cabinet. The SSC, which is headed by Lt. General P.W. van der Westhuizen, a hardliner who was formerly chief of South African military intelligence, is now viewed by many analysts as the most important decisionmaking body in the country. At the regional level, the NSMS consists of 11 Joint Management Centres (JMC); below that are 60 sub-JMCs and 448 mini-JMCs. Each of these JMCs consists of three committees: a joint intelligence committee; a political, economic, and social committee; and a communications committee. Although these bodies are limited to dealing with "security" matters, there are very few issues of any importance in South Africa today that do not bear on security as it is defined by government officials.

Can Pretoria's tougher stance succeed in quelling internal unrest and dampening international opposition? Will parliamentary politics continue to become less and less important as a determinant of government policy? Will the influence of the military continue to grow? These are the critical questions to be answered in 1987.

Mozambique: The Crisis Deepens

The year 1986 was tragic for Mozambique. On October 19, President Samora Machel and several of his closest aides, including two—Fernando Honwana and Aquino de Braganca—who had played key roles in improving Mozambique's relations with the West, were killed in a plane crash on South African territory. Machel's death came as the security situation in Mozambique was worsening and the fragile accommodation reached with South Africa in March 1984 was in serious danger of collapse. By early 1987, the nation's new president, former Foreign Minister Joaquím Chissano, appeared to have stabilized the situation somewhat, but the future still appeared bleak.

The roots of Mozambique's troubles are many and tangled. They include the failure of the Portuguese colonial rulers to develop the country's potentially rich human and economic resources, the shock caused by the sudden exodus at independence of hundreds of thousands of Portuguese settlers, the collateral damage inflicted by the final bitter years of the independence struggle in neighboring Rhodesia (Zimbabwe), the mistakes caused by a too-hasty embrace of socialist economic strategies, the whims of nature that have seen the country alternately ravaged by drought and flood, and the effects of South Africa's regional strategy of destabilization. In a bold effort to reverse his fortunes and stem the tide of a mounting insurgency, President Machel shifted his previous course in the early 1980s. Efforts were made to encourage a return to capitalism in some sectors of the economy and to attract Western investment. At the same time, Maputo, which had signed a treaty of friendship and cooperation with the USSR in 1977, sought a diplomatic accommodation with Western governments, especially the United States. When Machel signed the Nkomati Accord in March 1984, he had a twofold purpose. His primary objective was to end South African support for the Resistência Nacional Moçambicana (MNR) guerrillas; but he also hoped that the agreement would cement his developing ties with the West.

By the end of 1985 it had become clear that the Nkomati Accord was not the panacea that Machel and some of his advisers had hoped it would be. Western economic aid did flow in, but critically needed private capital was slow to follow. The most serious problem, however, was the failure of the accord to slow the spread of guerrilla activities throughout the country and thus stabilize the deteriorating security situation.

The MNR was conceived in 1974 and established in 1976 by Rhodesia's intelligence service as a means of gaining intelligence on Robert Mugabe's Zimbabwe African National Union (ZANU). When Rhodesia became the Republic of Zimbabwe in 1980, South Africa became the MNR's new patron. As a result of generous South African supplies and training, the Mozambican government's insensitivity to the needs and interests of large segments of the rural peasantry, and the incompetence of the Forcas Populares de Libertacao de Mocambique (FPLM), by early 1984 the MNR had unexpectedly become a serious insurgent force.

By cutting off the MNR's South African supply lines, the Nkomati Accord was supposed to set the stage for a withering away of the insurgency. This did not happen. Although it is nearly impossible to assess accurately the claims and counterclaims of the government and the MNR, the consensus among diplomatic and intelligence sources in early 1986 was that the military balance was shifting sharply in favor of the MNR. In mid-February, for example, MNR forces recaptured Casa Banana, their former headquarters in the Gorongosa National Park in Sofala province. Casa Banana had been captured in August 1985, at considerable cost, by troops from Zimbabwe that had been assisting Mozambique's counterinsurgency efforts. The inability of the FPLM to hold this position was demonstrative of its general military incompetence.

During the August 1985 capture of Casa Banana, diaries documenting continuing South African support of the MNR had been discovered, causing Mozambique to suspend a joint security commission with Pretoria. Throughout the first half of 1986, the two countries exchanged increasingly bitter recriminations. Foreign Minister Botha flew to Maputo in May and again in September in an attempt to defuse the situation. By this time, however, there were substantial grounds for doubting the "Pik" Botha's ability to speak for his government, especially the military, on the Mozambique issue.

Meanwhile, President Machel made several moves in an attempt to cope with the growing threat to his government. On March 30 Machel traveled to Moscow to explore possibilities of greater Eastern Bloc assistance, but received no new commitments. Just before leaving for Moscow he reorganized his government, giving sweeping powers to three aides—General Alberto Chipande, Armando Guebuza, and Jorge Rebelo. Then, in July, he named Mario Machungo as prime minister, freeing himself to concentrate on the war.

Machel's most urgent task was to secure increased military support from neighboring Zimbabwe. Some Zimbabwean military forces have been deployed in Mozambique since at least 1983. Until 1985, however, their mission was limited to guarding the railways and oil pipeline running between the two countries. In late 1985 crack Zimbabwean units assumed a more direct role in counterinsurgency operations. But in March 1986, after the MNR's recapture of Casa Banana, there were reports that Zimbabwe was reconsidering its involvement in Mozambique.

In June, a worried Machel traveled to Harare to meet with Mugabe. During this meeting Mugabe agreed to increase Zimbabwe's military involvement in an effort to defeat the MNR. The strength of this commitment, which is backed up by roughly 10,000–12,000 troops, was stated by Mugabe in a speech shortly after Machel's death: "Zimbabwe will never allow a situation in which the MNR takes over Mozambique. . . . We are prepared to die fighting to the last man in defense of the sovereignty of Mozambique, because the defense of that sovereignty is also the defense of Zimbabwe's sovereignty."

The situation in Mozambique became critical in October. On October 7, following a landmine explosion in South Africa near the Mozambique border, South African Minister of Defense Magnus Malan issued a strongly worded threat against Machel. The following day Pretoria announced that it would terminate the employment of the 58,000 Mozambicans working in South African mines. Mozambique responded by charging South Africa with organizing a massive MNR infiltration into Tete and Zambezia provinces from Malawian territory.

The MNR invasion was, in fact, the result of a September 11, 1986 confrontation between Malawi's President H. Kamuzu Banda and the leaders of Mozambique, Zimbabwe, and Zambia. In response to charges that he had allowed the establishment of MNR bases in Malawi, Banda expelled the MNR from the country. This resulted in a sudden exodus of a reported 10,000 guerrillas into Mozambique. By mid-October the MNR was for the first time in control of several border towns.

As these events were transpiring, a plane carrying President Machel crashed in the Lebombo Mountains along the border between South Africa and Mozambique. Suspicions immediately arose that South Africa had deliberately caused the crash. As of July 1987, international aviation experts had still been unable to identify definitively the cause of the crash. Charges that the plane had deliberately been led off course by a South African beacon remained highly speculative.

The death of Machel, a popular figure in Mozambique despite the country's woes, raised fears of an imminent crisis. Instead, the situation stabilized somewhat following the selection of Foreign Minister Chissano, a well regarded pragmatist with considerable political experience, to head the country.[10] Chissano's smooth and timely selection put to rest concern about a struggle for power between pragmatists and ideologues within Frelimo, Mozambique's ruling party. After Chissano expressed his intention to live up to the Nkomati Accord and asked six ANC political operatives to leave the country, South Africa eased up pressures on Maputo. And the MNR's new offensive appeared to stall somewhat. Whether this stabilizing trend will continue remains to be seen.

The key to Mozambique's future will be its ability to end the MNR insurgency. Four important indicators to watch for in 1987 will be (1) whether a British program to train Mozambican officers in Zimbabwean camps that began in early 1986 improves FPLM effectiveness; (2) whether Zimbabwe substantially increases its direct involvement in counterinsurgency operations; (3) whether the amount of South African support for the MNR changes; and (4) whether the MNR is successful in its efforts to win political support in the United States and other Western nations.

Zimbabwe: Signs of Progress

The internal security situation in Zimbabwe improved significantly in 1986. At year's end, the Zimbabwe African National Union (ZANU), President Mugabe's ruling party, which has the support of the country's Shona-speaking majority, and the Zimbabwe African People's Union (ZAPU), the largest opposition party that is supported by Ndebele speakers representing roughly 20 percent of the population, appeared to be working out the final details of an agreement to merge the two parties.[11] A reconciliation of the two former allies in the struggle to end white rule would eliminate the principal cause of unrest in the country and clear the way for the establishment of a one-party system at a future date.

Several factors are at work in causing the two parties to seek an agreement after six years of political squabbling and deadly fighting. The Mugabe government's interest in an accommodation was greatly increased by concerns about developments in Mozambique and South Africa. Since 1982 Zimbabwean military forces had been engaged in an often brutal campaign in Matabeleland to crush armed dissidents loyal to ZAPU. The need to maintain a military presence in Matabeleland acts as a constraint on efforts to assist Mozambique. Moreover, the Shona-Ndebele rift represents a serious source of vulnerability that could be exploited by South Africa. With tensions between South Africa and Zimbabwe growing, Mugabe can ill afford to allow the Matabeleland problem to fester. Moreover, in the past, the brutal nature of the campaign against the ZAPU dissidents has been a source of tension between the Mugabe government and the Western powers upon which it depends for economic and military support.

On the other hand, the willingness of ZAPU and its leader Joshua Nkomo to consider accepting a clearly subservient role in a united ZANU reflects a more realistic assessment of Zimbabwe's political algebra. Efforts to achieve unity in 1980–1981 failed largely because of Nkomo's insistence that ZAPU be given an equal share of power in the government despite the fact that his party could claim the support of no more than 20 percent of the population. Mugabe's ability to consolidate his domestic and international political position and the military's increasingly successful suppression of dissident activity appear to have caused Nkomo and his advisers to conclude in mid-1986 that it was time to cut a deal.

Hints of a possible agreement began to surface in March, but it was not until October that the two parties began to work out the details. An important indication that a deal had been reached was the November release of Dumiso Dabengwa, ZAPU's chief military commander during the liberation struggle, who had been detained since 1981.

Three possible barriers to a unification agreement remain. First, doubts remain about Mugabe's personal commitment to such an agreement. Second, some elements within ZANU might resist pressure to step aside in order to make room for ZAPU officials who would be given posts in the government. Even without this added complication, intra-ZANU tensions are a serious problem for Mugabe. In April 1986 these tensions erupted into the open in a conflict between Transport Minister Herbert Ushewokunze and Justice Minister Eddison Zvobgo, who come from rival Shona clans. A final threat to a unity agreement could come from younger ZAPU dissidents who might refuse to follow Nkomo's conciliatory lead and instead seek support from Pretoria or elsewhere to carry on their antigovernment campaign in Matabeleland.

Prime Minister Mugabe's June 1986 decision to increase his country's military involvement in Mozambique was based on a calculated judgment that Zimbabwe would have great difficulties resisting South African pressure if an MNR government were to come to power in Maputo. The seriousness of Harare's military commitment to Mozambique was underlined by reports in October that it would train a new elite 4,000-man Sixth Brigade. This brigade, which will be commanded by Colonel Lionel Dyke, a former Rhodesian officer who played a key role in crushing the Matabeleland resistance, is being trained to become a mobile, airborne force.

A critical factor in Zimbabwe's ability to assist Mozambique will be the response of the Western powers. Since independence, Zimbabwe has depended on the British and other Western powers for almost all of its military training and arms. The British show no signs of lessening their commitment in this area. Relations with the United States have been more problematical. In July 1986, all U.S. aid was suspended following an anti-U.S. statement by a junior government minister at a Fourth of July reception in Harare attended by former U.S. President Jimmy Carter. By year's end, however, U.S.-Zimbabwe relations had grown less tense, a result in part of the arrival of a new U.S. ambassador, former Union Carbide executive James Rawlings, who was strongly committed to improving ties between the two countries. On the other hand, if Zimbabwe significantly expands its military role in Mozambique, or if the United States moves to support the MNR—as some, notably Senator Jesse Helms, have proposed—tensions between Mugabe and the Reagan administration could take another turn for the worse.

Zimbabwe's relations with South Africa are almost certain to worsen in 1987. Zimbabwe is likely to be a prime target of Pretoria's efforts to demonstrate that sanctions, which Mugabe actively lobbied for, will damage the neighboring states to a greater extent than South Africa. Exactly how far the Botha government will go to make this point remains to be seen.

Angola: A Stalemate?

In 1986 Angola began its second decade of independence with the ethnic and political tensions that had plagued it throughout its first decade of existence still unresolved. But the tide on the battlefield now appears to be shifting in favor of the MPLA government in Luanda. Whether this military trend will continue in 1987, and whether it leads to any progress on the political front, remains to be seen.

The principal protagonists in Angola are the MPLA led by President Jose Eduardo dos Santos and UNITA led by Jonas Savimbi. The MPLA has ruled the country since emerging victorious in a three-way struggle for power at independence in November 1975, and UNITA has survived its defeat in 1975-1976 to become a formidable military and political force. Although the MPLA has been able to broaden its political base somewhat since independence, it remains dependent primarily on the active support of residents of Luanda and other northern cities and of the Mbundu peoples who represent roughly 25 percent of Angola's population. UNITA, on the other hand, attracts its greatest support from the Ovimbundu peoples of south-central Angola, who represent roughly 37 percent of the population. Ethnic arithmetic can be misleading, however. The struggle in Angola has become a highly personalized stuggle between the MPLA leadership and Savimbi, the outcome of which will be determined less by popular support than by the vagaries of international and regional politics.

A major turning point in the Angolan conflict occurred in late 1983, when the Soviet Union, which along with Cuba has provided direct military support to the MPLA since the 1975 civil war, decided to increase its commitment to the MPLA's survival. This decision, which was reaffirmed in April 1986 during a visit by President dos Santos to Moscow, led to an inflow of as much as $2 billion in increased military equipment in 1984-1986. This assistance and the continuing support of roughly 25,000–30,000 Cuban troops allowed an increasingly experienced and well-trained Angolan army to launch a major offensive against UNITA in the summer of 1985. The offensive culminated in September 1985 in a major battle at Mavinga just north of Jamba, UNITA's headquarters.

Although UNITA was able to turn back the government assault, it needed direct South African air support to do so. More important, the picture of UNITA forces on the ropes ended talk of an imminent Savimbi victory. Luanda's strategy appears to be twofold: The first objective is to bring under control Moxico, a thinly populated province with a salient into Zambia and Zaire, thus cutting UNITA's north-south communications lines; the second is to capture UNITA-held towns in the southeast, gradually forcing Savimbi's troops back toward Jamba in the far southeast corner of the country. Following the setback at Mavinga, however, Luanda apparently decided to give priority to the northern prong of this strategy. After several delays, government forces went back on the offensive in June 1986. Although advances have not been as dramatic as in 1985, when Savimbi's supply base at Cazombo was seized shortly before the battle for Mavinga, the offensive does seem to be making gradual headway. The government now appears much more patient than in 1985, allowing itself perhaps as much as two or three years before it attempts to push directly toward Jamba.

The deterioration in UNITA's military position has occurred despite the arrival in early 1986 of the first installments of covert assistance, including shoulder-fired ground-to-air missiles, from the United States. Reports in late 1986 indicated that U.S. arms were flowing to UNITA through Zaire. After having labored for four years to achieve a diplomatic accommodation with Luanda that would end the Cuban military presence in Angola and clear the way for a settlement of the conflict in Namibia, the Reagan administration in late 1985 decided to align itself with UNITA. This decision was made possible by the U.S. Congress's 1985 repeal of a decade-long restriction on covert aid to UNITA. Paradoxically, it was taken at a time when the majority of U.S. intelligence analysts were coming to the conclusion that UNITA could not win its war against Luanda.

Despite UNITA's setbacks, however, there is little prospect of a government victory in the short term. The more likely outcome is an ongoing military stalemate. Unfortunately, there appears to be even less prospect of a break in the diplomatic stalemate surrounding the issue of Cuban troops that has blocked a settlement in Namibia since the two issues were "linked" in 1981.

During a visit to Luanda by the Reverend Jesse Jackson in October 1986, President dos Santos reiterated his interest in renewed negotiations with the United States and issued a personal invitation to President Reagan to visit Angola. This "goodwill" gesture aside, three barriers to a settlement remain in place. First, both political and military considerations make it impossible for Luanda to agree to a Cuban troop withdrawal as long as UNITA and South Africa remain a military threat. Second, by deciding to provide support to Savimbi, the Reagan administration has seriously undercut its ability to play a mediator role in the conflict. Finally, neither the Soviet Union nor Cuba appears likely to reduce its commitment to ensure the MPLA's survival.

The only elements in the Angolan equation that might change in 1987 are the level of U.S. and South African support for UNITA.[12] In the United States, the Democratic party's victory in the November 1986 Senate elections and the controversy created by the Reagan administration's dealings with Iran may yet lead to congressional moves to block future aid to UNITA. In South Africa, growing internal pressures and concerns about the situation in Mozambique, which will have a much more direct impact on South African security than developments in Angola, could cause the SADF to reduce its support of UNITA. If these outside sources of support for UNITA were to dry up, it might open up possibilities for the MPLA to seek out a political solution with some groups within a militarily weakened UNITA—but this would be a solution that would not involve Jonas Savimbi. Over the longer term, a reduction in aid to Savimbi would also create a greater possibility of a military victory by government forces. But neither a negotiated settlement nor a military victory is likely to occur in 1987—or in the remaining years of this decade.

Implications for the United States

The year 1986 marked the demise of the Reagan administration's six-year-old strategy of "constructive engagement." In its assessment of that policy, the Secretary of State's Advisory Committee on South Africa concluded that constructive engagement "had failed to achieve its original objectives." In a passage alluding to an article written by Assistant Secretary of State Chester Crocker shortly before he entered government,[13] the Advisory Committee wrote:

> The situation inside South Africa has also moved in a direction sharply at odds with the hopes and expectations of the architects of constructive engagement: (1) The slow, halting, and circumscribed nature of the reforms so far enacted by Pretoria has largely discredited the argument that fundamental change can be brought about through a process managed and led by a National Party government. (2) The sustained intensity of

unrest and violence in the townships and "homelands" has raised doubts about the ultimate significance of the enormous disparity that exists in the physical power of the South African government and its opponents. No longer can it be assumed that this imbalance provides whites with an indefinite check on political disintegration. (3) The political shock caused by the international banking community's 1985 refusal to turn over South Africa's loans has forced a reassessment of Pretoria's vulnerability to international economic pressures. (4) Evidence of increasingly bitter anti-Americanism among South African blacks has heightened awareness of the long-term damage to U.S. interests that can result from policies and rhetoric that create an impression of a Washington-Pretoria "alliance." Many South Africans, black and white, have viewed recent U.S. policy as tacitly approving of the aggressive regional policies of the South African government and the limited character of its "reform" program.

By missing opportunity after opportunity to demonstrate a tangible commitment to end apartheid and instead resorting to increasingly brutal tactics to quell legitimate black protest, the Botha government has furthered the development of a growing political consensus in the United States in favor of stronger economic sanctions. Thus, in October 1986 the U.S. Congress voted, by overwhelming margins in both houses, to override a Presidential veto of the Comprehensive Anti-Apartheid Act of 1986, which imposes a package of economic sanctions stronger than any yet adopted by any of South Africa's other major trading partners.

In sum, U.S. policymakers now face a situation markedly different from that which existed in 1981. A new policy is now urgently required.[14]

There appears to be little prospect, however, that President Reagan will heed the Advisory Committee's urging that he assume a major leadership role in shaping a coherent, long-term U.S. policy toward South Africa and in winning support for a coordinated multilateral program of sanctions. The president's personal reluctance to take a tougher stand against apartheid was evidenced by two 1986 events. On July 17, in a speech that had received advanced billing as a definitive statement of administration policy, President Reagan reiterated his view that significant reforms had occurred in South Africa, castigated the ANC, and strongly criticized sanctions. Then, in September, despite the advice both of Richard Lugar, a strong Reagan supporter who was then chairman of the Senate Foreign Relations Committee, and of the Secretary of State's Advisory Committee, the president vetoed the Comprehensive Anti-Apartheid Act of 1986. These actions have caused a number of observers to question the sincerity of the Reagan administration's commitment to carry out the provisions of the 1986 act.

U.S. policy toward the rest of the region is in disarray. A major reason for this is the inconsistency between the Reagan administration's support of antigovernment forces in Angola and its efforts to shore up the government in Mozambique. This contradictory approach to the two "Marxist" states in the region has been attacked from both sides of the political spectrum in the United States. But neither liberals nor conservatives are in a position to force the administration to adopt a consistent approach.

Barring a major escalation of Soviet involvement in the region, which is highly unlikely, or a significant increase in the level of violence inside South Africa, which is possible but not probable, southern Africa will receive far less attention in Washington in 1987 than it did in 1986, and U.S. policy toward South Africa and the region is likely to remain incoherent and largely ineffective.

Notes

1. Canadian International Development Agency, "The Impact of Economic Sanctions Against South Africa on the SADCC States" (February 1986).
2. Ibid., pp. 16–17.
3. Ibid., pp. 18–20.
4. Leonard Spector, *Going Nuclear* (Cambridge: Ballinger Publishing Co., 1987), pp. 220–221.
5. "A U.S. Policy Toward South Africa: The Report of the Secretary of State's Advisory Committee on South Africa" (Washington, January 1987), p. 22.
6. Speech to the National Education Crisis Committee Convention, Durban, South Africa, February 1986.
7. See Michael Clough, "Beyond Constructive Engagement," *Foreign Policy* (Winter 1985–1986).
8. *Mission to South Africa* Report of the Commonwealth Group of Eminent Persons appointed under the Nassau Accord on Southern Africa, London, June 1986, pp. 63, 67–68.
9. See Nicholas Haysom, *Mbangalala: The Rise of Right-Wing Vigilantes in South Africa* (Johannesburg, South Africa: Centre for Applied Legal Studies, University of Witswatersrand, 1986).
10. Gillian Gunn, "Mozambique After Machel," *CSIS Africa Notes*, no. 67 (December 29, 1986).
11. See "Zimbabwe: A Sort of Unity," *African Confidential* (January 21, 1987).
12. See Michael Clough, "Coming to Terms with Radical Socialism," in Clough (ed.), *Reassessing the Soviet Challenge in Africa* (Berkeley, Calif.: Institute of International Studies, 1986).
13. Chester Crocker, "South Africa: A Strategy for Change," *Foreign Affairs* (Winter 1980–1981).
14. See "A U.S. Policy Toward South Africa," p. 38.

6
NATO's Southern Flank: A Troubled Region

Alan Platt

Historically, the Southern Flank of NATO—Spain, Portugal, Italy, Greece, and Turkey—has been taken largely for granted by U.S. policymakers. Although bilateral relations between the United States and the nations of the region have had periodic ups and downs in the postwar period, the relationships have typically been close. At the heart of these generally harmonious relations have been widely shared security concerns regarding the Soviet Union and the concomitant desirability of having the United States play a dominant role in the defense of the region. At the same time, these shared security perceptions and the often quiescent state of the region have combined to allow Washington to pursue for most of the postwar period a policy of "benign neglect." It has really only been at unusually troubled times—during the 1973 Middle East War, the veering to the left of the Portuguese, Greek, and Italian governments in the mid-1970s, the periodic Greek-Turkish crises over Cyprus, and the 1986 U.S. raid on Libya—that U.S. policymakers have focused particularly on the region.

In 1986, U.S. security relations with the countries of the Southern Flank were increasingly under pressure, as a number of the major events of this past year graphically bear witness. The aftermath of the *Achille Lauro* affair, the U.S. raid on Libya of April 1986, Greek Prime Minister Andreas Papandreou's periodic anti-American posturing, Spanish reluctance to integrate its military forces in NATO's command structure, and the Gonzalez government's simultaneous insistence on reducing the U.S. presence in Spain—all of these constitute symptoms and precursors of significant strains in U.S. security relations with the countries of the Southern Flank. And, of course, to these particular strains must be added a range of broader political and economic problems that currently cloud overall U.S.-European security relations and increasingly portend to divide U.S. and European interests in coming years.

This chapter focuses on the most salient factors and events in 1986 that affected U.S. security relations with the countries of NATO's Southern Flank. In a number of instances, these relations were perceptibly strained by a combination of political, economic, and regional pressures. Perhaps nowhere was the combination of these pressures more discernible than in the bilateral negotiations over U.S. and NATO military bases that the United States has been and is carrying on with the different countries of the region. Accordingly, these base negotiations are examined in detail in an effort to shed light on the direction and concrete nature of the growing strains in the usually harmonious bilateral U.S. security relations with the countries of the region. The chapter concludes with a brief discussion of what developments in 1986 may portend for future U.S. security relations with the countries of NATO's Southern Flank.

Spain

The year 1986 was truly a landmark for Spanish foreign policy. Since 1982, when the Spanish Socialist Workers party (PSOE) came to power, membership in both the North Atlantic Treaty Organization and the European Economic Community (EEC) have been issues of the highest priority for the government of Felipe Gonzalez. During this past year, both issues were resolved, happily from the United States' point of view, in favor of augmented Spanish participation in the Western community of nations.

In the period immediately following the 1982 elections, the focus of the new Spanish government was on gaining entry to the EEC. This was seen by the Socialists as critical to having Spain participate in a common Western European destiny, and as a starting point for a new, more active foreign policy that would be less isolated from Western European economic and security arrangements.

In early 1984, when prospects for Spanish entry to the EEC brightened despite economic objections by France, Italy, Greece, and the United States, Prime Minister Gonzalez began to focus on the NATO membership issue. This was a particularly thorny issue for Gonzalez and his party inasmuch as the Socialists had argued in principle against membership in the 1982 election campaign, changing their minds about the desirability of Spanish membership in NATO only after gaining power. In an effort to buy additional time to shore up popular support for NATO membership and, ultimately, to resolve the issue positively, Gonzalez chose in late 1984 to ask in his annual address to the Spanish Parliament that Spain hold a referendum on NATO, indicating that Spaniards would be asked to vote for NATO in "a political sense," without military integration. In the same speech, in an effort to appease the Left wing of his own

Socialist party, which had long opposed Spain's joining the alliance, Gonzalez indicated that he would simultaneously seek to reduce the U.S. presence in Spain, a presence that uncomfortably reminded many Spaniards of the United States' earlier close ties with the Franco regime.

In the spring of 1985, with EEC entry officially set for January 1, 1986, Gonzalez turned his full attention to the NATO issue and set March 12, 1986 as the date for the national referendum on continued NATO membership. Not surprisingly, NATO membership—and the related issue of future Spanish security relations with the United States—dominated Spanish politics for much of 1985 and early 1986. In the end, after a heated campaign in which the conservative, normally pro-NATO Popular Alliance party, led by Manuel Fraga, called for tactical reasons for abstention in the referendum, Gonzalez carried the day. In a surprise to most political observers and pollsters, the Spanish people approved continued NATO membership by 53 percent of the vote.

However, in an effort during the referendum campaign to enhance popular support for his pro-NATO position, Gonzalez agreed to add three significant conditions to Spain's NATO membership. These conditions are likely to strain in important ways prospective Spanish security relations with the United States, as well as with all the other members of NATO. First, nuclear weapons are to be banned from Spain. Second, the Gonzalez government committed itself to reducing the 12,500 U.S. troops currently authorized to be in Spain by the terms of a bilateral treaty. Third, Spanish forces will not be subject to direct NATO military command.[1]

In the spring of 1986, trying to take advantage of the Socialist government's strong political momentum created by entry into the EEC and the positive NATO referendum, Gonzalez moved to consolidate his power by advancing the date of national parliamentary elections to June 22, 1986. Facing a divided conservative opposition on the Right and a badly split Communist party on the Left, Gonzalez's Socialist party retained an overall majority in the June election, winning 184 seats in the 350-seat Parliament as compared to Fraga's Popular Alliance, which won 64 seats. In the election, the Socialists garnered 44 percent of the popular vote whereas the Popular Alliance got 26 percent of the vote; the rest of the popular vote was split among the eight other political parties. Despite an array of criticisms of the Socialists from the Left and the Right during the campaign, the generally positive results are likely to encourage the continuation of the pro-NATO, pro-EEC stance of the Spanish government into the foreseeable future.

Spanish participation in NATO, though, is likely to continue to be limited by the three conditions agreed to by Gonzalez in the NATO referendum campaign, a fact with important implications for U.S. security interests. For example, the condition pertaining to the size of the U.S. military presence in Spain has already seriously complicated the ongoing negotiations to renew the five-year U.S.-Spanish Agreement of Friendship, Defense, and Cooperation, which is due to expire in May 1988. The preliminary round of talks on renewal took place on July 10, 1986. No concrete progress was announced at that time, in large part because the Spanish negotiating team held firm to the idea of significantly reducing the U.S. military presence in Spain. Nor has any concrete progress been made in the several rounds of talks since then.

Moreover, following the preliminary round of talks, then U.S. Ambassador Thomas Enders declared that the United States was willing to replace roughly 500 U.S. military personnel at the Torrejon Air Base near Madrid with Spanish civilian personnel. Although the Gonzalez government welcomed this suggested cut, it showed no sign of being content to limit overall cuts in U.S. military personnel to this level or merely to transfer personnel and aircraft from one base to another in Spain. Indeed, in the subsequent rounds of negotiations held in late 1986 and early 1987, the Spanish government made it clear that the ultimate renewal of the U.S.-Spanish Base Agreement would have to go beyond "symbolism" and require "significant" U.S. personnel reductions. Even then, the Gonzalez government has made clear that it might be necessary to close or impose serious restrictions on operations at the Torrejon Air Base, where the 16th U.S. Tactical Air Force is headquartered, and at the Zaragoza Air Base, which is a critical facility for U.S. tactical fighter training in Europe. (See Figure 6.1.)

Foreign Minister Francisco Fernandez Ordonez made this point explicitly in a widely publicized speech to the Spanish Parliament in October. At the time, following Ambassador Enders's proposal of a symbolic cut, Ordonez declared that all U.S. bases would be closed if the United States did not come up with "adequate" reduction proposals. Ordonez then chose to underscore his government's seriousness on this point at the December meeting of NATO foreign ministers. At the time, he discussed the base negotiations privately with Secretary of State George Shultz and then repeated to a press conference that if the United States did not meet Spanish demands regarding the bases, there would be no future treaty. By the end of 1986, reports were circulating in the Spanish and U.S. press that the Spanish minister of defense was studying ways of taking over U.S. military installations and missions in Spain, including the stationing of thirty-six Spanish F-18A fighter bombers at Torrejon by 1988.

Although the Gonzalez government is primarily motivated by a campaign commitment and continuing domestic political considerations, its insistence on reducing U.S. military personnel in Spain also has a

FIGURE 6.1. Major U.S. Military Installations in Spain

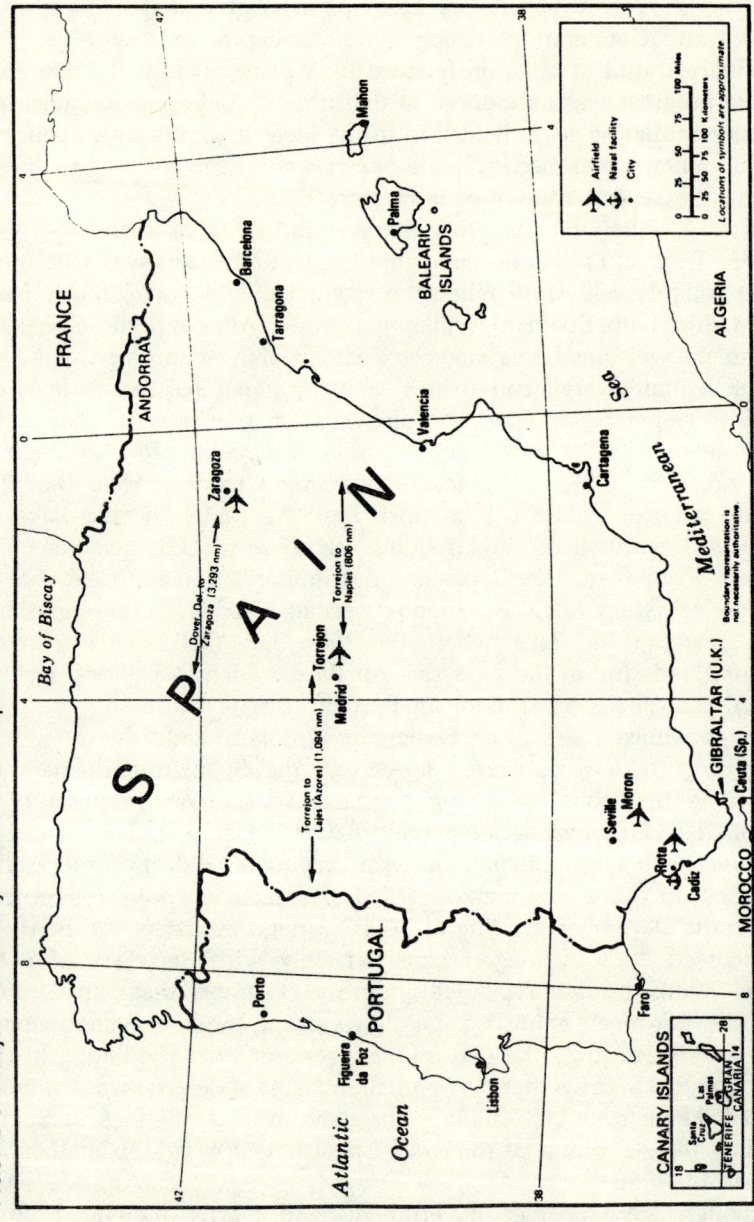

Source: U.S. Military Installations in NATO's Southern Region, report prepared for the Subcommittee on Europe and the Middle East of the Committee on Foreign Affairs, U.S. House of Representatives, by the Foreign Affairs and National Defense Division of the Library of Congress, October 7, 1986, p. 20.

significant domestic economic component. In 1982, candidate Gonzalez talked of creating a large number of new jobs. By 1986, however, the number of unemployed people in Spain had risen significantly; and in an otherwise bright economic outlook, unemployment has continued to be a serious, persistent problem. Accordingly, it is not totally surprising that as the reelected Gonzalez government studies new economic measures to create additional jobs, it will also continue to pursue base negotiations with an eye on achieving significant U.S. personnel reductions that will perhaps create new opportunities for Spanish employment.

In previous years, one avenue that might have offered the Spanish government hope regarding its domestic economic problems was the U.S. foreign and security aid program. Since the first bilateral Executive agreement permitting U.S. use of air and naval bases in Spain in 1953, the United States has provided billions of dollars in economic and military assistance to Spain to further a range of U.S.-Spanish political and security ties. However, in fiscal year 1987, the level of U.S. assistance to Spain was reduced from its customary $400 million level to only $105 million. The substantial congressional reduction in aid to Spain was partly due to the stringencies imposed by the Gramm-Rudman legislation. But it was also partly due to the anti-American statements emanating from Madrid in 1986 and early 1987 and the unwillingness of the Gonzalez government to allow U.S. planes to use Spanish airspace to carry out military activities directed toward Libya in April 1986. These developments have perceptibly undercut support for Spain in the Congress.

Although interest rates on past loans to Spain under the U.S. foreign military sales program are to be reduced in 1987, there is little prospect that U.S. aid levels will return to their customary levels in the near term. Trade disputes will continue between the United States and Spain over agricultural products, stemming from Spain's accession to the EEC. And Spain is not likely to concur soon with Washington's views on security challenges originating in North Africa, Central America, and other parts of the Third World. Rather, these issues seem sure to come together and to bring further strains to U.S.-Spanish security relations in the near term—strains that will undoubtedly be increasingly evident in the base agreement negotiations during the period leading to their planned conclusion in 1988.

Nevertheless, the reelected Gonzalez government appears to be firmly committed, overall, to a pro-American policy course; moreover, little is likely to come of the pleas of a number of candidates in the 1986 parliamentary elections to close all the bases and cancel entirely the agreement that has allowed up to 12,500 Americans to be stationed on Spanish soil. The base negotiations likely will result, ultimately, in highly visible, "significant" U.S. personnel reductions, perhaps closely calibrated with future U.S. aid levels. Leopoldo Calvo Sotelo, the former prime minister, might well have been speaking for Prime Minister Gonzalez when he observed, while summarizing the thinking in Spain on the U.S. presence issue: "Yanquis, go home—but not all of you."[2]

Portugal

Unlike Spain, Portugal was one of the founding members of NATO and has worked closely with the United States and other Atlantic alliance members throughout the postwar period on furthering common security objectives. This pattern of close security relations with the United States has characterized both the long postwar period of authoritarian rule of Antonio Salazar and his successor, Marcelo Caetano, and the roughly ten-year period of democratic rule since the bloodless ouster of Caetano and his immediate Communist successors in the middle 1970s.

That being said, Portugal in 1986, in the words of leading Portuguese academic, Alvaro Vasconcelos, is now "a more committed member of the Atlantic alliance than ever before."[3] For Vasconcelos and others, Portugal's current enthusiasm for commitment to the Western alliance is traceable in part to two major developments in 1986—the Portuguese accession to the European Economic Community in January, and the solid institutionalization of a pro-Western political-military orientation on the part of the government.

For roughly the last eight years, difficult negotiations have taken place concerning Portuguese entry to the EEC. France, Spain, and Italy, among other EEC members, have been worried about the trade ramifications of Portuguese accession, while the United States has long been concerned about what Portuguese accession would mean for the importation of U.S. soybeans into Portugal and the share of the Portuguese grain market reserved for Community suppliers. These were some of the problems complicating Portuguese entry into the EEC in earlier years, and they continue to be serious issues now that Portugal has joined the Common Market. For Portugal, though, although Common Market membership entails competitive and industry modernization problems during a seven-year transition period, entry to the EEC is likely to prove to be a landmark step in cementing Portuguese political, military, and economic ties with the Western community of nations.

On the domestic political front, 1986 was an important year for Portugal as well, with several developments reinforcing Portugal's commitment to the West. At present, the major political parties (save the Communists)—the Social Democratic party (PSD), the Socialist party (PS), and the Social Democratic Center (CDS)—all favor a pro-NATO position. NATO is viewed by these parties and most of their constituents as an antitotalitarian grouping in the post-Salazar era. In the October 1985 election, right-of-center Social Democrat Anibal Cavaco Silva campaigned vigorously on a pro-Western platform. In the balloting, his Social Democratic party won a plurality of 88 seats in Parliament, whereas the Socialists' share dropped to 57 seats and the pro-Moscow Communists to 38 seats. In June 1986, Prime Minister Cavaco Silva, thwarted legislatively on several key domestic proposals, asked for and received a parliamentary vote of confidence, getting a 15-vote majority. However, in April 1987, the government of Cavaco Silva fell because of domestic policy differences and new national elections were set for July 1987.

The institutionalization of a pro-Western political orientation at the highest political levels in Portugal was further advanced in 1986–1987 when Mario Soares was elected president. Campaigning on a pro-Western platform, Soares, a three-time former prime minister, surprised most Portuguese political observers by receiving 53 percent of the vote in a runoff election. Soares's election in 1986 probably went further in solidifying Portugal's pro-Western orientation than the election of his more conservative opponent would have done. For now and into the foreseeable future, the Portuguese political spectrum from the Socialists on the Left across to the parties on the Right all support a strong commitment to the Western alliance.

Central to the U.S. security relationship with Portugal is the Lajes base in the Azores, an island group located 800 miles west of Lisbon. The United States has had an air base there since 1944, helping to link the United States with Europe and the Middle East. This base received particular attention during the 1973 Middle East Yom Kippur War, when the Portuguese were the only country to allow U.S. C-5As to refuel while delivering supplies to Israel. Today, Lajes is not only an important refueling stop for military transports but also a highly important base for antisubmarine patrol activities; in addition, it is well situated to help tankers supporting various potential military operations. For example, Lajes allows U.S. antisubmarine aircraft to patrol the middle sector of the 4,000-mile sea-lane that links the U.S. Sixth Fleet in the Mediterranean with its major supply depots in the United States. It also allows for sustained surveillance operations over the key strategic area of Gibraltar.

In 1976, when the Communists were turned out of power in Lisbon, the Western powers promised substantial levels of economic assistance to the new Portuguese government. In fact, with few exceptions, Western aid levels to Portugal have been quite constrained during the past decade, and Portugal has remained relatively undeveloped, with a per capita income only 25 percent of the NATO countries' average. As with Spain, planned U.S. military assistance levels for fiscal year 1987 were significantly reduced by the Congress from $141 million to $83 million, due largely to the Gramm-Rudman legislation; and this development is bound to put pressure on U.S.-Portuguese relations, especially where the Lajes base arrangement is concerned.

U.S. aid levels and Lajes dominated the discussions held by Secretary of Defense Caspar Weinberger in Lisbon in May 1986, but the talks seemingly produced little concrete agreement. These issues were then taken to a higher level by Prime Minister Anibal Cavaco Silva in his September talks in Washington with President Reagan, Secretary Shultz, and Secretary Weinberger. While in Washington, the prime minister publicly endorsed the U.S. Strategic Defense Initiative and spoke warmly of U.S.-Portuguese ties. Nevertheless, he made it clear that future U.S.-Portuguese security relations would be closely linked to future U.S. aid levels and the modernization of Portuguese armed forces.

For the United States, this contingency presents a serious problem. On the one hand, Lajes is clearly one of the most important bases in Western Europe and Portugal is one of the United States' closest security allies, an ally that from time to time has helped U.S. interests outside of Europe. Most recently, for example, it was reported that Lisbon was a key place for the 1986 transshipment of U.S. arms to both Iran and Central America.[4] On the other hand, the U.S. Executive does not control the annual level of aid appropriations, and Congress does not seem inclined to earmark Portuguese aid funds to keep them at a level satisfactory to the Portuguese government. Indeed, the Congress currently plans to make significant cuts in aid to Portugal in each of the next few years, as compared to the level envisaged in the 1984 seven-year Lajes base agreement. The reduction in 1986 engendered noticeable ill-will in bilateral U.S.-Portuguese security talks; they loom as a serious irritant in 1987. If they are forthcoming, the cuts will not only strain normally close bilateral relations and increase pressures from the Portuguese to reopen the Lajes agreement; they also will jeopardize future U.S. efforts to expand the U.S. military presence in Portugal from Lajes to the Portuguese mainland, where a ground-based, deep-space surveillance station is currently planned and other installations might be sought, especially if the U.S. presence in Spain is substantially reduced in 1988.

Italy

Since the end of World War II, Italy has been among the United States' closest allies. More than any of the other countries on NATO's

Southern Flank, Italy has consistently shared with the United States a common geopolitical perspective on European security. Despite the fact that there is no aid-for-bases arrangement with Italy, such as those that exist with the other four countries of the region, Italy, an original signatory of the North Atlantic treaty, has provided a relatively large number of military installations for use by the United States and NATO during the postwar period. Most recently, pursuant to NATO's dual-track decision of December 1979, Italy agreed to accept 112 ground-launched cruise missiles on its soil; and in 1983, these deployments were begun on schedule in Comiso, Sicily. They are now well on their way toward completion.

In addition, as a result of its strategic location, Italy has long played a key role in supporting the U.S. Sixth Fleet and NATO operations throughout the Mediterranean area. In short, as Italian Communist leader Enrico Berlinguer has caustically noted, Italy is the "teacher's pet" of NATO.[5] Close political-military-economic ties with the United States, active participation in NATO and European Community institutions, and reliance on the United States' nuclear umbrella—all of these factors have been and are likely to remain central to Italy's foreign policy for the foreseeable future.

Nevertheless, two developments came together in 1985 that greatly complicated U.S.-Italian security relations. For most of the postwar period, successive Italian governments have been concerned primarily about the potential threat to its security from the northeast. The most likely scenario for Italian defense planners has involved the need to counter a Warsaw Pact offensive against NATO through Yugoslavia. In light of uncertainties in Libya, Greece, and Turkey, however, Italy has increasingly come to focus on problems to its south. In 1985, the Italian government issued its latest Defense "White Paper." Reflecting the first serious Italian governmental effort to rethink defense policy since the immediate postwar years, the White Paper explicitly acknowledged and discussed the reasons for which localized conflict in the Mediterranean was more of a real threat to Italian security interests in the near term than an attack from the north. Accordingly, the government proposed a number of measures concerned with reallocating Italian military expenditures to enhance the operational mobility and flexibility of Italy's armed forces in the context of various Mediterranean contingencies, rather than in the context of traditional U.S. and NATO threat scenarios.

In late 1985, this putative Mediterranean threat to Italian security interests—and the potential strains it may bring to U.S.-Italian relations—took on concrete meaning as a result of the *Achille Lauro* hijacking. After Palestinians seized the Italian cruise ship in October 1985, U.S. military aircraft intercepted an Egyptian commercial airliner carrying the hijackers to safe haven and forced it to land at the NATO air base at Sigonella in Sicily. Soon after the plane landed, a confrontation occurred over jurisdiction between the local Italian authorities and several U.S. officials present on the scene, including former National Security Council aide Lieutenant Colonel Oliver North. Following a late-night phone conversation between President Reagan and Prime Minister Bettino Craxi, the Italian government assumed jurisdiction over four of the hijackers. Despite U.S. pleas to the contrary, however, Prime Minister Craxi refused to hold the fifth, Abu Abbas, a well-known Palestinian terrorist thought to have masterminded the whole operation.

For the United States, the Italian government's decision not to detain Abu Abbas pending extradition proceedings was a most disconcerting development and an important setback not only to bilateral U.S.-Italian relations but also to U.S.-Middle Eastern antiterrorist efforts. The forcedown of the plane, the confrontation over jurisdiction, the dispute over Abu Abbas, the lack of U.S. governmental rebuke to the errant U.S. officers at Sigonella, the seeming trampling on Italian sovereignty—all of these events heightened nationalistic Italian sentiment and a growing resentment toward the United States and the use of U.S. bases in Italy.

These Italian sentiments returned to the surface in the spring of 1986, when the United States launched its much-publicized raid on Libya. At that time, Prime Minister Craxi not only refused the use of Italian airspace to U.S. planes, but his government openly criticized the wisdom of the American operation. In a public statement, Craxi observed that this U.S. action disregarded the principles underlying the U.S.-European "partnership;" he then reiterated the point that regarding such places as Libya, which were outside the NATO area, U.S. military actions were the exclusive responsibility of the United States. He added that NATO bases in Italy should not, and would not, be used in the future for such operations outside the framework of the Atlantic alliance.[6]

Partly in reaction to Libyan threats and partly out of pique with the United States following the U.S. raid on Libya, the Italian government opted in a highly publicized step to take command of the U.S. Coast Guard station on the southern most Italian island of Lampedusa. This station, which had been the target of a feckless Libyan missile attack immediately following the April 15 bombing of Tripoli, had for many years housed roughly two dozen U.S. Coast Guard personnel running a navigation station. In May, the Italian government decided that the U.S. personnel stationed at Lampedusa would be able to remain in place at least until 1988, when the current base agreement is to be renegotiated. Henceforth, however, instead of operating under autonomous U.S. command, they were to be placed under the command of an Italian Air Force officer.

Given the fact that Italian foreign-policy positions are often driven primarily by domestic political considerations, it is not surprising that the events of 1985 and 1986 concerning Libya and Lampedusa had important political ramifications in Italy. In mid-1985, the five-party coalition government of Bettino Craxi—composed of Christian Democrats (DC), Socialists (PSI), Republicans (PRI), Social Democrats (PSDI), and Liberals (PLI) became the longest-lasting cabinet in Italian postwar history. It had come into office in early 1983 and survived the 1984 European Parliament elections, the July 1985 election of Christian Democrat Francesco Cossiga as president of the republic, the 1985 regional elections, serious budget deficits and unemployment problems, and numerous tests of political strength in the Parliament. It came closest to falling in October 1985, when strongly pro-Atlanticist Defense Minister Giovanni Spadolini and the Republican party temporarily withdrew from the coalition to protest the government's handling of the *Achille Lauro*–Abu Abbas affair. However, the Republican party's resignation from the coalition was soon withdrawn after it received assurances about Italy's commitment to fight terrorism and about the future course of policies toward the Palestine Liberation Organization (PLO).

At the time, Craxi was resentful and publicly critical of U.S. actions. Accordingly, he chose to stand firm and ultimately prevailed as the defender of an Italian foreign policy that was somewhat less dependent on the United States and more focused on Italy's role as a Mediterranean nation. In June 1986, however, the Craxi-led coalition, which ultimately lasted one month short of three years, finally fell. The Christian Democrats triggered this development when their newly reconfirmed party chief, Ciriaco DeMita, chose to interpret favorable returns from local elections in Sicily as a mandate for returning the prime ministership to the DC and consequently brought down the coalition through a parliamentary vote of no-confidence.

The resulting governmental crisis lasted for thirty-five days during the summer of 1986, with Craxi staying on as a caretaker. In the end, the crisis was settled with a putative twenty-month agreement between the Christian Democrats and the Socialists, thereby providing for a second Craxi government that would stay in power until the spring of 1987. At that point, a DC-led government would take office until the next regularly scheduled national elections in June 1988. Accordingly, Craxi was sworn in as head of a second governmental coalition on August 1, 1986 with eight ministerial shifts and five new members of the cabinet. Craxi, however, refused to implement this plan to alternate the prime ministership and his government fell in March 1987, just as the Christian Democrats were to regain leadership of the coalition. New national elections were set for June 14–15, 1987. Moreover, the governing parties in Italy now all are seemingly committed to a future foreign policy that is pro-NATO and pro-European but somewhat less dependent on the United States and relatively more focused on Mediterranean security issues.

Not surprisingly, such an Italian policy course has become even more likely as a result of the recent disclosures about U.S. arms shipments to Iran. These disclosures have visibly upset Italian politicians across the political spectrum, especially inasmuch as the United States has often been critical of the perceived weakness in Italy's antiterrorist stance, and as the possibility was raised in November that Talamane, a small Tuscan port, was used for U.S. arms shipments to Iran without the knowledge of the Italian government.

Greece

U.S.-Greek relations have been warm for most of the postwar period. Long-standing historical ties between the two countries as well as the activism and prominence of Greek citizens in the United States, among other factors, have for many years provided the backdrop for generally harmonious bilateral political, economic, and defense relations.

This state of bilateral relations, however, has been under particular pressure in the period since 1981, when Greek Socialist leader Andreas Papandreou become prime minister. Indeed, during the past five years, relations between the two countries have been noticeably uneven and, at times, visibly stormy. In his 1981 campaign and again in his reelection campaign in 1985, Papandreou and his PASOK party referred to the United States as "the metropolis for imperialism" and called for changes in the status of the four major and twenty smaller U.S. military and intelligence-gathering installations in Greece, which have been there since the early 1950s and have come to symbolize close Greek security relations with the United States. During and immediately following the 1981 electoral campaign, Papandreou wanted to have all four of the major bases—Souda Bay, Nea Mkari, Iraklion, and Hellenikon—closed permanently. (See Figure 6.2.) Although Papandreou continued to insist rhetorically that this position remained unchanged, Papandreou eventually moderated his position; and in 1983, after months of tough negotiations, Greece and the United States signed a new five-year Defense and Economic Cooperation Agreement (DECA). With this document, the two sides struck a tacit bargain: In exchange for continuing high levels of U.S. aid, Greece agreed to keep the four bases open, at least until 1988. At the time of the conclusion of the 1983 DECA, however, Papandreou publicly reiterated his view that these bases served U.S. interests, not those of NATO or Greece. And in the DECA, at Papandreou's

FIGURE 6.2. Major U.S. Military Installations in Greece

Source: *U.S. Military Installations in NATO's Southern Region,* report prepared for the Subcommittee on Europe and the Middle East of the Committee on Foreign Affairs, U.S. House of Representatives, by the Foreign Affairs and National Defense Division of the Library of Congress, October 7, 1986, p. 41.

insistence, explicit language was incorporated calling for the termination of the United States' use of the bases in 1988.

In 1986, however, Greek foreign policy was characterized by ambivalence and ambiguity concerning the base issue, the DECA, and security issues more generally. On the one hand, Papandreou periodically criticized the operation of the U.S. bases as well as the policies of the NATO and EEC countries in regard to such issues as Cyprus, Poland, INF missile deployments, Afghanistan, and terrorism. On the other hand, though often assuming a high public profile in vociferously addressing these issues and stressing the independence of Greece, Papandreou pursued in practice a much more moderate course. In meetings with Secretary of State Shultz and other U.S. government officials in Athens in March 1986, for example, Papandreou conveyed the view that the U.S.-Greek base agreement was "state law" in Greece and that "state law" called for the closing of the bases in 1988. At the same time, he told Shultz that if the U.S. wanted negotiations on a new DECA, it had only to ask for them. Indeed, while implicitly recognizing the importance of these bases to Greece's long-term economic and security interests, Papandreou observed that the DECA might even be reviewed in 1988—if some of the bases were closed or, at a minimum, if restrictions were placed on some of the current operations at the installations. Shultz's March 1986 visit to Athens ended with a public declaration by the two nations that, regarding the bases and other outstanding problems, it was important for both sides to pursue actively a "step-by-step" approach to progress on outstanding bilateral problems.[7]

In 1986, uncertainty over the future of the U.S. military bases in Greece took on such importance that it clouded other aspects of the U.S.-Greek bilateral relationship. For example, in early May, U.S. Assistant Secretary of Commerce Harold Goldfield went to Athens for talks about future U.S. investment in Greece. Largely because of the base issue and associated uncertainties, the two sides, despite encouraging statements, failed to agree on a concrete plan for future U.S. investment in Greece. As U.S. investment in Greece is likely to be critical to Greece's economic future, and as large private-sector investment in Greece by American and European business people is likely to remain uncertain as long as the Athens government is ambivalent about the future of the bases, no major economic agreements between the United States and Greece were concluded in 1986; moreover, none are realistically in the offing in the period up to the termination, renewal, or modification of the DECA in 1988.

The October 1986 municipal elections in Greece seemingly did little to clarify the ambivalence of Greek foreign policy on the base issue or, more generally, toward the United States and NATO. Papandreou and his ruling PASOK party chose to downplay the national importance of these municipal elections, arguing that they were referenda on local issues, whereas the conservative opposition New Democracy party argued that the elections constituted a referendum on Papandreou's failed foreign and domestic economic policies. The other major party, that of the Communists, outraged at Papandreou's economic austerity program and foot-dragging on the base issue, campaigned against PASOK and seemingly voted in large numbers for New Democracy. Although PASOK retained control of virtually half the country's municipal governments in the elections, it lost the three most important cities—Athens, Piraeus, and Salonika. Overall, there was little doubt among political observers inside and outside Greece that PASOK and Papandreou lost the elections.

It is not clear as to what changes, if any, these local election results will bring about in 1987–1988 in the foreign and domestic policies pursued by the ruling Socialist government. As a result of developments in 1986, Papandreou would seem to be in the position of having to make certain tough policy choices. On the one hand, he could opt to make a major effort to win back the strong support that he enjoyed from the Communists in the 1981 and 1985 national elections. If Papandreou went in this direction, he would likely turn directly to the Communists for help in forming future cabinets. He might also make a highly visible, purposeful effort to further expand relations with the countries of the Warsaw Pact, especially the Soviet Union; and if he adopted this tack, he would undoubtedly adopt an unambiguous stance on closing the U.S. bases completely in 1988 and on ending Greek membership in NATO and the EEC. Although such a stance would serve to shore up PASOK's backing on the Left, it would likely be very costly to Greece in economic and defense terms, for the United States continues to be the major supplier of aid and weapons to Greece, despite the Papandreou government's tendency to support Soviet positions on disarmament issues and its disinclination to support the West's antiterrorist policies toward Libya and Syria.

Alternatively, Papandreou could make an effort to move toward the center of the political spectrum and to win back many of the voters who defected to the New Democracy party in the 1986 local elections, on the assumption that Leftist voters in the next national election would have little choice ultimately but to vote for PASOK. Such a policy posture might lead, among other things, to the renegotiation of the base agreement largely as is and to closer defense and economic ties with the United States and other countries of the Atlantic alliance.

There seemed to be some evidence of movement in this second, more pro-Western policy direction late in 1986. In November, Foreign Minister Karalos Papoulias visited Washington. His talks were described in the

Greek press as a "milestone," as the successful culmination of a series of contacts by Athens to reestablish U.S.-Greek relations of "normality, friendship, equality and mutual benefit."[8] It was also in November that U.S. Deputy Secretary of Defense William Taft visited Athens and, to the surprise of many, signed a defense and industrial cooperation agreement (DICA) that will give Greece's arms manufacturing industry unprecedented access to U.S. military technology. This DICA, the first separate defense-industry pact signed by the United States with a NATO ally, contains a specific provision for its premature termination if the U.S. bases are closed. The agreement itself is designed to encourage joint defense projects, transfer more advanced technology between the two countries, and permit industrial suppliers in the two countries to compete more actively for contracts. Specifically, it is aimed at helping to bring about a genuine two-way street between Greece and the United States. Under this new agreement, in 1987, Greece's M-48 tanks will be modernized, its A-7 attack aircraft will be upgraded, and U.S.-Greek cooperation in the electronics field will be significantly increased *inter alia*.

In addition, in early January 1987, the Greek government signed a final agreement to buy 40 U.S. F-16 aircraft in a deal worth roughly $1 billion. This deal, which had been delayed until Greece signed an agreement in late 1986 ensuring that there would be no leaks of F-16 technology to the Warsaw Pact, was hailed in Athens as presaging improved U.S.-Greek relations. At the same time, Prime Minister Papandreou cryptically informed the members of the Greek Parliament that he planned to keep Greece in NATO. However, he foresaw a "zero base" dialogue with the United States in 1987 that would start from the assumption that no military bases existed in Greece and hinted that a national referendum might be necessary. Finally, during a crisis with Turkey during the spring of 1987, the Greek government briefly ordered the closing of a U.S. naval communications facility and threatened the closing of the other U.S. facilities in Greece.

In light of these developments, the overall direction of prospective Greek foreign policy toward the United States remains unclear. On many East-West issues Papandreou continues to take a neutralist stance, and he is often highly critical of Washington. Among other things, he is a leading spokesman for the Third World in criticizing the United States's Strategic Defense Initiative and pushing such new disarmament plans as creating a nuclear-free zone in the Balkans. He also has refused to ally Greece with the West in its antiterrorist efforts, opting instead to emphasize the Turkish threat and to express solidarity with such countries as Libya and Syria. If, as expected, Papandreou receives and accepts an official invitation to visit Washington in 1987 and bilateral base negotiations with the United States are subsequently begun, then at least the thrust of Greece's near-term security policy should become clearer.

Turkey

Close U.S.-Turkish security relations date back to the late 1940s, but these relations have been intermittently strained in recent years. Recent strains have resulted from differences over Cyprus, which in turn have stemmed from the 1974 Turkish invasion of the island and the subsequent U.S. arms embargo. Moreover, since the arms embargo was lifted in 1978, there have been lingering hard feelings, and these feelings have been reinforced by what are judged in Ankara to be badly misguided U.S. policies toward Cyprus, Greece, the Middle East, and human rights in Turkey.

Reflecting differences over these issues, bilateral U.S.-Turkish security relations in 1986 were decidedly mixed. On the one hand, Turkey continued to make available to the United States and NATO a number of highly valuable military installations on the NATO front lines, thus permitting the forward deployment of U.S. forces. These bases, as well as associated early-warning and intelligence-gathering facilities, help Turkey to oversee the most direct air and overland routes among the Soviet Union and the Middle East and North Africa. They also help ensure the defense of the Bosporus and Dardanelles Straits, which are choke points critical to the Soviet Union's access to the Mediterranean Sea from the Black Sea. In 1986, these bases and their associated strategic value took on added importance to the West as the Soviet Union built up the Fifth Escadra and Black Sea Fleet and significantly expanded its strike aircraft based in the Crimea. These aircraft, which at the end of 1986 numbered more than 100 and included supersonic long-range Backfire bombers, potentially threaten NATO combatants in the eastern Mediterranean as well as airfields, shipyards, and resupply facilities.[9]

In exchange for the use of the vitally important military installations in Turkey, the U.S. government in recent years has agreed to pursue its "best efforts" to provide high levels of aid and arms to the Ankara government. Following extensive congressional hearings, these efforts led to $714 million in aid for Turkey in fiscal year 1986, $215 million in outright grants, and the rest in guaranteed loans. For fiscal year 1987, however, reflecting increasing general congressional skepticism toward foreign aid as well as the congressional tradition of giving Greece 70 cents in military aid for each dollar to Turkey, U.S. aid to Turkey was reduced dramatically by Congress from the requested $974-million level to $490 million.

Owing to serious dissatisfaction with this steep drop in U.S. aid—in combination with continuing, serious domestic economic problems—the Turkish government in 1986 visibly sought to draw some distance from the United States. It developed a range of new political and economic ties with the Soviet Union, culminating in July 1986 in the signing by the two countries' prime ministers of a long-term program of commercial, scientific, and technological cooperation. It reinforced links with a number of Arab countries in the Middle East, underscoring its long-standing independent posture on the Arab-Israeli conflict and its perceived identity as both a European and Middle Eastern state. It made carefully hedged remarks at the time of the U.S. bombing raid on Libya. It periodically emphasized, with an eye on Washington, that its military installations were to be used for NATO-area missions only. And it chose not to sign a new defense and economic cooperation agreement with the United States when the five-year-old 1980 agreement formally came up for renewal. Rather than canceling the automatically extended agreement, the Turkish government agreed to let the DECA continue; but it repeatedly made its unhappiness about current U.S. economic policies known to the highest levels of the U.S. government.

At the time of Secretary of State Shultz's trip to Turkey in March 1986, for example, the Turks expressed in the strongest terms their dissatisfaction with both U.S. aid levels in 1987 and the far greater access to the U.S. textile market. In response, Shultz publicly rebuffed these Turkish economic requests, leading the press to suggest that his visit to Turkey was "unsuccessful." On the textile issue, however, negotiators from both sides met behind closed doors over the next three months. In July, they reached agreement on a new bilateral textile accord. The new two-year agreement, though not satisfying all of Ankara's demands, does provide for the substantial growth of Turkish textile imports into the United States; even then, some quotas on a number of Turkish textile exports to the United States were retained.

This agreement, moreover, only partly satisfied the government's economic demands on the United States. And in early October, in a much-publicized interview in the *Washington Post,* Prime Minister Turgut Ozal again expressed his strong unhappiness over what he termed a lack of serious U.S. aid offers in exchange for the renewal of the expired 1980 DECA. He made clear his feeling that Turkey was providing the United States with much more than Washington was paying for and accepting a large number of risks to his country in the bargain. In particular, Ozal stressed the need for a major increase in U.S. aid to modernize the Turkish armed forces, the second largest standing army in NATO.[10]

Although the U.S. government clearly took Ozal's aid requests seriously, it was unable to satisfy fully his demands. For as in the case of Spain, Portugal, and Greece, the Executive is not able to set the appropriated aid level; this is done by Congress. However, in the case of Turkey, in addition to asking for more money for the Ozal government in a fiscal year 1987 supplemental aid request, the U.S. Executive in late 1986 found some ways around the problem: It came up with a variety of initiatives to help the Turkish armed forces, which are not subject to the congressional appropriations process. For example, in late 1986 the administration sought and received congressional approval to transfer excess equipment from Defense Department stocks to Turkey. Transfer candidates include F-4 fighter jets, A-7 attack aircraft, and T-33 trainer aircraft. In addition, the administration decided that up to ten U.S. ships may be transferred to Turkey on a no-cost lease basis and that the United States may help defray some of the cost of Turkey's purchase of Rapier missiles from the United Kingdom.

At year's end, these innovative measures had had a limited impact on U.S.-Turkish security relations. In late fall, the World War II, newly-refurbished *U.S.S. Missouri* paid highly publicized port calls in Turkey to commemorate its visit in 1946 and to underscore forty years of U.S.-Turkish friendship. And in December 1986, Assistant Secretary of Defense Richard Perle, after a year of tough negotiations, visited Ankara and reached tentative agreement with Turkey on extending the DECA. Though not totally happy with the projected level of future U.S. military aid, the Turkish government tentatively agreed to go forward with a new DECA in exchange for renewed promises of heightened U.S. aid levels and a number of other Executive initiatives to help with the modernization of the Turkish armed forces. However, in the spring of 1987, Prime Minister Ozal made it clear that the Turkish government would not adhere to a new DECA unless the U.S. fulfilled its promises on aid levels.

Conclusions

Since the formation of NATO in 1949, the major thrust of U.S. and Atlantic alliance defense efforts in Europe has been on the Central Front. Given the nature and character of the Soviet threat, this posture was understandable. In the immediate postwar years, the United States concluded bilateral agreements with the countries on NATO's Southern Flank, thereby providing for the construction and use of bases on their soil by the United States and NATO. In exchange for the use of these bases, U.S. policymakers, who only sporadically focused on this region, promised and consistently delivered relatively high levels of U.S. security assistance. And for most of the last thirty-five years, this aid-for-bases arrangement has gone forward without much fanfare.

As events in 1986 unfolded, these aid-for-bases arrangements, which have long been at the core of U.S. security relations in the region, were subjected to varying degrees of criticism and stress. In all five of the countries of the region, there were growing domestic and economic forces that increased pressures on the respective governments to be more independent of Washington on security issues. Where these pressures will lead in terms of security matters and, more specifically, in terms of the different ongoing base negotiations is unclear—especially where Spain and Greece are concerned. This is particularly so in the near term in light of current budget pressures in the United States and the seeming disinclination of the U.S. Congress to appropriate increasingly high levels of aid for either the same use or the reduced use of U.S. bases on the Southern Flank.

Overall, whether in regard to bilateral base negotiations or to such broader issues as international trade, relations with Third World countries, or terrorism, each of the countries of the Southern Flank seems poised to pursue a foreign-policy course in the near term that is likely to increase frictions with the United States. The pursuit of such policies does not necessarily signal closer relations with Moscow, although in the case of Greece, for example, it might. Such pursuit does, however, point toward relatively less congruent and less automatically pro-American security policies on the part of the countries of the Southern Flank. The lack of support from these countries for the U.S. raid on Libya graphically underscored this point to even the most ostrich-like observers of U.S.-European security relations on both sides of the Atlantic.

Given the wide-sweeping events and developments of 1986, at least one thing is certain: The United States's security relations with the countries of the Southern Flank are changing, and the region will likely be harder to take for granted and significantly more troublesome from the United States's perspective than it has been for most of the postwar period.

Notes

1. In October 1986, a "secret memorandum" on this condition was published in the Spanish press. The memorandum, whose validity has been unofficially acknowledged by the foreign minister, cited the government's readiness to find a way around the wording of the referendum so that Spain could cooperate with NATO's military forces. Initially considered too sensitive to be revealed to Parliament, the memorandum also indicated that the government was ready to make a significant military contribution to the alliance and to coordinate

Spanish military tasks with those of allied forces, especially in the large area between the Canary Islands and the Balearies. At the same time, according to the memorandum, Spain would formally remain "outside the integrated military structure," and, *inter alia*, Spanish forces would be commanded only by Spanish officers. For a detailed discussion of the conditions affecting Spanish membership in NATO, see *The Economist*, October 25, 1986, p. 49. See also *U.S. Military Installations in NATO's Southern Region*, a report prepared for the Subcommittee on Europe and the Middle East of the Committee on Foreign Affairs, U.S. House of Representatives, by the Foreign Affairs and National Defense Division of the Library of Congress, October 7, 1986, pp. 13–19.

2. Quoted in Jose Luis Gutierez, "The U.S. Can Trust Gonzalez," *New York Times*, June 25, 1986, p. 22.

3. See "Portugal and NATO," in *NATO Review*, (April 1986), p. 9. For further discussion of this point, see Thomas Bruneau, "Portugal After the Revolution: Decolonization and Democracy," in Howard Wiarda (ed.), *Southern Europe and the Mediterranean* (Washington: American Enterprise Institute, 1986), pp. 21–28.

4. *Baltimore Sun*, January 25, 1987, p. 1.

5. Quoted in Douglas Wertman, "Italian Foreign Policy in the 1980s: What Kind of Role?" *SAIS Review* (Summer 1982), p. 115.

6. *Foreign Broadcast Information Service, Western Europe*, April 16, 1986, p. 27; Douglas Wertman, "Italy's Durable Coalition Government," *Current History* (November 1986), pp. 383–385.

7. See *U.S. Military Installations in NATO's Southern Region*, pp. 38–39. See also *Foreign Broadcast Information Service*, March 31, 1986, p. S2.

8. *New York Times*, November 16, 1986, p. 9.

9. See Tom Lister and Bruce George, "Trouble on NATO's Southern Flank," *Jane's Defence Weekly*, April 26, 1986. And for a discussion of growing Soviet military capabilities in the Mediterranean region in the mid-1980s, see Arthur Moreau, Jr., "The Defense of NATO's Southern Region," *NATO Review*, (August 1986), pp. 13–20.

10. *Washington Post*, October 5, 1986, p. A-25.

7
Latin America: Political Progress, Economic Stagnation

Sally Shelton-Colby

Latin America in 1986 was marked by an expansion and consolidation of democratic trends in South America, though with some notable exceptions; by continued economic stagnation or deterioration in most countries, with modest but tenuous improvement in others; by new political and economic stresses in Mexico; by a deepening of U.S. military involvement in Central America; and by a strengthening of democratic processes in some countries of Central America.

The appearance of new, popular demands throughout Latin America for the resumption of economic growth and for relief from external debt also characterized 1986. These demands no longer emanated only from the extreme Left but also began to emerge from the political center and even the Right. Three countries unilaterally limited debt service, and others threatened to do so, as growing numbers of Latin Americans and even U.S. government officials began to question how the debt might affect democracy and political stability in the region. Indeed, Washington's interest in avoiding the formation of a debtors' cartel at the 1985 World Bank-IMF meeting in Seoul, Korea produced the Reagan administration's first effort to address the problem—the "Baker Plan." Premised on an assumption that increased commercial and development bank lending would lead to a resumption of growth in debtor nations, no steps were taken to implement the plan until the conclusion of a new emergency financing package for Mexico in November 1986. In the meantime, the serious toll taken on U.S. exports to the debtor nations resulted in growing calls in the Congress, echoed by some commercial banks, for selective debt relief. Although even some officials in the U.S. government began to consider the need for reducing the size of the debt, little consensus has yet developed as to whether and how that should be done.

The year closed with U.S. government policymakers focused overwhelmingly on the domestic- and foreign-policy repercussions of the controversy over providing Iran arms sales profits to the "Contras" fighting the Sandinista government in Nicaragua. One of the first effects appeared to be a strengthening of Honduran fears that the already weak U.S. domestic support for the Honduras-based Contras would erode further. Honduras's concern that Congress would once again cut off funds, thereby leaving the problem to the Hondurans to deal with alone, led Tegucigalpa to inform the U.S. government that the Contras had to be out of Honduran territory by April 1987.

Elsewhere, new regional efforts at political and economic cooperation outside the framework of existing institutions raised hopes for further progress in 1987. The newly formed "Group of Rio de Janeiro," composed of the Contadora nations (Mexico, Panama, Venezuela, and Colombia) as well as other democracies (Brazil, Argentina, Uruguay, and Peru) began a new campaign, supported by the heads of the United Nations and the Organization of American States (OAS), to defuse the Central America crisis. In December, moreover, two of the region's largest economic powers, Brazil and Argentina, signed more than twenty agreements on a series of political and economic issues; these agreements were meant to be the first steps toward a Latin American common market, which possibly would be joined by Uruguay as well. Over the long term, these measures toward closer cooperation among Latin America's leading democratic nations may be the most favorable sign of the region's emerging stability, development, and cooperation—factors critical to the solution of the mutual problems facing the region.

Following is a review of key developments in Latin America during 1986. They will be discussed on a country-by-country basis, with an emphasis on the political and economic context within which they occur and on the means by which trends are altered or strengthened by these developments.

South America

Argentina

President Raúl Alfonsín, Argentina's first civilian president in a decade, strengthened and broadened his popularity through an adroit series of bold political and economic initiatives. He resolved Argentina's long-simmering dispute with Chile over the Beagle Islands and continued to negotiate with the United Kingdom over the Falkland Islands conflict. During 1985–1986, he took advantage of the broad national revulsion against the military's involvement in the "dirty war" of the 1970s by strengthening civilian control over the military. He retired more than half the country's generals and admirals and vigorously prosecuted those accused of human rights violations. When the Supreme Military Council cleared several military officers of the charges in spite of evidence against them, Alfonsín boldly moved the prosecutions to the civil courts, which subsequently handed down judgments in a number of cases. Alfonsín also rescinded Argentina's doctrine of national security, one of the bases of the military's involvement in the internal counterinsurgency of the 1970s, and cut the military budget to almost one-half its previous size. Although the new high command has sworn its loyalty to Alfonsín, continuing unrest within the military was manifested dramatically in the May 1986 bombing at a military camp just prior to a presidential visit. A renewal of right-wing violence linked to a surge in kidnappings, robberies, and some disappearances of leftist activists raised concerns in the administration over military unhappiness. Legislation terminating prosecution of the military was enacted in December 1986 and the nation breathed a sigh of relief that the issue had finally been put behind it, though relatives of those who had disappeared were bitterly opposed to the move.

The split in Alfonsín's main opposition, the Justicialist (Perónist) party and the General Confederation of Labor (CGT), deepened during 1986 as reformers stepped up their battle against traditionalists for control of these groups. Some Perónists and the CGT were behind the almost daily strike activity and work slowdowns that plagued Argentina during the year, but efforts to bring down the government through national work stoppages, as in the previous years, failed. Contributing to Alfonsín's ability to resist such pressures was his bold promulgation in June 1986 of a new economic package, the "Austral Plan." Dealing with price and wage controls, deindexation, and the creation of a new currency, the program was aimed at reining in inflation, which had been headed toward an annual rate of 1,500 percent. By the end of 1986, however, the initial enthusiasm generated by the Austral Plan had waned as inflationary pressures reappeared, investment failed to pick up, the external debt continued to be a serious drain on Argentina's export earnings, and per capita income failed to recover. Moreover, the Argentines were embittered by Washington's decision in July 1986 to sell subsidized wheat to the Soviet Union, thereby depressing already-low grain prices and undercutting Argentina's own substantial wheat-based export earnings.

In spite of the economic malaise, neither the Perónists nor the military have thus far been able to provide a credible alternative program of government. However, the important gubernatorial elections due to take place in late 1987 will provide a key indicator of whether the traditionalists or the reformers are winning the internal battle for control of the Perónists. If the latter do well, especially if they recoup their now-eroded support in the industrial belt around Buenos Aires, they could pose a serious problem for the Radicals in the 1989 presidential election.

Economically, Argentina's prospects are mixed. The Austral Plan has cut inflation, although it still hovers around 6 percent per month. Annual real growth in 1986 was a healthy 5.6 percent, though investment was still stagnant, export earnings were down almost 20 percent, and Argentina's rigid industrial structure had not yet learned to compete internationally. The budget deficit has been reduced, although more through higher taxes than by cuts in government spending. The country's $49 billion external debt, the third largest in Latin America, takes up 68 percent of export earnings. The external debt issue has become highly politicized as Alfonsín continues to come under intense pressure from all major elements of the body politic, including his own party, to achieve economic recovery. The Argentines are using Mexico as a stalking horse for obtaining new concessions from the international banking community. Just as the Mexicans have attempted to link debt service to the price of oil, so are the Argentines trying to link debt service to the price of grain—probably a futile effort, but a necessary bow to domestic political exigencies.

The structural adjustment process has barely begun in Argentina. Yet the fact that it has begun at all is remarkable, given Argentina's history; and Alfonsín's success in avoiding systemic challenges to his administration may mark a turning point in Argentine political history. Still, both Argentina's future politics and its economic health must be considered highly uncertain, dependent both on the global economy and the evolution of the internal trends discussed.

Brazil

During 1986, Brazil plunged into its new democratic system with characteristic vigor as political parties and factions within parties formed and re-formed with dizzying speed. The press and Congress grew increasingly vocal; student and labor groups, traditionally weak, organized on a scale heretofore unknown in Brazil; and the Catholic Church, with a grass-roots organization unequalled in Brazilian society, intensified its activism on social issues, especially land reform. The military, closely and quietly consulted by President José Sarney on key decisions, remained seemingly relaxed over this political free-for-all.

The November 1985 mayoral elections and the November 1986 gubernatorial and congressional elections (the new Congress is intended to also act as a constituent assembly for the writing of a new Constitution) produced mixed political signals. Small left-of-center parties did better than expected in the mayoralty races, and the governing Brazilian Democratic Movement party (PMDB) did less well than expected. Subsequently, however, the gubernatorial and congressional races in 1986 produced an overwhelming victory for the PMDB, which won 22 of 23 governorships and a clear majority in the Chamber of Deputies. Especially significant were the PMDB victories that captured both the São Paulo and Rio de Janeiro governorships, the two most important states in the country in which the opposition had mounted challenges. The PMDB victory in Rio de Janeiro state also dealt a serious blow to the presidential ambitions of the charismatic populist, former Governor Leonel Brizola, bête noire of the Brazilian military.

The Achilles' heel of Brazil's political system, however, remains the economy. Facing 500 percent inflation and taking a cue from Argentina's Austral Plan, the Brazilian government announced the Cruzado Plan in February 1986: wage and price controls, deindexation of the economy, and creation of a new fixed-rate currency. Wildly popular, in part because wage controls had been sweetened by an 8 percent pay raise (thus injecting considerable new liquidity into the system), the Cruzado Plan generally succeeded in bringing down inflation to a degree. Nevertheless, Brazil was unable to control fiscal and monetary policy, reduce the large, often inefficient state sector, control new inflationary impulses, or revive business confidence in the economy.

In spite of these economic stresses, Brazil achieved 9 percent growth in 1986 and unemployment appeared close to only 3 percent, a sharp decline from the previous year. The International Monetary Fund (IMF) gave Brazilian economic policy its seal of approval so that Brazil was able to negotiate an unprecedented debt rescheduling with the Paris Club (a group of government, as opposed to private, creditors), without having to put into place an austerity program. By late 1986, however, underlying economic stresses could no longer be hidden. Faced with a serious plunge in October export earnings to one-fifth the usual level, inflation of about 5 percent a month (up to 8 percent by December), and no significant new investment, the government announced steep tax increases and a gradual phasing out of the price freeze as soon as the November 15 elections were over. Public reaction was unexpectedly hostile, cutting deeply into President Sarney's new-found popularity, and violence erupted in Brasilia as hundreds of demonstrators battled police for the first time ever in the Brazilian capital. PMDB leaders began to put as much distance as possible between themselves and the unpopular new policies, thus reinforcing the government's reluctance to implement more orthodox economic measures. If Brazil is unable to maintain its normally large export surpluses, it will no longer be able to service its external debt and grow. That situation in turn would create a profound dilemma for Brazil's new democratic government: Will it remain within the good graces of the international creditor community and be the first debtor to return to creditworthiness? Or will it put a priority on domestic growth, even if that has to occur at the expense of the foreign banks?

Pressures on Brazil to pursue the growth option are intensifying. President Sarney has underlined his commitment to economic growth under any circumstances, and his minister of finance has signaled that Brazil might have to reduce service on the external debt to 2.5 percent of GDP, almost half the existing level, in order to continue to achieve 5 to 7 percent growth. The policy of giving a higher priority to growth as compared to debt service is of course supported by the majority of Brazil's political parties. Underpinning the need for growth is a recognition that Brazil's newly democratic government will have to face that country's enormous social problems, the solutions to which will require the expenditure of substantial public funds. A report prepared for the government in the spring concluded that, although Brazil's economic progress has been dramatic, its social indicators put it among the hemisphere's least-developed countries. Brazil has long suffered staggering social underdevelopment; however, under a democratic administration, pressures to improve the plight of the poor will be more difficult to resist.

The extreme socioeconomic inequities in Brazil were manifested most clearly in the land reform issue, which turned violent in the spring of 1986. The government's consideration of land reform legislation (ownership of productive farmland is highly concentrated in the hands of a few) was triggered by broad unrest in the countryside. Clashes between armed peasants and landowners caused about 300 deaths in 1986. The influential Catholic Church attacked the Sarney Plan to redistribute untilled holdings as too timid; the landowners, by contrast, said it went too far. The issue, which has still not been fully resolved, holds the threat of additional violence in 1987.

In summary, the outlook for Brazil is mixed. Economic growth was buoyant and unemployment came down. However, the political exigencies of Brazil's new democracy and the need to provide jobs and social services resulted in only limited adjustment during 1986. In fact, fiscal policy was so loose that the public-sector deficit roughly doubled. Privatization of state-owned enterprises ran smack into the need to provide jobs to the regime's backers. Reserves dwindled as a result of a plunge in export earnings, soaring imports, and the financing of the current-account deficit out of reserves. Brazil's continued rejection of an IMF-monitored austerity program resulted in a situation whereby the country's commercial bank creditors were willing to agree only to a short-term roll-over rather than to a multiyear rescheduling. Inflation, though below 1985 levels, reached 65 percent (even with wage and price controls) by the end of the year. No significant new investment occurred. Hence Brazil, for the first time in some years, may face such a serious current-account deficit in 1987 that it will require "forced new money" from the commercial banks. If the banks insist, as they generally do, on an IMF program and austerity as the price of that new money, Brazil will have to make a tough choice between domestic growth and the foreign banks. In 1987 President Sarney will face a major political challenge in structuring an economic adjustment program acceptable to the fragile political coalition on which his administration is based. A needed maxi-devaluation of the cruzado as well is long overdue, major budget cuts may provoke additional popular turmoil and undermine the already shaky PMDB coalition.

Chile

Chile's political instability intensified during 1986. The September assassination attempt of President Augusto Pinochet by the extreme Left, the reimposition of the state of siege (although it was lifted in January 1987), Pinochet's publicly expressed interest in a new presidential term beginning in 1989, and the serious escalation of human rights abuses highlighted the fragility of Chile's political situation. The consequences of the assassination attempt and the discovery of huge arms caches (believed to have been brought into the country from Cuban and Soviet sources) were favorable for the regime in the short term but may turn negative over a longer period.

In the short term, General Pinochet's position was strengthened as the increasingly divided armed forces were obliged to rally behind him and, after some reluctance, to endorse the reimposition of the state of siege. His civilian support, which according to public opinion polls had averaged 15 percent or less in preceding months, rebounded. Pinochet clamped down hard and jailed many critics of his regime, especially labor union, student, church, and non-Communist political party leaders. Santiago's slums, the strongholds of anti-Pinochet sentiment, were swept regularly by security forces in an effort to crack the extreme Left's extensive organizational network.

Another short-term consequence, with important longer-term policy implications, was the democratic opposition's decision to distance itself from the Left by rejecting electoral alliances with the Communists. The specter of such cooperation, reminiscent of the major role played by the Communists in the pre-1973 political system, had long weakened the democratic center's standing, not only with the Chilean populace but also with the military. An end to this tactical cooperation, if the agreement holds, should remove a major obstacle in the path toward an orderly transition.

Opposition to Pinochet included a broad array of political parties ranging from center-Left to center-Right (including elements of Pinochet's old support base). Grouped under the National Accord (an umbrella organization formed at the urging of the Catholic Church to prepare for the 1989 transition), the democratic parties tried to carry their effort at cooperation one step forward by agreeing on a common candidate for the presidency and on the development of a national political campaign for free elections. Such efforts were unsuccessful, however, as philosophical and tactical differences continued to divide the parties. At times, their factiousness seemed to outweigh their cooperation, denting the effectiveness of their efforts to push for a transition.

Further reflecting support for a transition were the various social, trade union, labor, and professional organizations that joined together in a loose grouping called the "Civic Assembly" in the spring of 1986. Its purpose was to demonstrate that not only the old-line political parties but also the Chilean citizenry more generally wanted a transition. Its creation reflects the broadening disenchantment with the Pinochet regime.

One of the most striking developments of 1986 was the bold assassination attempt on President Pinochet. The strength of the Moscow-leaning Communist party of Chile, the Revolutionary Left Movement, and the Manuel Rodriguez Patriotic Front (FPMR), the guerrilla arm of the Communist party, had been underestimated by many prior to the assassination attempt and subsequent discovery of large weapons caches in remote rural areas. These groups appeared to have substantially greater Cuban (and possibly Soviet) technical and financial support than had been thought, although their strategy probably is a long-term one, focused on the post-Pinochet era under a possibly weak democratic government. The strongest Latin American Communist party outside of Cuba, the Chilean Communist party is believed to control about 20 percent of Chile's voting-age population and to be especially strong in urban slums and universities, though increasingly in rural areas as well. The extreme Left was unable to mount a serious military challenge to the Chilean security forces during 1986, but the organization and financing of the FPMR and its ability to sustain a sharply increased number of terrorist incidents caused some military analysts to conclude that it was beginning to pose a more serious threat to the government than in the past.

Restiveness and concern over Pinochet's political management were particularly evident in the military during 1986. The commanders of the Navy, Air Force, and the Constabulary, all of whom are in the governing junta (in addition to the Army), publicly articulated their concerns about Pinochet's possible presidential candidacy in 1989. Hence, a modicum of dialogue between the military and the democratic opposition began. Even in the Army, normally considered the most pro-Pinochet of all the services, there were signs at the senior-command level of uneasiness over the lack of movement toward a transition. Nevertheless, the military remained disturbed by the lack of unity in the democratic opposition, which it believed could lead to a repeat of the instability of the Allende years, as well as to the possibility that a vengeful civilian successor to Pinochet would follow Argentina's example of prosecuting the military for its involvement in Chile's own "dirty war." They also feared that a democratic government would be less than serious about dealing with the extreme Left. Pinochet manipulated these concerns and continued his successful strategy of removing those commanders suspected of disloyalty. In October he retired nine commanders, replaced one junta member, and promoted twelve senior military officers believed to be strongly loyal.

U.S. pressures on Pinochet also escalated during 1986. The U.S. government publicly criticized the heightened political repression in Chile, supported a UN resolution critical of Chilean human rights performance, and strengthened its ties with the democratic opposition. It abstained on critical World Bank and other loans for Chile, however, in recognition of Chile's successful, orthodox economic management.

Chilean economic performance during 1986 was robust. Downward trends in oil prices and interest rates, plus successful government efforts to diversify the economy beyond copper, helped produce a 5 percent growth rate (almost double that of 1985). Inflation fell from 26 percent to 17 percent, and the public-sector deficit fell from 3.5 percent to 2.5 percent. A highly attractive debt-to-equity conversion model resulted in the conversion of approximately $1.3 billion of Chile's debt into equity in local industry. Per capita consumption, however, has yet to recover significantly from the disastrous economic performance in previous years.

The year 1987 will be an important test of the opposition's ability to demonstrate more effective unity and its credibility as an alternative to Pinochet. Promulgation of electoral laws, following the January 1987 legalization of political parties, were widely criticized by the opposition as inadequate. Pinochet began to appear more and more like a candidate himself.

Peru

In Peru, President Alan García, enormously popular for his efforts to attack Peru's years-long economic and social crisis, faced mounting challenges from the Maoist guerrilla group Sendero Luminoso. For the first time, the growing Sendero-instigated violence was targeted during 1986 not at the countryside but at urban areas, including Lima, as García's initial efforts to deal with the problem through increased economic aid to the Andean sierras, the creation of a commission to negotiate peace with the rebels, and the punishment of officers involved in massacres of guerrilla sympathizers proved unsuccessful. In the face of public and armed forces discontent over spiraling criminal violence and a wave of bombings, assassinations, kidnappings, and sabotage attributed to the Left, García imposed a state of emergency in some areas in the spring.

García's government was further shaken in June by a coordinated uprising by Shining Path prisoners in three Lima jails. Bloodily repressed by the military, about 100 of the almost 300 rebel dead were found to have been shot, and he ordered the detention of those military personnel alleged to have been involved. The García government also purged more than 1,000 police officers suspected of corruption and drug trafficking, rejected certain naval modernization programs, and cut an Air Force purchase of Mirage jet fighters from 26 to 12, thereby exacerbating his shaky relationship with the security forces. In spite of the government's belief that the Sendero was decimated by the prison massacre, the level of violence almost doubled in the following three months. By late 1986 García appeared to have recognized the need for more military action against the guerrillas and stepped up counterinsurgency activities in the mountains. Allegations of a renewal of human rights abuses began soon thereafter in the sierras.

The November municipal elections resulted in a resounding victory for García's party, the American Popular Revolutionary Alliance (APRA), which won the race in Lima against even its popular Communist-backed United Left mayor and in other traditionally Marxist strongholds. García's popularity is due partly to his style and charisma and partly to his adoption of populist economic policies. García alienated the international creditor community shortly after his inauguration by declaring that Peru would unilaterally limit payments on its $15 billion foreign debt to 10 percent of its export earnings. Since then he has refused to negotiate with the banks, has rejected the IMF, and has called on the rest of Latin America to impose a political solution on the debt problem. Although international credit has just about dried up and even the IMF has declared Peru ineligible for further borrowing, García's go-it-alone strategy has given Peru the breathing space in which to stimulate its economy. In 1986 economic growth was 9 percent, purchasing power in the private sector was at least 7 percent higher than in 1985 (this improvement is even more dramatic if seen against the backdrop of the

40 percent contraction between 1980 and 1985), and inflation fell to 65 percent (from 140 percent) because of price controls and a decline in interest rates.

The year 1987 will pose greater difficulties for Peru. With reserves dwindling, it will probably not have sufficient foreign exchange to import the raw materials needed to grow at the same rate as in 1986. Foreign-exchange controls, including a ban on profit remittances and the price freeze, will be a deterrent to new investment (although some foreign oil companies are exploring in the Peruvian jungle). Key guideposts in 1987 will be García's ability to contain if not reduce the Sendero threat and criminal violence while maintaining control over the security forces. In addition, he will have to take steps to normalize his frosty relations with international creditors in order to resume the flow of credit necessary to sustain an adequate level of growth.

Colombia

The March 1986 congressional elections and the May 1986 presidential elections in Colombia produced a sweeping victory for the Liberal party, in spite of the break-off of a splinter group, the New Liberals. The August 1986 inauguration of Virgilio Barco as president of Colombia launched the first Colombian government in years to shun coalition rule with the opposition Conservative party. In spite of Liberal dominance of the Congress, however, Barco got off to a slow start at governance, and a sense of policy drift quickly set in. Conservative party leaders, unaccustomed to being in the opposition, were scarcely in a position to challenge the government effectively.

Although Colombia has a long tradition of violence, the first few months of the Barco administration witnessed a sharp escalation in the level of violence amidst concern over a breakdown of the fragile two-year-old truce negotiated by Barco's predecessor, Belisario Betancur, with the country's largest guerrilla group, the Revolutionary Armed Forces of Colombia (FARC). The FARC formed a political party, the Patriotic Union, and ran candidates throughout the country in the March elections (winning 14 Congressional seats). Other smaller guerrilla groups pulled out of the truce, charging the government with failure to comply with the terms of the agreement; these elements are now in almost daily battle with the Colombian armed forces. The truce, even a partial one, has been viewed as a potential model for other democratic countries with serious guerrilla problems.

The assassinations of almost three dozen members of Congress, local elected officials, and union leaders in late 1986 were generally attributed by leftist parties to right-wing paramilitary groups and/or to guerrilla organizations determined to sabotage the truce. Some of this violence was undoubtedly related as well to drug traffickers, who cooperated in some regions with guerrilla groups for the maintenance of security, seeking to undermine the Colombian government. Violence has been leveled especially at members of the Colombian judiciary in an attempt by drug traffickers to stop implementation of the U.S.-Colombia extradition treaty. Other elements of Colombian society, including the police and the press, have also been the target of the growing violence, which, however, does not appear to have deterred the Colombian government from its strong commitment to drug eradication.

Against this worrisome spiral in violence is Colombia's long history of working through its problems. The Colombian political establishment's strong commitment to the rule of law and the democratic system stands in stark contrast to the country's growing lawlessness. The future stability of the Colombian government will depend on its ability to rein in the violence and to demonstrate that the system's institutions and legal and political processes are stronger than those who would seek to destroy them.

Key signposts in 1987 will be President Barco's ability to check the spiral of violence in Colombia before it endangers not only Colombian democracy but also economic growth. This solution will require a continued commitment to drug eradication as well as an effort to deal with the sources of violence against the political system. Barco will be challenged to keep the FARC in the political system and to ensure that the $1 billion he committed (over four years) in economic assistance to depressed regions (in which the guerrillas are active) is well disbursed.

The Colombian economy grew at a healthy 3.5 percent in 1986 due to expanded oil and gas production, coffee, and manufactures. Inflation was a manageable 20.9 percent, and the fiscal deficit was a low 2.6 percent of the GDP. Some private capital was repatriated and fiscal policy was relatively tightly managed. In 1986 Colombia began production and export from its huge new coal fields, reputed to be the purest in quality and among the cheapest to develop in the world. Colombia was able to avoid many of the debt servicing problems of other Latin American countries owing to its traditionally cautious borrowing and spending policies. However, Colombia's economy is still too dependent (almost 50 percent) on coffee exports, the prices of which are subject to the vagaries of nature and international markets. Another potential economic difficulty would arise if Colombia became excessively dependent on oil exports, whose prices also depend on external factors beyond Colombia's control.

Bolivia

Bolivia, a country heading toward social and economic anarchy in preceding years, to everyone's surprise was a stunning success in 1986. Under President Victor Paz Estenssoro's audacious new economic policy, inflation—moving toward 23,000 percent (the world's highest) in 1985—fell to 66 percent by the end of 1986 (with a mere 10 percent projected for 1987). Unlike the situations in Argentina and Brazil, where prices were frozen, Paz abolished price controls and almost all trade restrictions (although he froze public-sector wages). He also eliminated the official exchange rate, overhauled the tax system, and in August began to reduce some state-owned enterprises, including the important government-owned tin corporation. He also concluded an IMF agreement and began to negotiate a normalization of Bolivia's relationship with commercial banks, ignored since 1984. The political opposition's reaction was relatively muted, although workers and miners threatened a general strike in the summer. In response, President Paz declared a state of siege and sent almost 200 labor leaders to internment camps until they agreed to end the strike.

In July 1986 U.S. troops joined with Bolivian security forces in "Operation Blast Furnace," a joint attack on Bolivian coca production that lasted for the next six months. With Americans ferrying Bolivian police and military personnel in U.S. military helicopters, a number of cocaine-processing laboratories were destroyed; the industry apparently bounced back, however, once the Americans had withdrawn. Bolivia remained the number-one supplier of cocaine to the U.S. market and itself began to develop a serious internal drug abuse problem.

Given the considerable amount of concessional aid flowing into Bolivia and the relative acquiescence of the political opposition to the government's economic adjustment effort, the short-term prospects for Bolivia, at least through 1987, seem relatively healthy. Key indicators for economic and political stability, however, will be the government's ability to obtain some level of growth in 1987 (against a 3 percent decline in 1986), to keep a lid on inflation, and to diversify away from Bolivia's excessive dependence on tin for export revenues. In addition, the government's ability to create alternative jobs for politically powerful tin workers will be a test of its ability to deal with this potentially destabilizing element.

Central America

Economic conditions in Central America continued to deteriorate in 1986 as most countries faced severe foreign exchange shortages, no new investment took place, commodity prices generally remained depressed, and pressures from international creditors to push forward with economic adjustment measures increased.

Resolution of the imbroglio in Nicaragua, by either political or military means, advanced not at all during 1986. Contadora, the regional effort to arrange a political solution, foundered as both Nicaragua and Washington threw obstacles into the path of negotiations. Furthermore, internal changes within some Contadora governments made the negotiating process more difficult. Panama threw out its elected president and Mexico was subjected to widespread charges of electoral fraud by opposition parties; the credibility of these two countries in regard to strengthening democracy in the region badly eroded. Furthermore, deteriorating economic conditions in Mexico produced a change in foreign-policy priorities as Mexico backed away from its deep involvement in Contadora in order to focus on the management of its debt and achieve greater support from Washington vis-à-vis the international creditor community. The two remaining Contadora members, Venezuela and Colombia, were preoccupied with their own internal political and debt management processes and, in any event, grew newly concerned over alleged Sandinista connections with regional guerrilla organizations.

Meanwhile, the Contadora talks went nowhere. With a new stalemate reached in December 1985 and no progress in 1986, eight Latin American governments, together with the secretaries general of the United Nations and the Organization of American States, formed a new initiative in December to revive the negotiations. Organizing themselves into a new, permanent organization, the Group of Rio de Janeiro decided as well to address regional economic issues, especially the debt, in an effort to assert Latin America's voice more effectively than either the OAS or the Cartagena Group (an informal club of Latin American debtor governments that has called for more liberal terms for servicing the external debt) had done to date. There was little hope, however, that any meaningful political settlement could be reached without dramatically changed views on the part of the key parties to the conflict—Nicaragua and the United States.

At the same time, Central American governments grew increasingly skeptical about the efficacy of the Contra program and the constancy of the U.S. government's support of it. President José Napoléon Duarte of El Salvador was embarrassed by charges that Contra resupply flights originated from Salvadoran air fields; he moved to suspend them, at least for the time being, as advisers pressured him to come to political terms with Managua. Similarly, the Hondurans asked the U.S. government to move the Contras out of Honduran territory by April 1987. Costa Rica and Guatemala reasserted their neutrality. All governments in the region grew more disillusioned with the Sandinistas as well. The crisis in Washington over Iran arms sales and alleged links to Contra aid reinforced concern in Central America over the weakness of U.S. support and the possibility that a Democrat-controlled Congress plus a weakened White House would result in a cut-off of funds, thus leaving the Contras—and the Sandinistas—for local governments to deal with.

Mexico

Mexico's economic crisis deepened and political turmoil intensified during 1986, causing many analysts to predict the beginning of a breakdown of Mexico's traditional system of political management. Although such forecasts generally ignored important signs of resilience in the system, there is little question but that Mexico in 1986 faced political and economic challenges unprecedented in recent Mexican history.

A partial catalyst of the political turmoil was the fourth straight year of economic stagnation: Mexico's GDP fell by 3 percent in 1986, inflation was 120 percent, and workers' purchasing power declined by 40 percent by year's end. The peso weakened further against the dollar and capital flight resumed during the first half of the year. The collapse of oil prices in the spring of 1986 cut Mexico's foreign-exchange earnings roughly in half, provoking an internal political crisis over economic policy in the Mexican cabinet. After intense discussions with U.S. government officials, particularly Chairman of the Federal Reserve Board Paul Volcker, the Mexican government fired its minister of finance, Jesús Silva Herzog, an advocate of greater economic austerity and structural adjustment, but also an individual who had threatened to interrupt debt service payments to the banks. Instead, the Mexican government convinced Volcker that Mexico had to resume economic growth, even if that meant slowing the process of adjustment. Such a shift in economic priorities would require the acquiescence of the IMF, which previously had suspended its agreement with Mexico over the latter's failure to meet key targets. The U.S. government leaned hard on the IMF to agree to an unprecedented, more relaxed program with Mexico. Washington also pressured commercial banks not only to pump in $6 billion in new money, but also to make additional funds available if Mexican economic growth did not resume in 1987.

In spite of its unfavorable standing with the international creditor community, the Mexican government took significant steps forward in the adjustment process. In June, Mexico entered the GATT, a move of historical importance that will open up Mexican industry to international competition. The government also began the process of reforming Mexico's cumbersome trade regime and selling off or closing a number of inefficient state-owned enterprises, including Fundidora, a steel-making plant employing 6,000 workers whose protests significantly damaged the governing Partido Revolucionario Institucional (PRI) in the July elections. The government continued its efforts to cut government spending, although the budget deficit was expected to rise to 17 percent (as opposed to the 5 percent envisioned in Mexico's earlier IMF agreement).

In the latter half of 1986, these efforts began to show some success. The maintenance of a highly competitive exchange-rate policy produced a healthy growth in nonoil exports of 33 percent. Extremely high interest rates drew some flight capital back into the country, and an unprecedented stock market boom took place.

Still, the failure of the Mexican government to pull out of the debt crisis and engineer a resumption of economic growth in 1986 contributed to a sense that Mexico was also suffering a political crisis. Following the July 1985 gubernatorial and congressional elections, the opposition—dominated by the National Action party (PAN)—led widespread demonstrations alleging that the PRI had rigged the elections. Whether such actions actually took place is not clear, but the PRI's nationwide vote declined to 65 percent of the total vote, from a high of 90 percent in the 1960s. This plunge was due partly to voter apathy and partly to the growing disillusionment among the urban middle class with the PRI's economic and political management. Although the right-of-center PAN has benefited more from this voter frustration than have left-of-center parties, it failed to develop a national party structure or to repair its own serious internal divisions. Nevertheless, it became increasingly clear during 1986 that the northern part of the country, especially, was unhappy with the Mexico City government and supportive of a more orthodox approach to economic policy.

As most of the Latin American countries (except Chile and Paraguay) have elected democratic governments, a new international focus was directed to the Mexican political system during 1986. Within the PRI, a Movement for Democratic Renewal emerged to call for a more open system of selecting PRI candidates, and President Miguel de la Madrid talked of the need for greater openness within the party. Opposition parties on both the Left and the Right made efforts (with limited success) to form an alliance for seeking a liberalization of the political process. U.S. congressional hearings during 1986 focused on allegations of Mexican electoral fraud and governmental involvement in drug trafficking (thus leading to Mexican charges of interference in that country's internal affairs). Even the Catholic Church, whose public role has traditionally been extremely limited, began pressuring the government to demonstrate greater respect for the popular will. Yet important elements within the PRI continued to resist pressures for political relaxation. The year 1986 closed with the PRI locked in an internal wrangle over how much political liberalization, if any, was desirable.

Although the PRI is facing an unprecedented period of internal turmoil during 1987, it will remain the dominant political force in Mexico. The economy, while stagnant, has not (yet) shrunk to socially unbearable levels, and Washington will continue to lean on the commercial and multilateral banks to provide enough capital for Mexico to achieve a modest level of economic growth. Moreover, no other group or party has yet been able to develop a national organization with sufficiently broad appeal to present itself as a viable alternative. In addition, the PRI has demonstrated that it will not hesitate to utilize the range of instruments available to it (including electoral manipulation) to maintain itself in power. The threat to stability comes instead from the potential for paralysis in government—from the inability to make tough decisions, regardless of the consequences—as Mexico approaches the autumn 1987 announcement of the successor to Miguel de la Madrid. A key signal of Mexico's future political and economic course will be the extent to which the government is able to sustain the economic adjustment process, specifically in the areas of privatization of state-owned enterprises, the reining in of fiscal and monetary policy, the reduction of the budget deficit, and resistance to labor demands for wage increases above the rate of inflation.

Guatemala

Guatemala was the newest democratic success story in Central America in 1986 because of the inauguration in January of Christian Democrat President Vinicio Cerezo, the country's first civilian president since 1970. Battling skepticism from all sides, Cerezo made a slow and cautious start, avoiding moves that might alienate the military and the powerful private sector. For instance, aware that the military remained a powerful force behind the scenes, Cerezo declined to investigate its role in the disappearance of thousands of Guatemalans during the 1960s and 1970s and moved gingerly as well in the area of land reform. Instead, he concentrated on consolidating democratic rule and dealing with Guatemala's severe economic crisis through modest spending cuts and tax increases. Meanwhile, problems of violence persisted; more than 700 persons were reported by the government to have been killed by the middle of the year (as compared to the approximately 300 civilian deaths in 1985, according to the Department of State).

In spite of Cerezo's generally cautious start at governing, he did move boldly to disband the controversial Department of Technical Investigations, a part of the police force widely believed to have been deeply involved in political repression and corruption. He also resisted the appointment of General Rodolfo Lobos, also believed to have been heavily involved in political killings, as minister of defense. In turn, Cerezo had to allow the army free rein in its continuing prosecution of the war against Guatemala's guerrilla forces, which had been reduced to approximately one-half their former level. In fact, he had little choice in the matter given that, prior to his assumption of office, the military enacted legislation that extended its control over almost all rural reconstruction and development programs as well as, of course, over the massive program of civil patrols and protected villages. It also established a State Security Council to manage national security policy; although this body is composed of both civilians and military, the head must be the Army's secretary of intelligence, thereby ensuring for the military an on-going, up-front role in the decisionmaking process on security issues.

Key indicators for 1987 will be the Cerezo government's ability to enact socioeconomic reform (especially land reform), achieve a renewal of economic growth after several years of decline, and manage an end to the still-high level of disappearances and killings. He will also have to prove that successful prosecution of the war against the guerrilla Left is not inconsistent with a strengthening of democratic processes and the rule of law.

Honduras

Honduras, in 1986, took a step closer to democracy when Jose Azcona was inaugurated as president in January. Even then, however, he faced an uphill battle to exercise power effectively vis-à-vis the Honduran military. Having failed to achieve even a plurality of the votes in the November 1985 elections, he won the presidency essentially because of a quirk in the election laws. In addition, the Honduran Armed Forces remain the dominant political element in the country, along with the continuing heavy influence of the U.S. government. Moreover, since Azcona's faction of the Liberal party controls only about one-third of the seats in Congress, he was forced to negotiate a coalition with the Nationalist party, thereby giving this coalition the presidency of the Congress and the Nationalists the presidency of the Supreme Court.

Reflecting growing Honduran military as well as civilian ambivalence over the presence of anti-Sandinista Contras on Honduran soil, candidate Azcona campaigned against their presence in Honduras but once in office seemed to acquiesce to their continued operation out of Honduran bases. In December, however, under heightened domestic political pressure from coffee growers who were protesting that they could not work their land and from peasants turned into refugees by the war, Azcona informed the U.S. government that the Contras would have to be out of Honduras by April 1987. Many in official Washington believe that timetable to be flexible; in the meantime, Azcona has allowed the U.S. supply effort of the Contras, blocked by his predecessor, to resume.

Armed clashes inside Honduras between Popular Sandinista Army forces and Contra units escalated significantly during 1986 as Nicaraguan efforts to prevent infiltration grew bolder. Since spring 1986, Sandinista units have maintained fixed outposts along the border; they have also carried out frequent patrols in the region of the Contra training camps. One cross-border incursion, in March, was described by Washington as an "invasion" of Honduras, thus temporarily raising the possibility that Washington might go to Honduras's aid. When it became apparent that Honduran army units were in fact not involved, Washington backed down. In August, President Azcona announced that Honduras would not permit U.S. personnel to train Contra forces in its territory, prompting a U.S. announcement that they would instead be trained in the United States.

Although the Nicaraguans generally avoided contact with the Honduran Army, the frequent Nicaraguan incursions into Honduras nevertheless heightened the danger of conflict between the two countries. Indeed, in December, Honduran military aircraft strafed two villages inside Nicaragua near a military staging area as a clear signal of Honduras's impatience with the Nicaraguan presence on its territory. Washington reinforced its commitment to Honduran national security by announcing its willingness to supply F-5 fighters to the Honduran Air Force.

Costa Rica

In February 1986, Liberation party candidate Oscar Arias, who at times was critical of the U.S.-backed Contra program, was elected president of Costa Rica. He argued that Contra aid should be directed at getting Nicaragua to the negotiating table and that only a political solution, including a strengthening of democratic, free enterprise-oriented neighboring countries, could be an enduring solution to the Nicaraguan problem. Arias's new approach marked a clear change, at least rhetorically, from the previous administration of President Luis Alberto Monge, which had lobbied the U.S. Congress in support of the Contras. Although Arias allowed members of the anti-Sandinista Southern Opposition Bloc (BOS) to continue to operate out of Costa Rica, he shut down a secret Contra airstrip, denied some Contras visas to enter the country, and beefed up the border security in order to deny the Contras new bases. Costa Rican public opinion, though strongly anti-Somoza, also turned strongly anti-Sandinista; public opinion polls identified Nicaragua as the country's greatest security threat. Still, support for Costa Rica's policy of neutrality also stayed strong. Concern over some Nicaraguan incursions into Costa Rican territory led the Costa Ricans to participate in a strengthening of its currently modest security forces by the United States in the form of training and equipment.

Nicaragua

Nicaragua's political system grew substantially more repressive during late 1985 and 1986. Arguing that U.S. economic, diplomatic, and military pressures were responsible for Nicaragua's problems, the Sandinista government in October 1985 promulgated "emergency measures" that suspended most civil liberties, including the freedoms of speech, press, and assembly. During 1986, the Nicaraguan government escalated its pressures on the Catholic Church through personal attacks on Cardinal Miguel Obando y Bravo and the detainment and deportation of a number of priests. The government also cracked down on opposition political parties, labor unions, the private sector generally, and human rights activists; moreover, it moved against the press and shut down *La Prensa*, Nicaragua's leading daily.

Nicaragua strengthened its military capabilities during 1986 with the help of 3,000 Cuban and more than 100 Soviet and Eastern European advisers; it increased its ground forces and improved its air capability as well through the addition of new Soviet-made attack helicopters, believed to be flown by Cubans. Nicaragua's armor exceeds that of the rest of Central America today by a ratio of almost two to one. The number of troop-carrying and attack helicopters in the Nicaraguan forces amounts to almost two dozen. Nicaragua's armed and security forces are 50 percent again as large as the next largest force in the region (that of El Salvador).

In 1986, the Soviet Union continued as Nicaragua's principal supplier of economic aid, and in late 1986 the Soviets renewed their commitment through 1987. Moreover, in March 1986 Nicaragua established diplomatic relations with the People's Republic of China, which granted trade credits in addition to the aid provided by West European countries.

While beefing up its strength along the Honduran border, including bold probes against Contra positions in the spring and winter of 1986, Nicaragua launched a campaign against the Miskito Indians along the Caribbean coast in March and April. The level of internal repression and growing anti-Sandinista sentiment, combined with seriously deteriorating economic conditions, enlarged the ranks of the opposition (FDN), along with cadres of the Costa Rican-based BOS and the Miskito-led Misurasata.

Severely limiting the effectiveness of the Contras as a political alternative to the Sandinistas was their inability to unite into an effective political force, in spite of heavy U.S. government pressure during 1986 to resolve their internal differences. Although internal opposition to the government was on the rise in Nicaragua, there was little evidence that the Contras had managed to translate anti-Sandinista sentiment into pro-Contra support. The Contras' military effectiveness was extremely limited, although approval by the U.S. Congress in late summer 1986 of $100 million in military aid provided an important shot in the arm. The shooting down of an arms resupply flight in October brought into the open the existence of a covert, private supply effort that probably had more impact on morale than on the Contras' fighting capacity. And the November discoveries that profits from arms sales to Iran were channeled to Contra support operations posed new obstacles to a renewal of U.S. military aid to the Contras in 1987.

The Democratic capture of the U.S. Senate in the November 1986 congressional elections, a weakened U.S. presidency as a result of the Iran-Contra scandal, and continuing limited support for the Contras at the level of public opinion have increased the chances that the Congress will reject sustained military aid. Nevertheless, opponents of Contra aid have yet to develop a credible alternative policy; moreover, sympathy for the Sandinistas in Washington has dwindled substantially while concern about them has spiraled. Moreover, the administration will argue that more time and money are needed for training the Contras and that one year's funding is inadequate. Another congressional appropriation of military aid during 1987 is therefore likely, though with a variety of restrictions attached. If, by the end of 1988, the Contras have succeeded neither in challenging the Sandinistas more effectively on the battleground nor in developing a more effective political strategy, the prospects for renewed congressional support in 1988 will be dim.

Panama

Panama suffered a setback in late 1985 in its slow move toward democratic governance. The head of the Panamanian Defense Force, General Manuel Noriega, ousted President Nicholas Ardito Barletta in September of that year and installed his vice-president, Eric Arturo Delvalle, as successor. Beyond a temporary withholding of some aid as a measure of protest, little was heard from Washington about Noriega's action. Washington's reticence was due largely to the strategic importance Washington attached to a close relationship with the Panamanian Defense Force (PDF) and its cooperation vis-à-vis the Panama Canal; it also reflected the importance of PDF support for U.S. activities elsewhere in Central America (e.g., reconnaissance flights and the rotation of military advisers in and out of Honduras and El Salvador).

Nevertheless, hearings chaired by U.S. Senator Jesse Helms and articles in the U.S. media produced a variety of charges that Noriega and the PDF were involved not only in corruption and drug trafficking but also possibly in gun-running and cooperation with Cuban intelligence. Noriega retorted with a series of blasts at the United States, accusing it of attempting to retain control of the Canal. (He did subsequently manage to push U.S.-backed economic reform legislation through the Panamanian Congress.) Panama became a more serious foreign-policy concern of the United States during 1986 in view of the continuing weakness of its institutions (especially the civilian parts of the government), growing charges of illicit activities by the PDF, violent confrontations between students and labor groups, and heightened social unrest. These problems persisted in 1987 as the United States grew more outspoken in its criticisms of Noriega and, in July, suspended economic and military assistance.

El Salvador

El Salvador, despite almost a decade of warfare, has proved a slowly emerging political and military success story. The guerrilla Farabundo Marti National Liberation Front (FMLN) was stalemated by a series of Salvadoran army successes, and general military trends were running in the government's favor. The FMLN even admitted its failures by suggesting that the war would go on for decades. Clouding the army's achievements, however, were persistent church and refugee reports of aerial bombardments of villages and large numbers of civilian casualties. Denied by the Salvadoran government, the charges have still not been satisfactorily clarified.

Politically, El Salvador continued its slow but steady pace toward emergent democracy. U.S. military and economic assistance remained an essential element in President José Napoléon Duarte's cautiously implemented but increasingly successful strategy of building up the center, weakening the extreme Right, moving militarily against the guerrillas, and getting the military out of politics. The Right was far less vocal than in the past and, under continued heavy pressure from the U.S. government, moved substantially toward accepting the rules of the new electoral game. The armed forces, as well, bowed to U.S. pressures to focus on their military role and eschew a political one. The extreme Left was routed militarily, although no successful effort was made to pursue a dialogue with the somewhat more moderate Left, as had occurred in previous years.

The picture has not been entirely favorable, however. Efforts to strengthen the center faltered as Duarte's unpopular program to adjust El Salvador's battered economy by devaluing the currency, cutting spending, and increasing taxes provoked serious protest from the business community and working class in mid-year demonstrations. The worrisome level of protest reflected the degree to which economic stagnation has replaced the guerrilla threat as the main Achilles' heel of Salvadoran democracy. In spite of renewed guerrilla pressures in early 1987, El Salvador has come a long way.

The Soviet Union and Latin America

The Soviets have long perceived Latin America as a potential source of major political instability and therefore as a potential threat to U.S. interests and security. At the same time, however, they have recognized the United States' concern, dating back to the nineteenth century, over external involvement in the area. In addition, the realities of geography and of U.S. political, economic, and strategic dominance in the region have made Latin America a lower priority for the Soviet Union than other areas such as the Middle East. Nevertheless, where the Soviets can take advantage of socioeconomic and political dissent in Latin America they will do so, primarily to distract U.S. attention from other areas more central to Soviet strategic interests.

The Soviet Union's priority in the Western Hemisphere is the Caribbean Basin (Central America, the Caribbean, and Mexico)—partly because of Moscow's stake in Cuba and partly because it believes that the area's socioeconomic inequities and years of political repression have made it ripe for exploitation. Turmoil in the basin would prejudice important U.S. interests in maintaining the security of the sea-lanes of communication through the area. It is well known that, in the event of conflict, more than one-half of the U.S. reinforcements to NATO would pass through the Caribbean Basin; almost half of all U.S. trade and more than half of U.S. oil imports transit the area as well. In addition, the United States can afford to project its military force into Europe and East Asia because it has not had to be concerned about a threat to its security from its southern flank.

Although it is worth emphasizing that the Soviets' interests in Latin America are not as great as their interests in other parts of the world, the Soviet Union will seek to take advantage of any opportunity to advance its influence. Latin America's move away from conservative military regimes toward more democratic government in 1986 coincided with the Communist party's adoption of a new policy at the CPSU Congress in February to improve relations with free market, democratic

Third World nations. Although the Soviet Union had little to offer Latin American nations in need of trade, technology, and capital, and although its economic model was fast losing its appeal to Latin American leftists, its interest in expanding diplomatic ties was attractive to those nations eager to assert their independence from the United States.

General Secretary Mikhail Gorbachev moved quickly to take advantage of percieved new opportunities by planning the first visit ever to South America by a Soviet leader. His trip, planned for 1987, will probably include Mexico, Brazil, Argentina, and undoubtedly Cuba. Shifting partly away from its earlier priority on relations with Third World Communist parties, the Soviet Union has sought to improve its relationship with major Third World actors in an effort to counterbalance the United States geopolitically. Washington has grown newly concerned at the prospect of a broadened Soviet presence in the Western Hemisphere in the form of new consulates and expanded commercial and diplomatic offices.

The 1986 discovery in Chile of large arms caches, which appeared to have emanated from Soviet sources, was dramatic evidence that Moscow would seek to maintain support for influence over Latin American Communist parties as part of a longer-term strategy premised on a future collapse of debt- and stress-riven Latin economic and political systems. Apart from Chile, the Soviet Union's profile in South America was low. The Soviets are still mired in their relationship with the Peruvian military and have gained little from the relationship.

In Central America the Soviet Union increased its military commitment to Nicaragua and has helped make that country by far the best armed in Central America. Washington sources have insisted that Sandinista military capabilities were strengthened substantially by a doubling of Nicaragua's arsenal of Soviet-made Mi-24 helicopter gunships and by the addition of SA-7 anti-aircraft missiles with a longer range and greater accuracy than Nicaragua's older ones. Nevertheless, the Soviets shipped most of their equipment through Eastern European or other friendly governments in an effort to keep their direct role limited, and the roughly 200 Soviet advisers present in Nicaragua are far fewer than in other Third World countries.

The Soviet Union's commitment to Nicaragua was an important part of the Soviet Union's foreign policy in the Third World, but Cuba has remained the centerpiece of Soviet priorities in Latin America. Significant changes in the international environment during 1986 affected Cuba's perception of its role in the hemisphere; moreover, new frictions may have developed in the Cuban-Soviet relationship, partly because of important Cuban economic failures during the year. Sugar exports fell by 25 percent as production failed to meet output targets, forcing Cuba to even buy sugar on the international market, at higher prices, to meet export goals in Eastern Europe. The foreign-exchange shortage that resulted prompted a temporary suspension of payments of Cuba's external debt, and Castro himself projected both a further decline of 50 percent in 1987 and a proportionate cut in imports. He also admitted that Cuba was earning less from sales of Soviet petroleum than before and that serious drought had damaged agricultural production. Surprisingly, Castro laid a good part of the blame for Cuba's problems on its own bureaucracy, but rather than calling for economic reform he preached the need for greater sacrifice. His appeals to the Soviet Union for additional assistance apparently fell on deaf ears.

Conclusion

The United States' tough stand against communism and international terrorism, including the spring 1986 U.S. air attacks on Libya and the approval of $100 million in aid for the Contras (not to mention the 1983 incursion into Grenada), reflected the beginnings of an emergence from its post-Vietnam withdrawal and a new willingness to use force to pursue its objectives. At the same time, the Soviets have clearly placed priority on their bilateral relationship with the United States, thus perhaps suggesting a slight de-emphasis on the Third World.

Beyond the Nicaraguan crisis, 1986 was marked by the intensification of two opposing trends: the deepening of the democratic process and a continued stagnation or deterioration of Latin American economic prospects. The main challenges of the newly elected democratic governments came not from conservative military forces or from leftist guerrillas but, rather, from the social and political stresses produced by economies that generally failed to recover. The total product of the region grew between 1.5 percent and 3 percent, only with per capita income still much lower than it was at the beginning of the decade in almost all countries. The economies of the oil-exporting countries declined significantly (except in Peru), whereas the non-oil-exporting economies registered higher growth rates than in 1985. These slight improvements, however, were due to short-term, consumer-led spending sprees in Brazil and Argentina rather than to new investment-led growth. The drop in oil prices resulted in a loss of more foreign exchange than was saved through lower interest rates. Inflation declined, but it did so through the imposition of wage and price controls, which are not sustainable except in the short term. Meanwhile, the Latin debt grew by 2 percent to $382 billion, whereas the terms of trade fell 8.7 percent during 1986.

The international creditor community's facade of unity began to crack as bankers publicly began to criticize forced new lending just to pay interest on old debt. In December, some leading bankers even called for debt relief in order to promote a resumption of growth in Third World debtors amid signs that the U.S. government, especially the Congress, was contemplating new policies for restraining the growth of debt and achieving earlier economic recovery in the region.

Most Latin American debtors (with some exceptions) continued to play by the rules of the international creditors' game. All debtors were intent, however, on obtaining reschedulings along lines at least as generous as those Mexico won from its creditors in the autumn of 1986. In effect, the process of debt relief was under way; it would be implemented during 1987 by protracted bank negotiations on a country-by-country basis rather than by a regional Latin American initiative. In addition, Brazil, with its shaky economy and growing public protest, was the first major debtor to suspend interest payments (since Mexico in 1982).

Potentially the most significant ingredient in the management of the debt during 1987 was the U.S. government's new awareness that there were political and economic limits to the ability of Latin America to service its external debt. Thus Washington actively supported substantially improved terms for Mexico vis-à-vis the IMF and the commerical banks, agreed to Brazil's insistence on excluding the IMF from its official aid rescheduling, and pushed for major new loans for Chile in spite of serious concerns over that country's human rights policy. The U.S. government began 1987 by looking more seriously at ways of lightening the debt burden and spurring the resumption of growth, partly out of concern over political stability in the region's new democracies, partly in order to avoid unilateral or coordinated debtor actions that would jeopardize the international financial system, and partly to stimulate U.S. exports, which had plunged dramatically during the debt crisis. The previous year closed and 1987 opened amid signs that alleviation of the Latin debt and containment of the Sandinistas in Nicaragua would be priorities for both Washington and the region.

References

The data in this chapter were based on the following sources: "Toward Renewed Economic Growth in Latin America" (Washington, D.C.: Institute of International Economics, El Colegio de Mexico, Fundacao Getulio Vargas, 1986); *World Development Report 1986* (Washington, D.C.: World Bank, 1986); Hearings on Third World Debt Legislation, Subcommittee on International Development Institutions and Finance of the Committee on Banking, Finance, and Urban Affairs, U.S. House of Representatives, March 1986; Abraham F. Lowenthal, "Brazil and the United States" (New York: Foreign Policy Association, 1986);

Richard A. Nuccio, "What's Wrong, What's Right in Central America, a Citizen's Guide" (Roosevelt Center for American Policy Studies, 1986); "Amnesty International, Report 1986"; and "The Impact of the Latin American Debt Crisis on the U.S. Economy," a staff study prepared for the Joint Economic Committee of the U.S. Congress, May 10, 1986.

8
South Asia in 1986

Stephen P. Cohen

The year 1986 saw the intensification of many trends already well under way in South Asia. In Afghanistan to the northwest the Soviets gained little ground against the Mujahiddin, despite the introduction of new strategies and new leaders. Pakistan continued its twofold resurgence, becoming militarily stronger and politically more open. India, the region's dominant power, expanded its military capabilities but found itself in a relatively weaker position vis-à-vis Pakistan and China. Perhaps because of this, but certainly because of widespread publicity surrounding the Pakistani nuclear program, the region seemed to have inched further toward nuclear weapons status during the year.

Everywhere in the region, states encountered strong centrifugal ethnic, linguistic, tribal, irredentist, and revivalist forces, which were particularly acute in Sri Lanka and India and increasingly so in Pakistan. Ironically, such forces have been stimulated by growing regional prosperity. (Many South Asian states are now net exporters of food, and even Bangladesh, once derided as a "basket case," looks forward to food self-sufficiency.) Both the poor and the rich have more money available to them for politics, and the generally open political systems of South Asia invite activism. And, despite all expectations, the new regional organization—the South Asian Association for Regional Cooperation (SAARC)—seems likely to thrive as well as survive.

These events, to be discussed in detail below, have hastened South Asia's movement toward greater strategic significance. Of course, that significance always existed in purely regional terms, but South Asia has become considerably more important for the United States, the Soviet Union, China, and other key states than it was six or ten years ago. Iran's downfall, the invasion of Afghanistan, the region's potential for nuclearization, and the reduced Indian military advantage over Pakistan (which is at least temporarily enhanced by the disturbances in India's Punjab) have led to the evolution of a "pentagon of power," a competition for influence between four adjacent states (two nuclear powers, the USSR and the PRC and two near-nuclears, India and Pakistan), plus the United States. Although none of these states are now at war with another, they do divide into hostile pairs: India versus Pakistan, Pakistan versus the USSR, the USSR versus China, and China versus India. This situation is historically unprecedented. No nuclear and near-nuclear cluster of hostile nations has ever existed on this scale before; it is complicated by the only loose connections that exist even among friendly pairs (there are no NATO-like ties here) and by the great disparity in economic and political structures among these five countries.

Oddly, only the two South Asian states, thought to be implacable enemies, share a common culture and political history; indeed, the very closeness of India and Pakistan have made it difficult for them to deal with each other on a business-like basis, although their shared nuclear and strategic problems as well as interlocking ethnic and irredentist movements necessitate a minimum degree of cooperation.

The Afghan War:
Old Strategy, New Tactics

After eight years of warfare (there were at least two years of heavy fighting in Afghanistan before the Soviet invasion on December 25, 1979), a political and military rhythm has been established in that country. The anniversary of the Soviet invasion is one occasion for proselytizing; another is the annual UN vote (held in mid-November) condemning the occupation. Indirect negotiations in Geneva between the Soviet Union and Pakistan have occurred with some regularity, and these have now been expanded to include a "shuttle" diplomacy by UN officials traveling between Moscow, Kabul, Tehran, and Islamabad.

The war itself follows a pattern influenced by weather and terrain. In early spring, both sides seek tactical advantage for that summer's fighting. By November, military activity usually slows down, except in those relatively small parts of the country in which movement is unimpeded by snow or climate, and both sides regroup and restock in preparation for next spring's battles. As the year 1986 saw a particularly mild early winter, with fog and cloud cover in the Kabul region, resistance forces were active there through December.

The same year saw the intensification of both the political/diplomatic contest and the military struggle between the Soviets and the official Kabul regime on the one hand, and the Mujahiddin and their supporters on the other. It was the Soviets who made the greatest changes in tactics, although by year's end this outcome seemed to have yielded little in the way of concrete gains.

A New Soviet Approach

Since 1984, the Soviets have been pursuing new military tactics in Afghanistan; the year 1986 saw the implementation of a new, complementary political approach. Both trends represent the abandonment of a fixed-point defense and the assumption that the Mujahiddin would quickly exhaust themselves politically and militarily. This approach, in turn, had replaced earlier Soviet expectations that the Mujahiddin would collapse once Soviet forces demonstrated their firepower after the 1979 invasion. Still, the Soviets operate within certain self-imposed constraints. Their manpower level totals about 150,000, of which 120,000 are in Afghanistan.[1] This figure represents a modest increase over previous levels (except for 1983, when there was no known increase); the Soviets have added about 10,000 soldiers each year since the invasion, and some 5,000 in 1985. Moreover, the quality of Soviet troops has improved significantly in recent years, as has the quality of their equipment.

The post-1984 military strategy was conceived for the long term and has several elements.[2] One is to cut the resistance off from its local Afghan support by attacking civilian villages, farms, and homes in areas of intense resistance activity. This strategy forces the Mujahiddin to supply their own food, thus aggravating their logistics and transportation problems. The Soviets also intensified their attacks on supply routes into Afghanistan, bringing the war closer to the Iranian and Pakistani borders and leading to an unprecedented number of air attacks on Pakistan.[3] Other innovations included the use of over 4,000 Soviet *Spetznaz* (Special Forces), the expanded use of armor-plated attack helicopters, the introduction of more sophisticated ground-attack aircraft (MiG 23s and MiG 27s, which replaced the MiG 21s), and more imaginative tactics.[4] Finally, the Kabul regime announced in 1986 that some 300,000 people would be moved from areas near the Pakistani border and relocated to the west.

These new military and counter-resistance steps did result in one major Soviet victory early in the year. The resistance had built up the mountain redoubt of Jhawar Killi (in Paktia province near Pakistan) as a major support facility. It was captured in late April, and "hundreds" of Mujahiddin were killed or wounded.[5] The base had been in use for six years and was laced with tunnels and workshops. The battle for Jhawar Killi was accompanied by the heaviest fighting of the year with substantial resistance casualties, although Mujahiddin representatives claim that the base was retaken after fighting died down in mid-June. Nor were the new Soviet tactics successful in Herat in the west or Kandahar in the south, or even north of Kabul, where Commander Ahmad Shah Masud operates. In each of these areas, fighting continued throughout the year, and Kandahar in particular remains a devastated city.

Expanded Soviet military activity also could not prevent direct Mujahiddin attacks on Kabul itself, and, in fact, it runs the risk of escalating the international dimensions of the war. Kabul is a city under siege, peppered with rocket attacks from its periphery and with Soviet armor patrols in its streets at night. The Afghan government remains under Soviet military protection, as few Democratic Republic of Afghanistan (DRA) units can be trusted. The same applies to the Afghan Air Force. At least two fighter and helicopter pilots defected to Pakistan in 1986, leading to still tighter Soviet controls over Afghan military operations. Perhaps a portent of things to come, moreover, was the shooting down on May 17 by Pakistan of two DRA aircraft that had entered Pakistani territory at Parachinar; one Sukhoi 22 crashed in Pakistan, the other on the Afghan side of the border. Pakistan's success was made possible by the forward deployment of Pakistan's U.S.-supplied F-16 aircraft and led to intensified U.S.-Pakistan discussions about additional steps to protect Pakistani airspace.

On balance, increased DRA/Soviet military activity did produce some early results, but by the end of the year these seem to have been largely eroded by greater Mujahiddin cooperation, better equipment, the international embarrassment of the Soviets, and the prompt response of Pakistan to Soviet/DRA cross-border attacks upon its territory. However, their military operations were only one component of their overall strategy, and the Soviets undertook important new political and diplomatic initiatives in 1986.

Politics and Diplomacy

The most sensational political development to occur in Afghanistan in 1986 took place on May 5, when Babrak Karmal was removed as secretary general of the Afghan Communist party, the People's Democratic party of Afghanistan (PDPA). Karmal was replaced by the 39-year-old Sayid Mohammad Najibullah, who had been in charge of Khad, Afghanistan's secret police. "Najib," as he is known, had originally been a medical doctor, but was long since associated with Afghan Communist politics. He came from the same Communist faction as Babrak Karmal (Parcham), but differed in that he was also from Afghanistan's dominant Pashtun tribe. As head of Khad, Najib had been active in wooing the Pashtuns along the Pakistan frontier, reportedly had masterminded terror bombings in Pakistan itself, and was directly responsible for the Kabul regime's assaults on human rights in Afghanistan, not excluding the widespread use of torture.[6]

Karmal was removed because he had made little headway in pursuing the war, had not been able to contain factionalism within the PDPA, and seemed to lack ideas for strengthening the regime. By year's end, Najib seems to be doing no better. His relocation plan remains vague, an expected revision of the Afghan constitution has been postponed, and there appears to have been no ground gained in wooing the Afghan people. Indeed, Karmal's removal generated another faction within the PDPA: When foreign journalists gathered to observe the "withdrawal" of Soviet forces from Kabul in October,[7] they also witnessed a public protest on behalf of Karmal—and were quickly hustled out of town. Perhaps to ensure Karmal's political burial, he was removed from the Afghan presidency and ruling politburo on November 20. Nevertheless, there now exists a "Karmal" faction within the Parcham branch of the PDPA, along with the ruling "Najib" faction, and both oppose the powerful "Khalq" branch of the party, the group that governed Afghanistan from the time of the 1978 revolution until the Soviets put Karmal in power after their 1979 invasion.

On the diplomatic front, the year began with considerable excitement over two events that occurred late in 1985. The first was the offer by the United States to serve as a "guarantor" of an acceptable peace settlement, including the withdrawal of Soviet troops;[8] the second was the sixth round of talks held from December 16 to 19, 1985 (Geneva VI).[9] There were also references made to Afghanistan in General Secretary Gorbachev's February 25 speech to the 27th Party Congress, emphasizing his desire to protect the Karmal regime and to withdraw Soviet forces from Afghanistan.

It was thus not surprising that by April there was considerable speculation about the terms of an eventual settlement of the Afghan problem. Feelings were running espcially high in Pakistan, where the opening up of the political process had led to major public debates over the issue and some detailed discussion of where Pakistan might make concessions to the Soviets.[10]

The heightened fighting along Pakistan's border, and the failure of Geneva VII (May 19–26) put a temporary end to speculation about an agreement. Formal UN-sponsored negotiations were concluded by mid-year, although the UN mediator, Diego Cordovez, resumed an informal shuttle among Islamabad, Tehran, Kabul, and Moscow in late November. Despite a new flurry of press reports, this shuttle proved as inconclusive as earlier formal and informal efforts had been.

At one level, the central issue dividing the two sides remains the timetable for the withdrawal of Soviet troops.[11] The Pakistanis speak in terms of months, the Soviets in terms of years. The two sides may move slightly closer in future negotiations, but there remains the fundamental question as to what kind of government will succeed the present Kabul regime. This regime could not survive the departure of the Soviets for many days, and would be forced to invite them back in to save itself. Other contentious issues include the fate of the nearly 5 million Afghan refugees in Pakistan and Iran, their participation in a future Afghan government, and the authenticity of Afghanistan's "nonaligned" status. Talks are likely to continue, and both sides have shown "flexibility and ingenuity in finding ways to keep them going,"[12] but a political solution acceptable to the Afghan people, the Soviet Union, and Afghanistan's other neighbors seems as distant as a military solution.

Pakistan: Enhanced Security and Stability

Although 1986 began under a cloud of uncertainty, Pakistan concluded the year with a markedly stabilized domestic political order and a clarified security situation. The two were linked in several significant ways.

First, Pakistan's enhanced democratization meant that the center of decisionmaking was significantly diffused. Eight years of martial law rule ended on December 30, 1985—although President Zia ul-Haq retained his position as head of the Pakistan Army. The prime minister, Mohammed Khan Junejo, soon began to assert his authority. On many issues of foreign and defense policy, it was not always clear whether Zia or Junejo was responsible for the final decision. It is certain that the Pakistan military has virtually retreated to the barracks, although it retains an obvious institutional interest in both domestic and foreign policies.[13]

Second, the greater openness of Pakistani politics in 1986 revealed certain issues that had not been fully discussed earlier. The pressures associated with hosting nearly 3 million Afghan refugees became a political issue, there was increased public outcry over the *dacoity* (organized crime) in rural Sind, and sectarian Sunni-Shia differences led to serious riots in Karachi. At the end of the year, extremely savage and violent riots occurred again in Karachi, this time between the city's Pathan and Muhajir communities (the Muhajirs are immigrants or descendants of immigrants from India). The army was called out to restore order, and the governor (a retired general) was fired early in 1987.

Despite the shock of the Pathan-Muhajir riots, the balance seems to be holding between expanded political participation and political stability. Under a civilian government it is easier to fix responsibility on a local or regional official, and regional crises do not become a test of the center's legitimacy or power.

The new openness also revealed that some issues are less volatile than previously thought (e.g., relations with the United States and the slow pace of negotiation with the Soviets over their departure from Afghanistan), and that the range of controversial issues is so great that Pakistani society does not divide neatly along any particular fault line. Finally, the new openness has led to a general rush to fill a perceived vacuum at the political center, particularly after the political weakness of some important politicians and movements was revealed during the year. The most important example of political decline involved Benazir Bhutto, the daughter of Zia's executed political predecessor, Zulfiqar Ali Bhutto.

Benazir's Arrival and Departure

Benazir's return to Pakistan on April 10 was triumphant, and for one month she drew crowds of unprecedented size in Pakistan's cities and during rural tours. She carefully avoided direct criticism of the Army (which could have put her back in jail, as the constitution had been modified to prohibit defamation or criticism of the armed forces) and offered general support of Pakistan's current foreign policy. Her ideological strategy was to retain her father's Left-wing supporters without alienating or frightening Pakistan's large middle class. Her political strategy was to drive wedges between Junejo and Zia, between Zia and the Army, and between the United States and Zia; and to offer herself and her Pakistan People's party (PPP) as a responsible alternative to the military and to the phlegmatic Junejo, whose conservative Pakistan Muslim League lacked a popular base.

However, the 33-year-old "Miss Benazir" did not fully control the PPP, which her father had badly split. A month after her return to Pakistan, a leading centrist, Ghulam Mustafa Jatoi, resigned as president of the Sind branch of the PPP. Many other party regulars had serious reservations about Benazir herself. Some could not accept a woman as their leader; others doubted her political skills (although not her temporary charismatic appeal); and many feared their displacement by a younger generation of enthusiasts.

The softness in Benazir's support was revealed on Pakistan Day (August 14), the celebration of Pakistan's independence from British rule. PPP rallies scheduled for Lahore were canceled by Junejo, leading to major riots and arrests (the government claimed that it had evidence of preparation for armed violence by PPP cadres). Benazir was arrested, and massive civil disorder and violence took place in the Sind—but not in Punjab itself. Thus revealed was a lack of enthusiasm for Benazir in Pakistan's most important province; when she was released from jail a month later, the steam had gone out of the PPP. Benazir postponed and then canceled a national protest scheduled for September (her goal was to force the government to hold mid-term elections before 1990). Jatoi's successor as PPP Sind president also quit, and Jatoi himself founded the rival National People's party in late August.

Benazir and the PPP were not the only political groups to suffer a setback during 1986. In the middle of the August riots, the pro-Soviet leftist Wali Khan departed for a trip to the Soviet Union, derided by those he left behind. The various religious parties, especially those on the Right, became preoccupied with sectarian issues, further limiting their national appeal (although Pakistan is an Islamic state, it has never been a sectarian one). The rise of militant Shiism in Iran has led to Shia activism in Pakistan; this situtation, in turn, has created a militant Sunni backlash, and the two forces have literally taken their differences to the streets of Karachi, where widespread violence has occurred throughout the year.[14]

By the end of the year it was clear that Benazir Bhutto and the PPP were no longer the dominant political forces in Pakistan, although most observers believe that the PPP remains the single most popular party. It suffers from organizational weakness, the memory of Zulfiqar Ali Bhutto's excesses, uncertainty about Benazir's leadership qualities, and, perhaps most important, the absence of an issue that would consolidate opposition to Junejo. Pakistan's economy is in excellent shape, most Pakistanis warily support both the U.S. tie and Pakistan's policy toward Afghanistan, and the Indian threat has not been convincingly turned into a domestic issue.[15] Meanwhile, Junejo is gradually mastering the art of democratic politics, although some observers speculate that Zia will eventually select the more dynamic Jatoi to replace him before new elections are held in 1990. This may or may not occur, but it is clear that Zia himself has gained in political stature as a result of Pakistan's return to democractic politics; not only did he keep his promise to restore democracy, but the gyrations of the politicians make him look increasingly statesmanlike.

Foreign Affairs and Defense Policy

Aside from the protracted negotiations with the Soviet Union over the fate of Afghanistan, the most important foreign-policy event of the year 1986 was the conclusion on March 24 of an agreement with the United States to renew the multiyear economic and arms assistance package. The agreement is as yet unimplemented: The U.S. Congress

TABLE 8.1

Annual Funding of the Post-FY 1987 Program (in millions of dollars)

	Annual	Total	Terms
Economic Aid			
Developmental assistance	$ 50	$ 300	grant
Economic support funds	250	1,500	grant
PL 480	80	480	loan
Foreign Military Sales	290	1,740	concessional loans
Total Program	670	4,020	

must once again, in early 1987, extend its waiver of the Symington amendment and also appropriate funds for fiscal year 1988, when the new program is scheduled to begin.[16] As the Senate has now come under Democratic control, the Pakistani package (and nuclear program) will receive close scrutiny, particularly in view of the exposure, in July, of yet another Pakistani effort to illegally acquire materials necessary for its nuclear weapons program. Congressional support for the administration's Afghan policy is strong and bipartisan, however, and as Pakistan figures prominently in that policy, the Congress will be reluctant to stop aid altogether. Much will depend on Pakistan's actions in August and September to reasure the United States about its nuclear ambitions.

The aid package itself would continue the modest modernization of the Pakistani armed forces begun under the 1981–1987 program as well as the support of several significant developmental projects. The overall funding level is projected at $4.02 billion for the six-year period, to be weighted in favor of economic assistance by a 57–43 percent ratio (the first program entailed $3.2 billion and a 50–50 percent balance).[17] The rationale for the second program remains the same as the first: to help Pakistan meet continuing political and military pressures from the Soviet presence in neighboring Afghanistan. It is also designed to ease Pakistan's security situation and thus remove or reduce the incentive to acquire nuclear weapons.

The annual funding of the post-FY 1987 program expected by U.S. officials[18] is shown in Table 8.1. As of July 1987, no firm decisions had been made concerning the major weapons to be purchased with the military aid. Given the sharp increase in air attacks on Pakistan from Afghanistan, air defense is a high priority. However, a sophisticated air-defense system, such as the E-3A Sentry (AWACS), would use up at least half of the military assistance package; lesser systems, such as the U.S. Navy's E-2C Hawkeye, have yet to be proven as adequate for terrain as mountainous as the Pak-Afghan border.[19] Other weapons discussed publicly include new armor. Some Pakistanis would like to acquire the M-1 Abrams tank to supplement their large (1,100-unit) fleet of obsolescent Chinese Type-59 tanks, and their lesser number (about 450 units) of refurbished M-48A5 tanks. Neither tank is a match for the Soviet T-72 scheduled to enter Indian inventories in large numbers.[20]

Following agreement on the overall size of the package, the United States and Pakistan concluded a Memorandum of Understanding (MOU) on the transfer of advanced technology. This MOU was in part inspired by the U.S.-Indian MOU of a year earlier. As Pakistan's defense production infrastructure is still very weak, the MOU is not expected to lead to any major defense production agreements, although there have been discussions about a joint Pakistan-China-U.S. program to produce in Pakistan a fighter based on a Chinese aircraft. The new package and the MOU were also followed by the high-profile visit of Prime Minister Junejo to the United States in mid-July. Though largely ceremonial, the visit demonstrated Junejo's desire to be seen (and treated) as a political force in his own right, not merely as "Zia's prime minister."

In 1986, no significant changes occurred in Pakistan's relations with its neighbors or with other states important to it. Relations with India cooled after the beginning of the year, and Pakistani officials blame the Indians for lack of progress on new transit and trade agreements and for the two nations' inability to formalize the Zia-Rajiv 1985 agreement not to attack each other's nuclear facilities. Indeed, the planned visit of Rajiv Gandhi to Pakistan in 1986 was postponed; Indian officials point by way of explanation to alleged Pakistani support for the Sikh terrorists and the Khalistani movement, to continued shooting along the Kashmir cease-fire line and in the Siachin glacier, and to published reports of Pakistan's nuclear program. The year ended with sharp recriminations between the two sides over the size and intent of Indian military maneuvers along the Pakistan border, known as "Operation Brass Tacks." Indo-Pakistani ties clearly dipped during 1986, but in this respect they are only following the pattern of ups and downs and the search for tactical advantage that has characterized the two countries' relations for at least eight years.

Elsewhere, Pakistan continues down its generally moderate foreign-policy path. Zia went on record early in the year as favoring Arab "realism" toward Israel, and gently criticized the PLO for being "unrealistic."[21] He pursued his earlier efforts as a go-between in the Iranian-Iraqi dispute: Although Pakistan has close relations with the Saudis, it also is a neighbor of Iran, has a large Shia population of its own, and thus maintains correct to good relations with the Iranian regime. Pakistan's relations with China continue to be very close, and the year saw at least one important nuclear agreement between the two countries, thus raising further questions about the Pakistani nuclear program.

Pakistan's Nuclear Program and Regional Proliferation

Although India's nuclear program is more advanced than that of Pakistan (India actually tested a device in 1974), public and governmental attention was focused on Pakistan's nuclear capabilities throughout the year. In April, the U.S. Special Ambassador for Non-Proliferation, Richard T. Kennedy, refused to answer questions about Pakistan's uranium-enrichment capabilities in open session. Two months later (just before Junejo's U.S. visit), the press carried reports of a Soviet demarche to Pakistan, allegedly threatening a Soviet response if Pakistan were to develop a nuclear weapon. These reports also described a stiff U.S. rejoinder to the Soviets, thus indicating some superpower divergence on nonproliferation strategies, at least as applied to South Asia.[22] The Pakistanis officially continue to deny any intention or capability of acquiring nuclear weapons, but one of their own leading nuclear scientists, A. Q. Khan, was permitted to state publicly that "the most essential item in making a bomb is a simple screwdriver."[23] Nevertheless, the U.S. government did certify on October 21, as required by the Congress for the release of aid, that Pakistan did not have a nuclear weapon and that U.S. military and economic assistance "contributed significantly" to nonproliferation; this certification was followed shortly by a detailed *Washington Post* article claiming that Pakistan had enriched uranium to bomb-grade levels (93.5 percent) and had conducted two tests of a triggering device.[24]

Earlier public reports have claimed that Pakistan received assistance on bomb design technology from the People's Republic of China. If it were to develop a nuclear weapon, Pakistan could use any of its fighter or light bomber aircraft as a delivery system. Such aircraft would be vulnerable to preemptive attack, giving rise to Indian fears that Pakistan might use its nuclear capability for strategic compellence. However, it is more likely that Pakistani strategists would see a nuclear weapon as a last-ditch deterrent, protecting the country from both the overwhelming conventional capabilities of its likely enemies as well as from potential nuclear threats.[25]

Whatever the accuracy of these revelations, they provoked extensive criticism of the U.S. nonproliferation policy both in Congress and in

India. Congress is likely to examine this policy carefully in 1987, especially inasmuch as the Symington waiver must be renewed to allow continued U.S. arms assistance to Pakistan after FY 1987. The previously mentioned incident of illegal activity antagonized several key senators and congressmen who earlier had supported U.S. aid, thus diminishing Pakistan's chances. Indian leaders have harshly criticized the United States for failing to restrain Pakistan, although India still refuses to discuss, let alone accept, any of the many proposals for regional nuclear restraint put forward by President Zia. India, like Pakistan, wants to keep its "options" open, a position that is popular in both countries. It remains to be seen whether Pakistan can sustain the nuclear program in the face of closer congressional scrutiny and whether Pakistan and India can manage their nuclear relationship at the pre-weapon level, given the high degree of uncertainty that surrounds the intentions and capabilities of both countries.

India: Domestic Agony, Strategic Uncertainty

Despite a highly publicized visit by Mikhail Gorbachev, the intensification of the nuclear debate, and major progress in the South Asian regional movement, Indian attention remained focused in 1986 on domestic political events especially the Sikh-Punjab crisis.

Domestic Developments: From Bad to Worse, and Better?

In September 1985, Rajiv Gandhi reached what was thought to be a comprehensive agreement on the Punjab with H. S. Longowal, a Sikh moderate politician. Immediately afterward, Longowal was assassinated. His successor to the chief ministership of Punjab, S. S. Barnala, was unable to begin the implementation of the agreement in 1986, partly because of extremist Sikh opposition, partly because of the opposition of the neighboring state of Haryana. Among other things, the agreement involved the transfer of the joint Harayana-Punjab capital city of Chandigarh to Punjab and the reallocation of water assets between Punjab and Harayana.

Rajiv's parallel attempt to improve the quality of intelligence and police forces in Punjab was somewhat more successful, although Sikh extremists still operate throughout the state and have expanded their activities to include the assassination of high officials throughout India. Indeed, they may or may not have been behind the failed October 2 assassination attempt on Rajiv. Early in the year, alleged Pakistani support for Sikh extremists and terrorists had become a major domestic issue in India and threatened to disrupt relations with Pakistan, but by mid-1986 informed Indian sources were characterizing such support as "rather low level."[26] The year ended with further Sikh atrocities against Hindus in the Punjab (in early December twenty-three Hindu passengers on a bus were systematically murdered), Hindu retaliation against Sikhs in New Delhi, and the arrest of uncooperative and extremist Sikh leaders. However, the terrorist Sikh strategy of forcing a transfer of population between Punjab and the rest of India, which they see as a step toward the creation of an independent Sikh Khalistan, seems not to be working, and the assassination and terror strategy may be a measure of the weakness of Sikh extremists—not of their strength.

India's ethnic separatist problem is not confined to the Punjab, however. The year saw significant progress on this front in one region and a significant setback in another. The success occurred in Mizoram (in India's northeast corner) on June 24, with the formal end to a twenty-year insurgency by Mizo tribals. Drawing on a pattern that successfully ended several other guerrilla struggles, the Indian government appointed the head of the rebel Mizo National Front, Laldenga, to lead a coalition Mizo government, and agreed to special constitutional protection for Mizoram. But the year also saw the full-scale emergence of a new regional ethnic protest, in the northern districts of the Communist-governed state of West Bengal. Here, Indians of Nepali origin (*Gorkhas*, usually spelled *Gurkha*) were demanding that a Nepali-speaking state be created. Despite widespread violence, the West Bengal and Indian governments are both unlikely to yield on this issue soon. The Gurkha agitation, like the Sikh separatist movement, has security implications for India. Not only are they both further manifestations of ethnic separatism, but like the Sikhs, Gurkhas are heavily represented in the Indian Army, which is often called upon to quell such movements when (as is often the case) local police forces and paramilitary units cannot cope.

Rajiv's failure to make significant headway in the Punjab further damaged his political reputation. Although he remains the most popular Indian leader today, a number of the party faithful have broken with him. In turn, he has purged members of the Congress party he thought were disloyal or incompetent. He has yet to hold elections within that party, and these were elections he has promised to resume (party elections were suspended in the early 1970s); he also seems increasingly frustrated with the task of running a country that will soon have 1 billion people.[27] There is little doubt that this frustration at home partly explains Rajiv's activism abroad.

Security and Foreign Policy: The Search for a Role

As in domestic politics, Rajiv has consciously molded his foreign policy more along the lines developed by his grandfather, Jawaharlal Nehru, than along those of his mother, Indira Gandhi. She took little interest in global disarmament and nuclear issues; Rajiv has put India at the center of a group of six nations seeking to restrain the superpower nuclear arms race. She made the Indian military very dependent on Soviet weapons; Rajiv has resumed Nehru's strategy of diversified sources by beginning a serious dialogue with the United States over the acquisition of advanced military technology. Indira was at best cool to normalizing relations with Pakistan and the idea of a regional South Asian association; under Rajiv there has been some progress in improving ties with Pakistan and India has cooperated fully in the SAARC. Finally, Indira saw the Soviets as India's chief ally against the threat from China; Rajiv is less sure of Soviet support, although Moscow may have concluded that India is less important than before as a factor in their own relationship with Beijing. In short, Indian foreign policy is undergoing a transition, one forced upon it by an altered strategic environment (especially the stabilization of Pakistan and the new movement of the Soviets toward China), but also one partially welcomed by Rajiv and his generation, who seem determined to strike out on their own without publicly rejecting the formulations of the recent past.

Delhi maintains that the regional security environment is more threatening than it has been for years. It sees Pakistan as continuing to acquire first-line equipment, and as having a nuclear weapons program under way; Indian and Pakistani forces face each other in Kashmir, and skirmishes between them have occurred regularly over the past year, especially on and near the remote Siachin glacier. To the northeast, there have been minor incidents along the contested MacMahon Line, and India has alleged that Chinese troops have crossed that line. To the south, Tamil guerrillas not only threaten Sri Lanka's integrity as a state, but a number of them are extreme revolutionary ideologues; New Delhi fears that if they succeed in Sri Lanka, South Indian politics could also be destabilized—yet because of the popularity of the Tamil cause, it is hard to clamp down totally on them.

Despite these regional concerns, the most publicized foreign policy event of the year was General Secretary Gorbachev's visit to India in the last week of November. Little was accomplished during the trip. Indeed, the spectacular welcome accorded to Gorbachev was criticized as excessive and did not mask the growing differences between India and the Soviet Union on critical issues, especially their relations with

China. Gorbachev was several times pressed in public on Moscow's policies toward Beijing and Afghanistan, but his answers were unconvincing to informed Indian observers.[28] Nevertheless, the Soviet Union is widely perceived by Indians as their best international "friend," Rajiv and Gorbachev apparently get on well with each other, and some significant new economic agreements were concluded during the visit.

Less heralded, but a milestone in its own right, was the first trip to India by a U.S. secretary of defense (Caspar Weinberger) on October 11–12. Weinberger informed New Delhi that the United States would sell a supercomputer to India for monsoon research (once assurances that the computer would not be used in India's nuclear program nor its technology be transferred to third nations). Some of the luster of Weinberger's trip was dimmed, however, by his subsequent announcement in Islamabad that the United States would meet Pakistan's airborne early-warning requirements; Weinberger's Indian hosts were bitter about the fact that the issue had not been discussed with them beforehand.

The Weinberger visit was the surface manifestation of growing defense production collaboration and military-to-military contact between the United States and India. Several areas of cooperation have been agreed upon, the most important of which concerns the development of a light combat aircraft (LCA). India faces block obsolescence of its LCA fleet (especially the MiG 21). If India produces its own LCA, its present 75 percent dependence on Soviet-designed or Soviet-supplied aircraft could sharply decline in five to ten years. A twenty-person Department of Defense team headed by Deputy Under Secretary Talbot Lindstrom made an unprecedented survey of Indian aeronautical design and production capabilities in February, and Delhi later agreed to purchase some GE 404 engines for the LCA. Several U.S. companies are discussing co-production and technology transfer arrangements with the government of India; the most notable of these is Northrop, whose canceled F-20 project would seem to be an ideal base for U.S.-Indo LCA cooperation.[29] In another defense production area, India contracted for co-production of the GE LN2500 naval ship turbine for its forthcoming corvettes, frigates, and fast patrol boats. Quite separately, defense cooperation is expanding in other areas, including enhanced Indian military training in the United States, visits to Indian military schools by U.S. briefing teams, the participation of the Indian frigate *Godavari* in the Fourth of July naval parade in New York, and U.S. Navy ship visits to Indian ports in October 1986 and January 1987. These activities are still modest, but nothing like them has occurred since the heady period of U.S.-Indian defense cooperation immediately following the 1962 Sino-Indian War.

Although the year also saw an agreement to purchase the Soviet MiG 29 (India will be the first country outside of the Soviet Union to receive it), the two most important Indian arms purchases involved Western countries. The Swedes entered into a $1 billion deal to sell and co-manufacture the 155 millimeter Howitzer, and the British agreed to refit and sell *HMS Hermes* as a "Harrier carrier." As a result, India will obtain two such carriers and, with its current airlift and sealift assets, the ability to project a modest degree of power throughout the Indian Ocean region. India's naval forces would be of only tactical importance in a war with Pakistan (possibly along the remote shoreline to the west of Karachi in southern Baluchistan), but they do add up to a strategic factor in relations with the weaker Indian Ocean littoral nations and the island nations of the region, including Sri Lanka. India's objective is to compete with and eventually supplant the expeditionary forces of the superpowers—France and Great Britain—in its own Indian Ocean backyard.

Perhaps because of India's sense of regional vulnerability and uncertain superpower support, the year saw the largest military exercises ever conducted in South Asia, "Operation Brass Tacks." These command and field exercises began in the summer and concluded in early 1987 with corps-level maneuvers and large-scale firing exercises near the Pakistani border. Brass Tacks was largely inspired by the new head of the Indian Army, General K. Sundarji, who has a reputation for professionalism and innovation. (In 1983 he had organized a symposium on nuclear proliferation and military strategy and written in favor of tactical nuclear weapons.) However, it can be assumed that more than miltary objectives were being met by Brass Tacks: The operation clearly sent a signal to Pakistan (and its outside supporters, such as the United States and China) that the Indian military could mobilize an overwhelming force on Pakistan's border at a time of the year when most of the Sino-Indian border is closed by snow.

The message was received and noted in Pakistan, where it led to a war scare. President Zia, more relaxed than most Pakistanis, noted that Brass Tacks involved an "unprecedented level" of concentration of forces for South Asia; he also speculated that such levels had "rarely" been seen in Europe and elsewhere. He ruled out the possibility of war between India and Pakistan and called for futher discussions on con-fidence-building measures between them.[30] Brass Tacks clearly revealed the need for such measures, inasmuch as it placed Indian forces in an ideal position to launch a surprise attack on Pakistan; this in turn forced Pakistan to reconsider its own force disposition and possibly draw units away from the western frontier with Afghanistan, thus weakening its defense against Soviet probes.

Finally, New Delhi remains wary of Pakistan's nuclear program. Indeed, the year 1986 saw considerable debate among Indian officials and commentators on the wisdom of militarizing India's nuclear program. This debate, which has actually raged for more than twenty years, was initially stimulated by the Chinese nuclear test. Successive Indian administrations have kept open the "option" (although Morarji Desai did pledge that *his* government would abandon any work on nuclear explosions). India has an advanced and largely indigenous civilian nuclear industry, a space exploration program that could produce a medium-range ballistic missile in the next few years, and a large stockpile of unsafeguarded plutonium. If it were to exercise its "option," India could become a minor nuclear weapon state very quickly—but it has thus far resisted this path. Because of India's advanced nuclear capability and the uncertainties surrounding the Pakistani program, the region runs a serious risk of slipping into a nuclear arms race that would enhance the security of neither country.[31]

Other Regional Issues

Important developments in two other South Asian countries and the region as a whole are worth noting. The regional state with the most critical internal problems remains Sri Lanka, which only four years ago had been South Asia's leading candidate as an economic and political success story. The bitter conflict between a segment of Sri Lanka's minority Tamils and the majority Sinhalese-dominated government continues unabated. The Tamils see themselves as a persecuted minority and have developed a stronghold in the northern districts of the island. The Tamils have also established bases in the Indian state of Tamil Nadu (although the previously enthusiastic support of their Tamil brethren had diminished greatly by late 1986). The Sinhalese see themselves as a Buddhist minority, threatened by the larger Indian Tamil population. Because several of the Tamil revolutionary groups are extreme Marxists or PLO-influenced radicals, India itself is wary of them; but it had tolerated some Tamil bases both because it would be politically unpopular to crush them and as a way of putting pressure on the Sri Lankan government to compromise with more moderate Tamil rebel groups. In turn, the Sri Lankan government has sought outside support against the insurgency, most notably from Israel and Pakistan. (The Israeli president, Chaim Herzog, paid a brief visit to Sri Lanka in November.)

The year was drawing to a close without any major breakthrough in Sri Lanka until, on November 8, the Tamil Nadu Indian state police rounded up a number of Tamil militants. This action triggered the movement of other militants back to Sri Lanka. Shortly afterward, Rajiv

Gandhi endorsed the Sri Lankan government proposals for a settlement.[32] The Sri Lankan strategy is to make a reasonable offer to the militants (in effect giving them political power in the northern and western segments of the island, which they already control) while crushing the groups that would not participate in such a settlement.

South Asia's second most populous state, Bangladesh, saw the lifting of martial law and the return of quasi-civilian government. On May 7 the party of President H. M. Ershad (the Bangladesh Nationalist party, or BNP) won the parliamentary elections. Ershad resigned as head of the Bangladesh Army in August and won a controversial election as president on October 15. Soon afterward he obtained parliamentary sanction for acts conducted under the martial law regime (the BNP controls more than the necessary two-thirds majority), and on November 10 martial law was formally ended. Ershad had governed for more than four years following a coup in 1982, but he still faces stiff opposition from various leftist, rightist, and centrist parties. Widely perceived as a competent but not exceptional leader, he has received considerable external foreign economic assistance; and despite staggering social and economic problems, Bangladesh is not quite the "basket case" that some had expected it to become. In addition, Ershad has not only skillfully managed relations with India but has also been in the forefront of the movement to promote a regional South Asian association (SAARC).

The year saw the full emergence of SAARC, the world's newest regional organization. Originally opposed by India and Pakistan (each suspected the other of being behind the idea), it has been embraced reluctantly by both, and Rajiv Gandhi was elected SAARC chairman at the mid-November 1986 annual meeting of regional leaders in Bangalore, India. A location for the SAARC Secretariat was agreed upon (Kathmandu, Nepal), as was a system of dues payments and a schedule for future meetings. SAARC will also sponsor and establish a number of regional centers (one for meteorology will be established in India, and an agricultural information center is to be located in Bangladesh). More than 200 seminars and meetings have already been held under SAARC auspices since 1984.

As important as these efforts are, SAARC's real significance lies in three other activities. First, as the Bangalore session demonstrated, periodic regional gatherings are useful places in which to conduct important bilateral political business. For example, Rajiv and Pakistan's Junejo had some discussions concerning the rising tensions between their countries and Rajiv and Sri Lanka's president J. R. Jayewardene conferred on the Sri Lankan insurgency. Second, SAARC has begun to interest itself in issues that have regional security implications, although its charter does not include military matters. Partly because of U.S.

encouragement, it has taken on narcotics and terrorism as subjects for regional cooperation; these will invariably lead to discussions concerning the ethnic and political irredentist movements that have spilled across the regional frontiers. Finally, SAARC members are considering ways in which they can forge a common position at various international fora. As an established regional organization, for example, SAARC may evolve a common position on GATT and other global negotiations.

Conclusion

Having emphasized the growth of South Asia as a strategically significant region, I foresee no dramatic breakdown of the evolving system through either pressures from without or forces from within. The year 1986 saw the intensification of trends that did not all run in the same direction. It also saw the maturation of both a regional and superpower understanding of the South Asian pentagonal strategic game and a willingness to play it for at least another round.

The United States and the Soviet Union both recognized the importance of dealing with India and Pakistan while retaining—or expanding—their ties with China. They have shared a desire to avoid an irrevocable commitment to any South Asian state: Secretary Weinberger's answers to the press on the United States' position on Indo-Pakistani relations were startlingly similar to Gorbachev's response to queries on the Soviet positionvis-à-vis India and China. Both men expressed the desire that friends would not quarrel and the belief that such quarrels would not lead to war.

Pressures from the region on the two superpowers to enhance their support were notable during 1986 and will continue into 1987 and beyond. Pakistan wants an enhanced commitment to its security from the United States and, failing that, would like to see a continuation of U.S. aid while its own nuclear program remains protected. India seeks—but has not gotten—reassurance from the Soviets on China and Pakistan, but it is also wary of Soviet pressures on Pakistan, given that these pressures will likely lead to enhanced U.S.-Pakistan ties. Finally, both South Asian powers fear that their importance to the superpowers has not yet reached the point where the superpowers could be counted on in a purely regional crisis; both also fear the havoc to the region in the event of a major crisis that did involve the superpowers.

The prognosis for the near term is more of the same. Despite a flurry of activity late in the year, the Soviet Union is unlikely to improve its position in Afghanistan. Nor is it likely to withdraw soon, leaving the country (and its clients) to their respective fates. The United States will continue to enhance its standing in India, which is likely to tolerate continued U.S. arms sales to Pakistan. That country, in turn, will probably not push its nuclear program to the point of no return (namely, a test or other firm evidence of possession of a nuclear weapon), which would mean a break with the United States and a nuclear arms race with India.

In short, South Asia is changing in significant ways. It will be only a matter of time until Pakistan and India can very quickly convert their nuclear programs to military purposes. There is as yet no sign of doctrinal development, which would be a clear indicator of India's and Pakistan's nuclear intentions. Not only will they both have to evolve a strategy for dealing with the threat each poses to the other; they must also take into account the strategies of existing nuclear powers (for Pakistan, this assessment must include Israel) and explore ways in which their nuclear military forces can be put to the service of their regional diplomacies. For both India and Pakistan, this expanded regional diplomacy could include a role in the Gulf region and elsewhere in the Indian Ocean littoral.

The other regional security development that will affect the superpowers' policies is the emergence of India as at least a modest supraregional power, with Pakistan trailing not far behind. India's power-projection capabilities are growing slowly but steadily; India and Pakistan now train at home and abroad a large number of Middle Eastern, Asian, and African officers; India sees itself as a source of relatively high technology for less-developed countries and as a source of middle-level technology for the more backward or inflexible Communist states, not excluding the Soviet Union. Ironically, the emergence of both India and Pakistan as strategic middle-level countries is chiefly hampered by their fixation on the threat that each sees in the other. Their hostile relationship has been destructive to broader ambitions. Indeed, whether it can be contained by such regional institutions as SAARC or successfully dampened by outside powers such as the United States and then transformed into a stable form of isometric state building remains to be seen.

Notes

1. See Zalmay Khalilzad, "The Soviet Union and Afghanistan," paper presented to the Second U.S.-Pakistan Bilateral Forum, Islamabad, October 27–30, 1986.

2. See Khalilzad, "The Soviet Union and Pakistan"; and *Economist*, October 25, 1986.

3. By year's end, almost 700 incursions into Pakistani territory had taken place; about one-third of these were classified as "serious," involving penetration of 5 kilometers or more or the release of ordnance.

4. For a summary of Soviet innovations, see Anwar Nasir, "New Soviet Gameplan," *Far Eastern Economic Review*, November 27, 1986.

5. *Washington Post*, May 12, 1986.

6. According to Amnesty International, Soviet officials were often present and directed the torture. See *Economist*, November 22, 1986. See also United Nations General Assembly, *Report of the Economic and Social Council, Report of Human Rights in Afghanistan: Note by the Secretary General* (Interim report by the Special Rapporteur of the Commission on Human Rights, Felix Ermacora), UN Document A/41/778, October 31, 1986.

7. The Soviets withdrew six regiments (8,000 troops) beginning on October 15 and arranged for heavy publicity. The timing of the withdrawal (just before Gorbachev's Rejkavik summit with President Reagan), the irrelevance of many of the units (some were air defense regiments, and the Mujahiddin have no aircraft), as well as suspicion that they were merely replaced by fresh units or had been introduced to Afghanistan solely for the purpose of public withdrawal, led most observers to regard the exercise as a publicity stunt—not as a signal of Soviet seriousness about a negotiated settlement and withdrawal.

8. This offer was contained in a letter to UN Assistant Secretary General Diego Cordovez on December 10, 1985.

9. For a comprehensive history of the Geneva negotiations through mid-1986, see Richard P. Cronin, "Afghanistan: United Nations–Sponsored Negotiations: An Annotated Chronology and Analysis," Congressional Research Service, Library of Congress, publ. 86-792F, July 23, 1986.

10. Some of the concessions, apparently inspired by the government of Pakistan, appear in *The Muslim* (Islamabad), April 3, 1986.

11. Pakistan refused to negotiate directly with the Afghan regime, which is represented by the Soviets. Iran has been consulted on the progress of these talks by several parties, including the UN negotiator Diego Cordovez.

12. Cronin, "Afghanistan," p. 24.

13. For background, see Stephen P. Cohen, *The Pakistan Army* (Berkeley, Calif.: University of California Press, 1984); and Hasan Askari Rizvi, *The Military and Politics in Pakistan* (Lahore: Progressive Publishers, 1986).

14. There has also been sharp disagreement in Pakistan's national assembly over the pending Shariat (Islamic law) bill and the degree to which it will follow Sunni or Shia legal practices.

15. There have been high growth rates for the economy over the past two years (between 7.5 and 8.5 percent), although the long-term prognosis is less promising, given Pakistan's high birth rate, increasing debt burden, and low literacy rate. Still, Pakistan may soon be a "middle-income" country.

16. The Symington amendment to the International Security Assistance Act (P.L. 95-92) requires, among other things, a cutoff of assistance funds to any country that receives materials or technology that could enrich uranium, if that country has not placed such items under inspection, or has not placed all of its nuclear establishment under inspection. (The parallel Glenn amendment restricts assistance to countries that have imported reprocessing technology that could yield plutonium—but this does not apply to Pakistan.) In 1981 Congress

voted a six-year waiver of the Symington amendment for Pakistan; it also required the president to certify in writing that the termination of assistance to Pakistan would have a serious, adverse affect on U.S. interests, that Pakistan would not acquire or develop nuclear weapons, and that continued assistance "contributed significantly" to nonproliferation objectives.

17. Pakistan had originally asked for a $6.5 billion follow-on program, arguing that because of inflation and Pakistan's rising debt burden this amount would match the earlier figure. For complete details, and for a concise history of the U.S.-Pakistan security relationship, see Herbert G. Hagerty, "United States Assistance to Pakistan," paper presented to the Second Bilateral Seminar on U.S.-Pakistan Relations, Islamabad, October 26–30, 1986.

18. Hagerty, "United States Assistance," p. 30.

19. For a survey of available systems, see Ashley J. Tellis, "Hawkeyes for Pakistan," *Journal of South Asian and Middle Eastern Studies* 10, no. 1 (Fall 1986), pp. 36–66.

20. There are several useful studies of the regional military balance, all of which conclude that India is decisively ahead of Pakistan. See Robert G. Wirsing, "The Arms Race in South Asia: Implications for the United States," *Asian Survey* 25, no. 3 (March 1985), pp. 265–291; and Jerrold F. Elkin and W. Andrew Ritezel, "The Indo-Pakistani Military Balance," *Asian Survey* 26, no. 5 (May 1986), pp. 518–538.

21. For Zia's remarks, see Foreign Broadcast Information Service (FBIS), *South Asia* March 19, 1986.

22. For press accounts, see *Washington Post* July 15 and 21, 1986.

23. *Dawn* (Karachi), October 6, 1986.

24. See the article by Robert Woodward in *Washington Post*, November 4, 1986.

25. For an analysis based on interviews with senior Pakistani military strategists, see Cohen, *The Pakistan Army*.

26. See the editorial and article in *Times of India* August 16, 1986 and the inteview with the notably professional head of the Punjab police, Julio Rubeiro, in *Gentleman* (Bombay), October 1986, in which Rubeiro is quoted as saying that "I do not think they [the terrorists] are going to Pakistan anymore on a big scale."

27. An informed evaluation of Rajiv and his cohort can be found in Steven R. Weisman, "The Rajiv Generation," *New York Times*, April 20, 1986.

28. The text of the Gandhi-Gorbachev news conference of November 28 is in FBIS, *USSR International Affairs*, December 2, 1986.

29. India and United States had signed a Memorandum of Understanding on defense-related technology in 1984; implementation procedures and nuclear assurances language were completed in 1985; and a large variety of items were subsequently cleared for commercial sale to India. These items included tubes for radar sets, night vision technology, and a co-produced Garrett jet engine (for dual military and civilian use in India's new Dornier aircraft); the Indians are also seriously considering licensed production of LN2500 General Electric gas turbine engines for use in their new patrol craft and frigates.

30. Quoted in *Dawn* (Karachi), November 13, 1986.

31. One of the few original ideas on containing the Indo-Pakistani nuclear arms race was offered by the distinguished Indian scholar R.V.R. Chandrasekhara Rao, who proposed that the two states agree to a time-bound "no first make" pact. Thus, the region's nuclear arms race could be deferred for at least three years, until the end of Rajiv's and Zia's terms of office in 1990. See *Chicago Tribune*, November 13, 1986.

32. *New York Times*, November 18, 1986.

Acronyms

AASU	Aviation Armies of the Soviet Union
AAW	anti-air warfare
ABL	Armored Box Launcher
ABM	antiballistic missile
ADs	Airborne Divisions
AFB	Air Force Base
ALCM	Air-Launched Cruise Missile
AMRAAM	Advanced Medium Range Air-to-Air Missile
ANC	African National Congress
ANZUS	Australia New Zealand United States (Treaty)
ARDE	Revolutionary Democratic Alliance
ASAT	anti-satellite
ASDF	Air Self-Defense Force
ASEAN	Association of Southeast Asian Nations
ASW	Air-to-Surface Weapon; Anti-submarine Warfare
ATB	Advanced Technology Bomber
ATM	anti-tactical missile
AWACS	Airborne Warning and Control System
BAOR	British Army of the Rhine
BMD	Ballistic Missile Defense
BMP	armored personnel carrier
CD	Committee on Disarmament
CDD	Coastal Defense Division
CDE	Conference on Disarmament in Europe
CDR	Conseil Democratique Revolutionaire
CG	Guided Missile Cruiser
CGN	Guided Missile Cruiser, nuclear
CIA	Central Intelligence Agency
CMEA	Council for Mutual Economic Assistance
CMRN	Comité Militaire pour le Renouveau National

COMECON	Council for Mutual Economic Assistance
CPSU	Communist Party of the Soviet Union
C^3I	command, control, communications, and intelligence
DARPA	Defense Advanced Research Projects Agency
DDG	Guided Missile Destroyer
DEW	Distant Early Warning System
DIVAD	Division Air Defense
DMZ	Demilitarized Zone
DoD	Department of Defense
DSCS III	Defense Satellite Communication System, phase III
EC	European Communities
ECM	electronic counter measures
EFA	European Fighter Aircraft
EHF	Extremely High Frequency
ELF	Eritrean Liberation Front; Extremely Low Frequency
EMP	electromagnetic pulse
EMT	equivalent megatonnage
EPDM	Ethiopian Peoples Democratic Movement
EPLF	Eritrean Peoples Liberation Front
ERIS	Exoatmospheric Reentry Vehicle Interceptor Subsystem
ET	emerging technologies
FAAD	forward-area air defenses
FAL	Armed Forces of Liberation
FAR	Force d'Action Rapide
FARC	Colombian Revolution-Armed Forces
FARN	Armed Forces of National Resistance
FDN	Nicaraguan Democratic Force
FMLN	Farabundo Marti Front for National Liberation
FOFA	Follow-on Forces Attack
FPLM	Forças Populares de Libertação de Moçambique
FRG	Federal Republic of Germany
FROG	Free Rocket Over Ground
GATT	General Agreement on Tariffs and Trade
GDP	Gross Domestic Product
GDR	German Democratic Republic
GLCM	Ground-Launched Cruise Missile
HML	Hard Mobile Launcher

HOE	Homing Overlay Experiment
IADB	InterAmerican Development Bank
ICBM	Intercontinental Ballistic Missile
IFF	Identification Friend or Foe
IMF	International Monetary Fund
INF	Intermediate-Range Nuclear Force
IRBM	Intermediate-Range Ballistic Missile
JCS	Joint Chiefs of Staff
JSTARS	Joint Surveillance and Target Attack Radar System
JTACMS	Joint Tactical Missile System
KAL	Korean Air Lines
LAF	Lebanese Armed Forces
LCC	launch control center
LDP	Liberal Democratic Party
MBFR	Mutual and Balanced Force Reduction
MIA	Missing in Action
MIRV	Multiple Independently-Targetable Reentry Vehicle
MLRS	Multiple Launch Rocket System
MNF	Multi-National Force
M-19	Movement of 19 April
MNR	Resistência Nacional Moçambicana
MPLA	Popular Movement for the Liberation of Angola
MRDs	Motorized Rifle Divisions
MSBS	Mer-Sol Balistique Stategique
MSDF	Maritime Self-Defense Force
MX	Missile, Experimental
NATO	North Atlantic Treaty Organization
NORAD	North American Air Defense
NUM	National Union of Mineworkers
OAS	Organization of American States
OAU	Organization of African Unity
OLF	Oromo Liberation Front
OMG	Operational Maneuver Group
OPEC	Organization of Petroleum Exporting Countries
OSD	Office of the Secretary of Defense
OTA	Office of Technology Assessment

OTH-B	Over the Horizon Backscatter (radar)
PAC	Pan-African Congress
PACAF	Pacific Air Force PGT Guatemalan Labor Party
PLO	Palestine Liberation Organization
PNC	Palestine National Council
PRC	People's Republic of China
PRTC	Revolutionary Party of Central American Workers
R&D	research and development
RAP	reliable acoustic path
RDF	Rapid Deployment Force
RFP	request for proposals
ROK	Republic of Korea
RPV	Remotely Piloted Vehicle
RSAF	Royal Saudi Air Force
RSI	rationalization, standardization, interoperability
RVs	reentry vehicles
SADCC	Southern Africa Development and Coordination Conference
SADF	South African Defense Force
SALT	Strategic Arms Limitation Talks
SAMs	surface-to-air missiles
SDF	Self-Defense Force
SDI	Strategic Defense Initiative
SDIO	Strategic Defense Initiative Organization
SEAL	sea-air-land
SICBM	Small Intercontinental Ballistic Missile
SLBM	sea-launched ballistic missile
SLCM	sea-launched cruise missile
SOF	Special Operations Forces
SPD	Social Democratic Party
SPLA	Sudan Peoples Liberation Army
SPLM	Sudan Peoples Liberation Movement
SRAM	Short-Range Attack Missile
SSBN	Fleet Ballistic Missile Submarine, nuclear-powered
SSN	submarine, nuclear-powered
START	Strategic Arms Reduction Talks
SUBAC	Submarine Advanced Combat System
SWAPO	Southwest African People's Organization
TDs	Tank Divisions
TEL	transporter-erector-launcher

TLAM/N	Tomahawk land attack missile/nuclear
TOW	Tube-Launched, Optically Tracked, Wire-Guided
TPLF	Tigray Peoples Liberation Front
UDF	United Democratic Front
UNITA	National Union for the Total Independence of Angola
URNG	Guatemalan National Revolutionary Unity
VLF	Very Low Frequency
VLS	vertical launch system
Voyska-PVO	National Air Defense Troops
VSTOL	Vertical/short take-off and landing
WEU	Western European Union
WTO	Warsaw Treaty Organization
ZANU	Zimbabwe African National Union
ZAPU	Zimbabwe African People's Union

About the Contributors

Barry M. Blechman and **Edward N. Luttwak** are senior fellows in strategic studies at the Center for Strategic and International Studies. Dr. Blechman is also president of Defense Forecasts, Inc., a research and analysis enterprise in Washington, D.C. They have each written about foreign affairs and national security issues for more than 20 years.

Michael W. Clough is senior fellow for African Studies at the Council on Foreign Relations, New York. In 1986 he served as the study director of the Secretary of State's Advisory Committee on South Africa. He was the American director of the United States–South Africa Leader Exchange Program. He has taught at the University of Wisconsin and the U.S. Naval Postgraduate School.

Stephen P. Cohen is a professor of political science and director of the Regional Security Project (Program in Arms Control, Disarmament, and International Security) at the University of Illinois, Urbana. Professor Cohen was a member of the Policy Planning Staff, U.S. Department of State, from 1985 to 1987.

Kimberly Ann Elliott is a research associate at the Institute for International Economics. She is the coauthor of *Economic Sanctions Reconsidered, Trade Protection in the United States: 31 Case Studies* and *Auction Quotas in United States Trade Policy.*

Gary C. Hufbauer is the Wallenberg Professor of International Financial Diplomacy at Georgetown University. Hufbauer was formerly deputy assistant secretary for international trade and investment policy of the U.S. Treasury, the director of the international trade staff at the U.S. Treasury, and professor of economics at the University of New Mexico.

Herbert S. Levine is a professor of economics at the University of Pennsylvania and a specialist on Soviet economic planning and growth.

He has traveled extensively and lectured in the Soviet Union, Eastern Europe, and China. He is the chairman of the Board of Directors of Plan-Econ, Inc. (a Washington-based research firm), a trustee of the National Council on Soviet and East European Research, and a member of the ACLS-SSRS Joint Committee on Soviet Studies.

Alan Platt is a former chief of the arms transfer division of the U.S. Arms Control and Disarmament Agency and a former senior specialist on Europe at The RAND Corporation. Platt now works as a consultant on international and security affairs in Washington, D.C.

Sally Shelton-Colby is presently a consultant to Bankers Trust Co. and formerly a U.S. ambassador and deputy assistant secretary of state for Latin America. Ms. Shelton-Colby has focused on political and economic affairs in Latin America for almost 20 years.

James J. Townsend is president of Information Strategies, a Washington-based defense consulting firm, and an adjunct fellow at CSIS. He is a specialist in U.S. and Soviet military forces and coauthor of *The Future of Military Aviation*.

Other Titles Published in Cooperation with the Center for Strategic and International Studies

Northern Europe: Security Issues for the 1990s, edited by Paul M. Cole and Douglas M. Hart

Making Government Work: From White House to Congress, edited by Robert E. Hunter, Wayne L. Berman, and John F. Kennedy

NATO—The Next Generation, edited by Robert E. Hunter

Modern Weapons and Third World Powers, Rodney W. Jones and Steven A. Hildreth

The Emerging Pacific Community, edited by Robert L. Downen and Bruce J. Dickson

The Cuban Revolution: 25 Years Later, edited by Hugh S. Thomas, Georges A. Fauriol, and Juan Carlos Weiss

The U.S. and the World Economy: Policy Alternatives for New Realities, edited by John Yochelson

Bioenergy and Economic Development: Planning for Biomass Energy Programs in the Third World, William Ramsay

Forecasting U.S. Electricity Demand: Trends and Methodologies, edited by Adela Bolet

U.S.-Japanese Energy Relations: Cooperation and Competition, edited by Charles K. Ebinger and Ronald A. Morse

National Security and Strategic Minerals: An Analysis of U.S. Dependence on Foreign Sources of Cobalt, Barry M. Blechman

Index

Abbas, Abu, 174, 175
ABM. *See* Antiballistic missile
Achille Lauro, 85, 164, 173-174, 175
Afghanistan, 66, 76, 178, 213, 214-218, 220, 221, 231, 233(n7)
Afghan War, 214-218. *See also* Afghanistan
African National Congress (ANC), 143, 147-148, 149, 151
Aganbegyan, Abel, 5
Airborne warning and control system (AWACS), 65, 222
Alfonsin, Raúl, 187-188
Alma Ata riots, 9
ANC. *See* African National Congress
Andropov, Yuri, 120-121, 124, 127
Angola, 136, 137-138, 141, 143, 159-161
Antiballistic missile (ABM)
 systems, 33, 53
 Treaty, 47, 53, 54
 See also Ballistic missile(s), defense
Antisatellite system(s) (ASAT), 53
Argentina, 97, 109(n18), 187-189, 209, 210
Arias, Oscar, 204
Arms control, xi, 10-13, 27, 44, 54-55, 57, 92, 111(n41)
ASAT. *See* Antisatellite system(s)
Aspin, Les, 22, 33
Assured survival policy, 32
ATB. *See* Bombers, Advanced Technology

Attrition warfare, 28
Australia, 97
Austral Plan, 188-189, 190
AWACS. *See* Airborne warning and control system
Ayatollah Khomeini. *See* Khomeini, Ayatollah
Azcona, Jose, 203, 204

Baker, James, 99, 102. *See also* Baker Plan
Baker Plan, 186
Balkans, 180
Ballistic missile(s), 10-13, 40, 42, 45-46
 defense (BMD), 11, 29, 32, 44. *See also* Antiballistic missile; Strategic Defense Initiative
 elimination of, 54
 Galosh, 53
 intercontinental (ICBM), 11-12, 32-34, 37, 39, 43(table), 46, 56, 58(table)
 intermediate range (INF), 13, 178
 Minuteman, 33
 MX, 32-33, 37
 Pershing II, 25, 36, 55
 SS-20, 36, 41-42
 submarine-launched (SLBM), 34, 40, 43(table), 58(table)
 Trident, 34, 37, 44-45, 47
 See also Cruise missiles; Nuclear weapons
Banco, Virgilio, 196, 197
Banda, H. Kamuzu, 156

Bangladesh, 213, 230
Barletta, Nicholas Ardito, 206
Barnala, S. S., 224
Beagle Islands, 187
Beira corridor project, 138
Belgium, 36
Bentsen-Gephardt-Rostenkowski surcharge bill, 94
Berlinguer, Enrico, 173
Betancur, Belisario, 196
Bhutto, Benazir, 219–220
Bhutto, Zulfiqar Ali, 219, 220
BMD. *See* Ballistic missile(s), defense
Bolivia, 198
Bombers
 Advanced Technology (ATB), 35, 37. *See also* Stealth aircraft
 and arms control, 57
 B-1, 32, 34, 37
 B-52, 34
 U.S. vs. Soviet Union, 58(table)
Bosporus and Dardanelles Straits, 181
Botha, P. W., 136, 142, 152, 153
Botha, Roloef "Pik," 143, 155
Botswana, 137, 143, 150
Bradley, Bill, 100
Brasilia, 99, 190
Bravo, Cardinal Miguel Obando y, 205
Brazil, 94, 97, 98, 99, 187, 189–192, 209, 210, 211
Brezhnev, Leonid, 7, 84, 119

Canada, 26, 94, 95, 96, 103
Cartagena Group, 199
Carter, Jimmy, 30, 158
Casa Banana, 155
Castro, Fidel, 210
Catholic Church, 189, 191, 193, 201, 205
Cerezo, Vinicio, 202, 203
Challenger, 49
Chemical warfare, 62
Cherednichenko, M., 84

Chernavin, Vladimir, 68
Chernenko, Constantine, 121
Chile, 187, 192–194, 201, 209, 211
China. *See* People's Republic of China
Chissano, Joaquim, 143, 154, 156
Chun, 18
CIA. *See* United States, Central Intelligence Agency
Clancy, Tom, 24
Clausewitz, Karl von, 29
Cocaine, 198
Colombia, 196–197, 199
Command, control, communication, and intelligence systems (C^3I), 64–65, 72
Common Market, 170
Commonwealth nations, 136, 139
 Eminent Persons Group (EPG), 149, 150–151
Communist Party
 in Afghanistan, 216
 in Chile, 192–193
 and CPSU Congress, 208
 in Europe, 13
 in Greece, 179
 in People's Republic of China, 16
 in Portugal, 171
 in Soviet Union, 7–8, 9
 in Third World, 209
Contadora, 187, 199
Contras, xii, 187, 199, 203, 204, 206, 210. *See also* Iran-Contra affair; Nicaragua
Cordovez, Diego, 217
Cossiga, Francesco, 175
Costa Rica, 204–205
Craxi, Bettino, 174
Crocker, Chester, 145, 161
Crowe, William J., 54
Cruise missiles, 25, 35, 36, 41, 42, 52, 54, 55, 72. *See also* Nuclear weapons
Cruzado Plan, 190
C^3I systems. *See* Command, control, communication, and intelligence systems

Cuba, 20, 159, 160, 161, 208, 209–210
Cyprus, 178, 181
Czechoslovakia, 53

Dabengwa, Dumiso, 158
Darman, Richard, 96
de Braganca, Aquino, 154
Debt crisis
  in Latin America, 4, 186, 210
  in Third World, 93, 98–100, 102, 211
DECA. *See* Defense and Economic Cooperation Agreement
Defense and Economic Cooperation Agreement (DECA), 176, 178, 182, 183
de la Madrid, Miguel, 201
Delvalle, Eric Arturo, 206
DeMita, Ciriaco, 175
Dense pack deployment plan, 33
Desai, Morarji, 229
Deterrence, 29, 30, 55, 72, 85
DIA. *See* United States, Defense Intelligence Agency
Directed-energy weapons, 50. *See also* Laser weapons
DoD. *See* United States, Department of Defense
Dollars, xiii
  decline of, 103, 110(n26)
  devaluation of, 2
  overvaluation of, 101–102
dos Santos, Jose Eduardo, 159, 160–161
Duarte, José Napoléon, 199, 207, 208
Dyke, Lionel, 158

East Germany. *See* German Democratic Republic
Economic Recovery Tax Act, 101
EEC. *See* European Economic Community
Egypt, 14
El Salvador, 205, 207–208

Enders, Thomas, 167
England. *See* Great Britain
EPG. *See* Commonwealth nations, Eminent Persons Group
Ershad, H. M., 230
Ethiopia, 20
European Economic Community (EEC), 95, 97, 107
  and Greece, 178, 179
  and Portugal, 170
  and South Africa, 136, 151
  and Spain, 165
Export-Import Bank, 94

Falkland Islands, 29, 187
Farnborough Air Show, 66
Federal Republic of Germany (FRG), 4, 13, 14, 30, 36, 93, 95, 101, 102, 103, 104, 106, 107
Fraga, Manuel, 166
France, 44, 97, 228
  and NATO, 75–76
  and Portugal, 170
  and SDI, 76
  strategic forces of, 45–46, 48(table)
FRG. *See* Federal Republic of Germany
Fundidora, 201

Gabriel, Charles A., 65
Gandhi, Indira, 226
Gandhi, Rajiv, 222, 224, 225, 226, 229–230
García, Alan, 194–195
Gates, Robert M., 52
GATT. *See* General Agreement on Tariffs and Trade
GDR. *See* German Democratic Republic
General Agreement on Tariffs and Trade (GATT), 92, 98, 231
  member countries of, 97, 200
Geneva talks, 12, 217
German Democratic Republic (GDR), 53

G-5. *See* Group of Five
Godavari, 227
Goldfield, Harold, 178
Goldwater-Nichols Defense
    Reorganization Act, 2
Gonzalez, Felipe, 165
Gorbachev, Mikhail, 1, 23, 44, 54,
    85, 107, 127
  administrative changes of, 123,
    126
  and Afghanistan, 76, 77, 217. *See
    also* Afghanistan; Afghan War
  foreign initiatives of, xii
  growth acceleration policy of,
    122–123
  and India, 224, 226–227, 231
  and People's Republic of China,
    77, 231
  reforms of, xii, 5, 8–10, 120,
    122–127, 133, 134
  South American trip of, 209
Gramm-Rudman legislation, 63, 93,
    169, 172
Great Britain, 13, 91, 101, 228
  and African National Congress,
    149
  Alliance party in, 44
  and Argentina, 187
  defense spending, 22
  economic decline of, 3
  Labour party in, 44
  nuclear forces, 30, 34, 36, 44–45,
    48(table)
  nuclear targeting policy, 45
  Trident program in, 44–45
  and Zimbabwe, 159
Greece, 176–181
Grenada, 85
Ground Wave Emergency Network,
    35
Group of Five (G-5), 93, 94, 102,
    108(n4)
Group of Rio de Janeiro, 187, 199
G-2 initiative, 103
Guatemala, 202–203
Gurevich, Mikhail, 80
Gurkhas, 225

Hackett, Sir John, 24
Helicopters, 61, 66–67, 141, 205,
    209, 215
Helms, Jesse, 159, 207
Herzog, Chaim, 229
Herzog, Jesús Silva, 200
Honduras, 187, 199, 203–204
Hong Kong, 17, 95
Honwana, Fernando, 154
Howe, Sir Geoffrey, 151
Hungary, 9, 53
Hussein, Saddam, 15, 16

ICBM. *See* Ballistic missile(s),
    intercontinental
IMF. *See* International Monetary
    Fund
India, 24, 47, 97, 213–214, 222,
    224–229, 230, 231, 234(n29),
    235(n31)
Indian Ocean, 228, 232
INF. *See* Ballistic missile(s),
    intermediate range
International Monetary Fund (IMF),
    99, 109(n18), 186, 190, 191–
    192, 195, 198, 200, 211
Iran, 14–16, 77, 130, 213, 218, 223.
    See also Iran-Contra affair;
    Iran-Iraq War
Iran-Contra affair, xii, 1, 107, 172,
    176, 187, 199, 206. *See also*
    Contras
Iran-Iraq War, 14–16, 21, 76, 222.
    See also Iran
Iraq, 14–16. *See also* Iran-Iraq War
Israel, 81, 94, 96, 229
  nuclear capabilities, 46–47,
    48(table)
  Shin Beth, 47
Italy, 36, 103, 170, 172–176

Jackson, Jesse, 160
Jane's Fighting Ships, 40
Japan, 4, 14, 26, 94, 95, 96, 101,
    102, 103, 104, 106, 107
  Defense Agency, 77, 78

Defense Principle of 1976, 78
  economy of, 18
  Liberal Democratic party (LDP)
    in, 19, 20
  taxes in, 110(n29)
  unemployment in, 18–19, 20
Jatoi, Ghulam Mustafa, 219
Jayewardene, J. R., 230
J-curve analysis, 102
Jhawar, Killi, 215
Joint STARS. *See* USAF/Army Joint
  Surveillance Target Attack
  Radar System
Jordan, 14
Junejo, Mohammed Khan, 218, 219, 222, 230

Kabul, 214, 216
Karmal, Babrak, 216, 217
Kashmir, 226
Kennedy, Richard T., 223
Khad, 216
Khan, A. Q., 223
Khan, Wali, 220
Kharg Island, 15
Khomeini, Ayatollah, 16
Khuzestan, 77
Kiichi Miyazawa, 103
Kinetic-energy weapons, 50, 51
Kissinger, Henry, 4
Koeberg nuclear power reactor, 148
Kohl, Helmut, 55, 62

Lajes base, 171, 172
Lampedusa island, 174, 175
La Prensa, 205
Laser weapons, 53–54. *See also*
  Directed-energy weapons
Latham, Donald C., 41
LDP. *See* Japan, Liberal Democratic
  party in
Lebanon, 14
Lesotho, 137, 139, 143
LIBOR. *See* London Inter-Bank
  Offer Rate
Libya, 85, 130, 164, 169, 174, 175, 179, 180, 182, 184, 210

Lindstrom, Talbot, 227
Lobos, Rodolfo, 203
London Inter-Bank Offer Rate
  (LIBOR), 99, 109(n18)
Longowal, H. S., 224
Long-Range Theater Nuclear Forces, 36
Lugar, Richard, 162
Lusaka Accord, 136

Machel, Samora, 154, 155, 156
Machungo, Mario, 155
MacMahon Line, 226
Macmillan, Harold, 3
Malan, M. P. Weynaud, 152, 156
Malawi, 137
Mandela, Nelson, 148. *See also*
  African National Congress
Mansfield, Mike, 107
Masud, Ahmad Shah, 215
Matabeleland, 157, 158
Mbundu peoples, 159
Mexico, 93, 98–99, 186, 199, 200–202, 209, 211
Mikoyan, Artem, 80
Mil, Mikhail, 66, 80
Mil Design Bureau, 66
MilStar satellite system, 36
MIRV. *See* Multiple independently
  targetable reentry vehicle
Miskito Indians, 205
MNR. *See* Resistencia Nacional
  Mocambicana
Monge, Luis Alberto, 204
Mongolia, 77
Moore, John, 40
Morskoi Sbornik, 68
Mozambique, 136, 137–138, 143, 154–157
MPLA. *See* Popular Movement for
  the Liberation of Angola
Mugabe, Robert, 154, 157, 158, 159
Mujahiddin, 213, 214, 215, 216, 233(n7). *See also* Afghanistan;
  Afghan War
Multiple independently targetable
  reentry vehicle (MIRV), 46, 57

Muzorewa, Abel, 142

Najib. *See* Najibullah, Sayid Mohammad
Najibullah, Sayid Mohammad, 216, 217
Namibia, 137, 141, 160
National Command Authority, 35
National Forum (NF), 146
National Union for the Total Independence of Angola (UNITA), 143, 159, 160–161
NATO. *See* North Atlantic Treaty Organization
Net assessment, 24, 28, 29, 59
Netherlands, 36
New Nation, 147
New York Times, 152
New Zealand, 97
NF. *See* National Forum
Nicaragua, 20, 187, 199, 204, 205–206, 211. *See also* Contras
Nkomati Accord, 136, 148, 154, 155, 156
Nkomo, Joshua, 157
Noriega, Manuel, 206, 207
North, Oliver, 174
North Atlantic Treaty Organization (NATO), 22–23, 25, 36, 54, 66, 92, 208
  and chemical warfare, 62
  combat aircraft, 73(fig.)
  defense spending, 26, 72
  and deterrence, 31
  Follow-On Forces Attack concept, 26
  and Greece, 176, 178, 179, 180
  and Italy, 173, 174, 176
  Maritime forces, 74(fig.)
  and Portugal, 171
  and SDI, 51, 72
  and Spain, 164, 165, 166, 184–185(n1)
  and Turkey, 181
  and U.S. nuclear guarantee, 72
  vs. Warsaw Pact, 71–75
  weaknesses of, 70
North Korea, 78
Norway, 22
Nuclear weapons, xi, 29, 42, 226
  and conventional weapons systems, 71
  and India, 223, 229, 235(n31)
  inventories of, 56(fig.)
  and NATO, 55
  and Pakistan, 221, 223, 229, 232, 234(n16), 235(n31)
  U.S. vs. Soviet concepts of, 55
  Western consensus on, 30
  See also Arms control; Ballistic missile(s); Cruise missiles
Nunn, Sam, 107

OAS. *See* Organization of American States
Ogarkov, Nikolay V., 5, 66
O'Neill, Tip, 94
Operation Blast Furnace, 198
Operation Brass Tacks, 222, 228
Ordonez, Francisco Fernandez, 167
Organization of American States (OAS), 187, 199
Ovimbundu peoples, 159
Ozal, Turgut, 182, 183

PAC. *See* Pan-Africanist Congress
Pakistan
  and Afghan refugees, 218
  and Afghan War, 215, 216, 217, 232(n3)
  and economic growth, 233(n15)
  funding for Post-FY 1987 Program, 221(table)
  and India, 213–214, 224, 228, 229
  nuclear capabilities, 47, 221, 223–224, 229
  and SAARC, 230
  Shia in, 220
  and United States, 216, 219, 220–222, 234(nn16, 17), 235(n31)
Pakistan Muslim League, 219

Pakistan People's party (PPP), 219–220
Palestine Liberation Organization (PLO), 14, 175, 222, 229
Pan-Africanist Congress (PAC), 148
Panama, 199, 206–207
Panama Canal, 206, 207
Panamanian Defense Force (PDF), 206, 207
Papandreou, Andreas, 164, 176, 178–179, 180
Papoulias, Karalos, 179
Paraguay, 201
Paris Club, 190
Partido Revolucionario Institucional (PRI), 201, 202
Pashtuns, 216
Pathan-Muhajir riots, 218
Pave Paws radar systems, 35
Paz Estenssoro, Victor, 198
PDF. *See* Panamanian Defense Force
PDPA. *See* People's Democratic party of Afghanistan
Peacekeeper. *See* Ballistic missile(s), MX
People's Democratic party of Afghanistan (PDPA), 216, 217
People's Republic of China (PRC), 24, 77
  Communist party in, 16
  and India, 226, 227, 228
  liberalization in, 8, 16–17
  military acquisitions of, 78
  modernization in, 16–17
  and Nicaragua, 205
  nuclear forces, 46, 48(table)
  and Pakistan, 223
  People's Liberation Army, 46
  and South Asia, 213–214
  and Soviet Union, 77, 231
Perle, Richard, 183
Perónists, 188–189
Peru, 187, 194–196, 209, 210
Philippines, 16, 17
Pinochet, Augusto, 192, 193, 194

PLO. *See* Palestine Liberation Organization
Poland, 178
Popular Movement for the Liberation of Angola (MPLA), 159
Portugal, 170–172
PPP. *See* Pakistan People's party
PRC. *See* People's Republic of China
PRI. *See* Partido Revolucionario Institucional
Punjab, 224

Rawlings, James, 158
Reagan, Ronald, 34, 44, 54, 85, 94, 95
  and *Achille Lauro* hijacking, 174
  and chemical weapons, 62
  and Portugal, 172
  and South Africa, 150, 162
  and tax increases, 104
  See also Reagan administration
Reagan administration, xii, xiii, 2, 5, 100, 108(n3)
  and ABM Treaty, 47
  and arms control, 10
  and constructive engagement, 161
  defense buildup, 60, 84, 106
  and defense spending, 22. *See also* United States, defense spending
  and Iran-Contra affair, 107. *See also* Iran-Contra affair
  and Mozambique, 163
  and SDI, 12. *See also* Strategic Defense Initiative
  strategic modernization program, 35
  trade policy of, 94–96
  and UNITA, 160, 162
  and U.S. dollar, 102. *See also* Dollar
  See also United States
Recession, world, 103, 104
Red Storm Rising (Clancy), 24

254   Index

Resistencia Nacional Mocambicana (MNR), 138, 154, 155–156, 157
Reykjavik summit, 1, 23, 54, 233(n7)
Rhodesia, 138, 154. *See also* Zimbabwe
Rogers, Bernard W., 36, 55

SAARC. *See* South Asian Association for Regional Cooperation
SADCC. *See* Southern African Development Coordination Conference
SADF. *See* South Africa, Defense Force
Sakharov, Andrei D., 8
Salazar, Antonio, 170
SALT. *See* Strategic Arms Limitation Talks
Sandinistas. *See* Nicaragua
Sarney, Jose, 99, 190, 191, 192
SASOL coal-to-oil facilities, 148
Saudi Arabia, 14, 222
Savimbi, Jonas, 143, 159
SDI. *See* Strategic Defense Initiative
Sendero Luminoso, 195
Shia, 218, 220, 223
Shultz, George, 149, 167, 172, 178, 182
Siachin glacier, 226
Sicily, 175
Sikhs, 222, 225
Silva, Anibal Cavaco, 171, 172
Sinhalese, 229
Sisulu, Zwelakhe, 147, 152
SLBM. *See* Ballistic missile(s), submarine-launched
Snowcroft, Brent, 32
Snowcroft Commission, 32, 33, 34
Soares, Mario, 171
Sotelo, Leopoldo Calvo, 170
South Africa
   anti-Americanism in, 162
   apartheid in, 136, 146–147, 149, 151
   arms industry, 141
   black township councils in, 144, 146
   black trade-union movement in, 144, 145, 147
   boycotts in, 146, 147
   Coloured and Indians in, 146
   Crossroads, 151
   Defense Force (SADF), 141, 142, 143, 150, 161
   economy of, 137, 138(table), 139(table)
   foreign workers in, 137
   Freedom Charter, 148
   and homelands, 145, 151–152
   identity documents in, 145
   Internal Security Act, 152
   and media, 149, 152
   military forces, 140–141, 142(table)
   National party in, 152, 161
   new constitution of, 136, 144, 146, 153
   nuclear capability of, 47, 141
   population (racial composition), 144(table)
   reforms in, 144–146, 149
   and regional interdependence, 137–144
   sanctions against, 136, 139, 140, 150, 151, 159
   State Security Council, 153
   states of emergency in, 136, 146, 151
   Suppression of Communism Act, 152
   tricameral parliament, 136, 146
   violence in, 146, 148(table), 150
   and Zimbabwe, 154
South Asia, 213–214, 231, 232
South Asian Association for Regional Cooperation (SAARC), 213, 226, 230, 231, 232
Southern African Development Coordination Conference (SADCC), 137

economic data, 138(table), 139(table)
economic dependence on South Africa, 140(table)
military forces of, 142(table)
See also South Africa
South Korea, 16, 17–18, 78, 94, 95, 96
Southwest African People's Organization (SWAPO), 143
Soviet Military Power, 25
Soviet Union
  and Afghanistan, xi, 214, 215–216, 221, 231, 233(n7). *See also* Afghanistan; Afghan War
  agriculture, 113
  aircraft design, 79–82
  air defenses, 54
  air forces, 62, 64(fig.), 69–70, 181
  alcoholism in, 120, 123, 129
  and arms race, xi
  ballistic missiles, 10–13, 29, 37, 39(fig.), 40, 41–42, 43(table), 55
  ballistic missile defense, 52–53
  bombers, 41, 42, 43(table)
  and Caribbean Basin, 208
  censorship in, 8
  civil aviation in, 83
  Communist party in, 7–8, 9
  and Cuba, 208, 209–210
  economy of. *See* Soviet Union economy
  foreign military facilities of, 68
  Gosplan in, 6, 7, 123. *See also* Soviet Union economy, centralized planning of
  and Greece, 179
  ground forces, 66
  helicopters, 66–67
  and India, 226, 231
  and Iran, 77
  and Iran-Iraq War, xii, 20–21
  KGB, 120
  military-industrial complex, 86
  and MPLA, 159, 161
  natural resources in, 116
  naval forces, 67–69, 77, 181
  and Nicaragua, 205, 209
  nuclear targets in, 57
  and Pakistan, 214, 231, 232
  and People's Republic of China, 77, 231
  procurement system of, 82
  and SDI, 11–12, 55, 134
  and South Asia, 213–214
  and Southwest Asia, 77
  space program, 52
  strategic forces, 37, 39(fig.), 40–41, 56(fig.), 58(table)
  submarine force, 40–41, 43(table)
  and Third World, 210
  and Turkey, 182
  27th Party Congress, 5, 23, 123, 217
  vs. U.S. military technology, 79–82, 84
  and Warsaw Pact, 72
  weapon systems, 59(table)
  See also Gorbachev, Mikhail; Soviet Union economy
Soviet Union economy, xii, 6, 85
  and arms sales to Middle East, 130
  capital stock in, 117–118, 126, 132, 134(n1)
  centralized planning of, 116–117, 119, 121–122, 126. *See also* Soviet Union, *Gosplan* in
  data for 1986, 128–130
  and defense spending, 24, 26, 27(fig.), 52, 115, 133–134
  discipline in, 119, 121, 127
  disillusionment with, 120
  extensive growth strategy in, 112. *See also* Gorbachev, Mikhail, growth acceleration policy of
  factor productivity in, 112, 114, 117, 134(n1)
  five-year plan for 1986–1990, 123, 125, 126, 130, 131(table), 133
  and foreign trade, 7, 126, 129–130, 132
  and Foreign Trade Bank, 126

and Fuel-Energy Bureau, 126
and gold prices, 114
and gross national product, 113–114, 127
growth rate deterioration in, 112, 113(table), 114–120
indebtedness in, 130, 132
and investment expenditures, 115, 125, 129, 131–132
and labor brigades, 121
and Machine-Building Bureau, 125
machinery in, 115, 117–118, 126, 129, 132
and Ministry of Foreign Trade, 126
output and productivity in, 113(table), 128(table)
policy decisions in, 115–116
and price system, 125
private economic activity in, 6, 7, 119, 127
production vs. productive capacity in, 116
and recession in the West, 114
reforms in. *See* Gorbachev, Mikhail, reforms of
and State Agro-Industrial Committee, 125
wage/productivity increases in, 121
and weather, 114, 127
and worker morale, 114
and world economy, 114
See also Gorbachev, Mikhail; Soviet Union
Spadolini, Giovanni, 175
Spain, 95, 165–170, 184–185(n1)
Spear of the Nation, 148
Spector, Leonard, 141
Sputnik, 10
Sri Lanka, 213, 226, 229–230
Stealth aircraft, 63–64. *See also* Bombers, Advanced Technology
Strategic Arms Limitation Talks (SALT), 22, 34, 35, 37, 41, 57
Strategic balance, 55, 56(fig.), 59

Strategic Defense Initiative (SDI), 2, 10, 11–12, 22, 32, 47, 49–51, 111(n40)
and France, 76
and Greece, 180
and isolationism, 72
and Portugal, 172
Submarines
Poseidon, 34
Trident, 34, 40, 44, 62
Typhoon, 40
See also Ballistic missile(s), submarine-launched
Suez Canal, 14
Sukhoi, Pavel, 80
Summit of Western Industrial Nations, 62
Sundarji, K., 228
Sunday Times (London), 47
Sunnis, 218, 220
SWAPO. *See* Southwest African People's Organization
Swaziland, 137, 143
Sweden, 228
Switzerland, 95
Syria, 14, 81, 130, 179, 180

Taft, William, 180
Taiwan, 17, 19, 94, 95, 96, 108(n9)
Tambo, Oliver, 149
Tamils, 226, 229
Technology, military, 79–82
Terrorism, 76, 173–174, 175, 178, 184, 210, 222, 225, 231
Thatcher, Margaret, 44
Third World, 98–100, 102, 169, 180, 184, 209, 210–211
Third World War, The (Hackett), 24
Tishenko, Marat, 66
Tokyo Economic Summit, 102
Torrejon Air Base, 167
Torture, 216, 233(n6)
Tower Commission report, xii
Tupolev, Andrei, 80
Turkey, 180, 181–183

UDF. *See* United Democratic Front

ul-Haq, Zia, 218, 219, 220, 222, 224, 228
Umkhonto we Sizwe. *See* Spear of the Nation
UN. *See* United Nations
UNITA. *See* National Union for the Total Independence of Angola
United Arab Emirates, 14
United Democratic Front (UDF), 146, 148, 151
United Nations (UN), 214, 217
United States
  and Afghanistan, 217
  and African National Congress, 149
  air defense of, 51–52
  air forces, 63–64, 65
  antisatellite systems of, 51
  and arms race, xi. *See also* Arms control
  Army AirLand Battle concept, 26, 65
  aviation programs, 61, 62
  ballistic missile defense, 49. *See also* Ballistic missile(s), defense; Strategic Defense Initiative
  ballistic missiles, 10–13, 36, 37, 38–39(table). *See also* Ballistic missile(s)
  and Bolivia, 198
  and Brazil, 211
  budget deficit, xiii, 2, 92, 93, 101, 103, 104–105(table)
  and Central America, 186
  Central Intelligence Agency (CIA), 24, 42
  and Chile, 194, 211
  and Colombia, 197
  Comprehensive Anti-Apartheid Act, 162
  Congressional Caucus on Competitiveness, 96
  and Contras, xii, 187, 204, 206, 210. *See also* Iran-Contra affair
  countervailing strategy of, 31, 32, 85
  defense buildup, 60, 84, 104, 106
  Defense Intelligence Agency (DIA), 24, 37
  defense spending, 22, 26, 27(fig.), 49(table), 104–107, 110–111(n35), 111(n41)
  Department of Defense (DoD), 25, 34, 51, 64, 79, 105
  and directed-energy weapons, 11
  and El Salvador, 207
  and Greece, 176, 177(fig.), 178, 180–181, 184
  gross national product, 3, 93
  and Honduras, 203–204
  House of Representatives, 94
  and India, 224, 226, 227, 231, 234(n29)
  and International Monetary Fund, 200, 211
  and Iran, xii, 77. *See also* Iran-Contra affair; Iran-Iraq War
  and Iran-Iraq War, xii, 20–21
  and Italy, 173, 176
  Joint Chiefs of Staff, 41, 62
  and Libya, 164, 169, 174, 182, 184, 210
  Marine Corps, 60–61
  and Mexico, 200, 201, 202
  National Security Council, xii
  and NATO, 165, 183
  Naval Air Systems Command, 61
  naval forces, 62–63, 67
  nonproliferation policy of, 223–224
  nuclear forces, 38–39(table), 56(fig.), 58(table)
  nuclear targets in, 57
  and Pakistan, 216, 220–222, 227, 231, 234(n17)
  and Panama, 206–207
  and People's Republic of China, 231
  and Portugal, 171
  President's Chemical Warfare Review Commission, 62
  public debt of, 2
  recession of 1982–1983, 102
  Senate, 206

Sixth Fleet, 171, 173
  and South Africa, 136, 149–150, 151, 161–162
  and South Asia, 213–214
  and Southwest Asia, 76(table)
  vs. Soviet military technology, 79–82, 84
  and Spain, 165–167, 168(fig.), 169–170, 184
  strategic triad, 30, 31(fig.)
  and Third World, 99, 102, 169, 184
  trade deficit, xiii, 92, 93, 94, 101–102, 103, 104
  trade policy of, 93–96
  troops in Europe, 107, 111(n41)
  and Turkey, 181–183
  weapon systems, 59(table), 60(table)
  and world economy, 2
  as world power, 3, 91
  and Zimbabwe, 158–159
Uruguay, 97, 187
Uruguay Round negotiations, 93, 94, 95, 96, 97–98, 107–108
USAF/Army Joint Surveillance Target Attack Radar System (Joint STARS), 64–65
Ushewokunze, Herbert, 158
U.S.S. Missouri, 183
USSR. *See* Soviet Union

van der Westhuizen, P. W., 153
Vanunu, Mordechai, 47
Vasconcelos, Alvaro, 170
Venezuela, 199
Vietnam, xi
Volcker, Paul, 102, 200

Warren Air Force Base, 32
Warsaw Pact, 23, 26, 53
  combat aircraft, 73(fig.)
  and Greece, 179
  maritime forces, 74(fig.)
  vs. NATO, 71–75, 173
  weaknesses of, 70
Washington Post, 63, 182, 223
Weinberger, Caspar W., 2, 78, 172, 227, 231
West Bank and Gaza, 14
West Germany. *See* Federal Republic of Germany
World Bank, 99, 186, 194
Worrall, Dennis, 152

Yasuhiro Nakasone, 107
Yeutter, Clayton, 94
Yom Kippur War, 171
Yonas, Gerold, 79

Zaire, 137
Zambia, 137, 138, 139, 141(table), 150, 156
ZANU. *See* Zimbabwe African National Union
ZAPU. *See* Zimbabwe African People's Union
Zaragoza Air Base, 167
Zia ul-Haq. *See* ul-Haq, Zia
Zimbabwe, 137, 138, 139, 141(table), 142, 143, 150, 154, 156, 157–159
Zimbabwe African National Union (ZANU), 154, 156, 158
Zimbabwe African People's Union (ZAPU), 157, 158
Zvobgo, Eddison, 158